TOP CLASS MANAGEMENT

Lessons for Effectiveness

Richard Graham has been a senior manager in a large nationalised industry, a government economic adviser, Director of Ashridge Centre for Transport Management, an independent consultant and now a director of a successful private company. He has written and broadcast on transport management and policy.

Edwin Singer is an independent consultant specialising in the problems of people at work and has worked for both public and private organisations. His publications include *Effective Management Coaching*. Recently he has become a County Councillor and Committee Chairman, gaining insights into the management of public services.

TOP CLASS MANAGEMENT

Lessons for Effectiveness

Richard Graham

Edwin Singer

INSTITUTE OF PERSONNEL MANAGEMENT

First published in 1993

Phototypeset in Times by
The Comp-Room, Aylesbury
and printed in Great Britain by
The Cromwell Press, Melksham

British Library Cataloguing in Publication Data

Singer, Edwin J.
  Top Class Management: Lessons for
  Effectiveness. – (Developing Skills
  Series)
  I. Title II. Graham, Richard III. Series
  658.3

ISBN 0-85292-530-1

ipm

INSTITUTE OF PERSONNEL MANAGEMENT
IPM House, Camp Road, Wimbledon, London SW19 4UX
Tel: 081-946-9100   Fax: 081-946-2570
Registered office as above. Registered Charity No. 215797
A company limited by guarantee. Registered in England No. 198002

Contents

Acknowledgements

Usually there are many people involved in the writing of such a book, but strangely this one has been written through many hours of discussion and agony at the word-processor by the two of us. There has been no typist and we have done our own research. However, we must both express gratitude to our wives for their patience and encouragement.

There was a third member of the team involved in the creation of this learning technique. Brian Ellison of Ashridge Management College was an essential participant in a large number of the programmes we ran and we must acknowledge his contribution. Of course, we must also acknowledge the encouragement and support of all the staff at Ashridge, whose very special facilities made the original development programmes so successful.

Without our clients all this would not have happened. In particular we would wish to place on record our appreciation of the positive encouragement of British Rail Midland Region management, whose active promotion of management development led to the original commission and who gave us active assistance in the development of the course by providing the research material used in constructing the learning framework. Many other clients contributed to our further development but most have preferred to remain anonymous. They came from many industries across the spectrum of manufacturing, distribution and transport, and we thank them for all their contributions.

Foreword

This book came about as a result of one of those happy chances in life. We had often talked about creating a management development programme based on businesses invented by the participants. Edwin had run training courses like that years earlier, but when Malcolm Ramage of British Rail approached Richard at Ashridge Management College to help with major changes in their management, we suddenly had the opportunity to work together. British Rail was being reorganised and this meant not only that managers had to do things differently but that the very culture of the railway had to change – from a concentration on railway operations to a positive emphasis on customers. Our client presented us with a set of training objectives and a target population of junior managers from all disciplines within the railway. Our brief was to design a programme which would introduce them to the many new skills they would need and which would also encourage this major behavioural change.

Each of us had different knowledge and skills to offer, but we needed a way of dramatically demonstrating the change from specialist- to customer-oriented management which would quickly introduce the relevant skills. We both felt strongly that traditional management training based on case studies was far from satisfactory and we disliked the straight lecture as simply inefficient. So we developed a general management course which required the participants, working in groups, to invent a railway and then 'run' it; all in the space of a week.

Obviously, we ourselves had to learn how to make such a course and how to lead it. Also, we had to understand the business from which the participants came. We had to decide how much information and structure was necessary in order to enable the participants to relax and enjoy tasks of a size and complexity with which they could cope. Above all we recognised that such an approach had to engage their enthusiasm, because without their wholehearted particpation the project would fail. More traditional courses of lectures and cases can at least take place even if the participants hate them. In our case, no co-operation – no course. In short, the whole thing had to be fun.

The courses were successful. We had much indirect feedback and one full-blown review conference. The London Midland Region of British Rail eventually commissioned 27 courses. We went on between us to create similar courses for 10 more clients. Throughout all of this, we discovered that we had concentrated our combined experience and begun to formulate a comprehensive view of management. As a result of this, when the opportunity came along to undertake some training at board level with directors, we decided to capitalise on our experience and adopt a similar approach. This time we did not need to ask them to invent a business; they already had one. We used the same combination of questioning, feedback, problem-solving and task-setting to develop these seminars. Again, the experience has broadened our understanding of the way businesses are managed, and those lessons have been incorporated in our thinking.

Our courses and seminars are designed to create learning situations. But training courses are only a practice pool, so to speak, where managers can learn their strokes under continuous supervision. Real management is learnt by jumping in at the deep end. Therefore advice, assistance and coaching must come from one's superiors, on the job. This we have also demonstrated throughout these courses, and many of the techniques can be used in training within businesses. In creating these programmes, we had to create all the supporting instructions and briefing material. We have decided to make this available. In the Appendices we reproduce the full material from two courses. Not only does this make it clear how they were organised, but we hope that others will build on our work.

Over the years that we worked together, we realised that we were redefining our own beliefs about management as a job and as an art. All the individual skills used by managers have to be combined in different degrees for almost every job. Furthermore, the skill of enabling those that work for us to learn how to do *their* jobs betters is perhaps the most important of all. We have come to the conclusion that management is not like many of the other professions, where an agreed syllabus of knowledge and skills can be acquired and, once a satisfactory standard has been attained, practised. Management itself is a practical skill, almost a knack, like swimming or riding a bicycle. You can explain what is supposed to happen, but until people actually do it, real learning will not take place.

These experiences persuaded us that we had developed something which was novel and effective, and we felt that others should know about it. The book could almost have been two books – one for trainers and one for managers. We have put it all together because we believe that learning is so central to good management that the actual processes of management and the development of management skills are indissoluble aspects of the same thing – an organisation which recognises that learning is an essential ingredient for success. Although we have both moved on, this book is our contribution to the literature of an activity which gave us both much pleasure in enabling many young managers to do their job better. Perhaps having jumped in at the deep end they will not sink but strike out for successful careers.

Richard Graham and Edwin Singer

Introduction

It is not enough simply to say what good management is; it is much more important to understand how to make managers good. This book describes in detail what happens when we stop trying to talk *at* managers and instead give them the opportunity to learn – when we create learning situations rather than just lecture on principles. The result has been a novel approach to the development of managers which also makes an important contribution to the way businesses are run. Our concern is what people achieve at work. Our interest is in personal goals which are consistent with organisational goals and therefore make for successful companies and public bodies. Our emphasis is on what people do at work and how managers make the doing turn into achieving. We are convinced that 'doing a worthwhile job' is good for both businesses and those that work for them.

We argue that management is a comprehensive activity in which many different techniques and knowledge sets have to be present at the same time. Most would agree that the whole of management consists in achieving the aims of an enterprise by organising the co-operative efforts of the people who work for it. Unfortunately, it is more often presented as a series of tasks and techniques which are described, taught and practised as individual activities. We believe that management is a coherent skill, like life itself.

At the heart of the manager's job is the need to make things happen far beyond his personal scope and ability. He or she needs others to accept the management of their time and talents and in return be provided with the means to do the job. Once this bargain has been struck the enterprise can begin. No matter how hard we focus on planning, recruiting, accountancy, production engineering, marketing and the rest, if that basic bargain has not been struck the enterprise will fail.

Managing a business is itself a process of learning. Those who operate a business must always be learning to improve

1

performance. This inevitably means people working in new ways. It is the manager who must enable that learning to take place. Therefore, the principles underlying the process of learning are the same principles that underlie the way people behave at work. If these are applied, the business becomes a learning organisation, which tends to heighten motivation and raise individual performance.

Motivation, though, is not just about wanting to do the job well. We believe that people at work also want to be part of a successful business. The measures of that success must be agreed and accepted; both the managers and the staff they manage must recognise success in the same way. We will argue that the only criterion to which they can all subscribe is the excellence of the product or service produced.

The only arbiters of that excellence are the customers. One of the key characteristics of a market, where people spend their own money to buy things, is that judgements are made every time a purchase is completed. It is the market which tells if you are any good. We believe that successful managers know how to reflect and magnify market views about the quality of what is sold so that those who produce the goods and services know that what they do is worthwhile.

Although making people feel good about what they do is the start of good management, it is not the whole of it. Good managers have clear goals. It is an essential task of those who manage the managers, their directors, to articulate the goals of the business and create the strategy for achieving them. Out of this comes style and policy, not, as some would have it, the other way round. Thus the directors set the agenda for the business. They must also give that agenda to the managers, who in turn pass it to the workforce, so that in the end it is owned by the whole business.

Even this is not enough. Hidden within any group of men and women is a vast repository of skill and experience. It is the management's task to mobilise this in the context of working groups. Problems are not solved by individual managers giving instructions. Rather they are tackled by the people closest to them being shown how to use their own resources to solve them. Furthermore, no matter how skilful a manager is in developing such an enterprise, the participants must know how successful they are.

This is the real message of Schumacher's *Small is Beautiful*: to feel real satisfaction and motivation to do a good job, the units of production must be small enough for those who work in them to *know* how they are doing. This knowledge of results must be in terms that the workers can understand. A skilful manager provides for this.

Managers are often portrayed as parental figures and we would not entirely demur at this. When things go wrong there must be such a presence. But problems and crises are the very times when management skill is most honed. It is no use developing participative management in the good times, only to revert to traditional ways when things get tough. We will argue that to develop the skill of management requires a change of behaviour and this cannot be taught. Only the circumstances in which such skill can develop can be created. Under these conditions each manager can learn what behaviours suit him best in stimulating positive motivation in his subordinates and colleagues. This book therefore describes in detail the way in which we have sought to create such circumstances.

Since we also believe that the process of learning is part of what is to be learnt, we shall describe that process as we develop our argument. Chapter by chapter we shall show how management skill is a continuum of activities built around a single set of principles. And within each chapter we shall describe the means by which such skill may be developed. Running alongside this will be an account of a course and a senior management seminar, developed by us, in which the circumstances for learning were created.

Before we start, two important points must be made. Throughout the book we shall refer to 'companies' and 'businesses' almost interchangeably. By these words we include both private and public enterprises, as well as a great deal of what might be termed 'administration', from government to charities. The principles of good management, we believe, are as valid in the public sector as the private.

Secondly, our argument depends on recognising some truths about the way we do business and are governed. This is a book about management and, as far as we are able, we make no value judgements about what we describe. Our central belief is

that poor management is still too common and it benefits nobody: good management not only makes successful businesses,
it also means enjoyment and satisfaction for both managers
and managed.

1

The Manager's Real Job

What managers do

When we were children we accepted that our needs would be met without question. Only as we grew up did we begin to question how the milk arrived at the doorstep or where the buses came from or how things got into the shop. Even then we tended to identify all the activities around us with the people who did the work. We assumed that the milkman, the driver and the shopkeeper were themselves responsible. We did not differentiate between the job and those who arranged for it to be done.

The reason is simple. At first, all a child's needs are satisfied by its parents. They are seen as producers as well as providers. They make things happen, almost, as it were, by magic, and the child accepts it. Only later do we realise that our parents relied on a whole array of people and businesses to run the household, and the act of co-ordinating all these efforts – some paid for, some voluntary – is management. Management is at heart a domestic activity directly concerned with people rather than pieces of paper.

We shall therefore define management as 'making things happen through people'. We all know what a manager has to do because we all have to do it for our families sooner or later. Parents decide what to do, plan how to do it, acquire the resources, recruit the people and check on the results. Notice that we have not mentioned payment. That is because while every manager, even father and mother, has limited resources and must work within them, actually trading the resultant output can be entirely separate. In fact, of course, the process of management can itself be paid for.

The key question for most laymen and many managers is not *what* managers do, but *how*. In a successful company all the familiar activities of management – planning, recruitment, control, monitoring and so on – are fitted together in harmony to achieve agreed ends. Those ends are known and understood by all who work there, and care will have been taken to obtain the understanding and commitment of all concerned. Everybody will know what part they have to play and how their work fits in with everybody else's. Each will need to exercise his or her individual skills as part of the total effort. This process by which goals are decided, work allocated, effort co-ordinated and skills developed is really what managers do. *Management is the skill of enabling others to understand group goals and work effectively to achieve them.*

A good example of this is the symphony orchestra. Its players individually possess a wide range of skills. They take pride in the exercise of those skills but recognise that their efforts are meaningless unless co-ordinated as a whole to create a single sound. They will therefore co-operate with the conductor and accept his discipline. He, in turn, knows that to get the sound he wants the players must all do the same things at the same time in the same way. A most effective way to achieve this is through the players wanting it.

The conductor must therefore bring into harmony the skills, desires and motivation of the players in order to create the symphony for their listeners, who will respond with applause for both the orchestra and its players. The production is delivered and the feedback of appreciation is immediate. The conductor acts as the enabler, exercising a range of interpersonal skills to make the whole thing happen according to his overall plan. But before he and his orchestra perform they have a rehearsal; and the purpose of this is not simply for the conductor to tell the orchestra what he wishes to happen, or even just to get their agreement – they are going to *learn* how to do it.

The usual response of managers to the learning needs of their staff is to reach for the nearest training course. *This is not what we mean.* The front line of staff learning must be in the office, on the job. And notice that we write of 'learning', not 'teaching'. To understand this distinction we need to look in some detail at how people learn.

The process of learning

Consider these four propositions:

- You only learn when you want to.
- You only learn when you see what is in it for you.

- You need to try out as you learn to make it work for you and develop your skills.
- You will only know if it works for you if you can demonstrate the results of what you have done.

You learn when you want to

Has a boss or supervisor leaned over your shoulder and told you not to bother about asking why, just to get on with the procedure? Far too often instructions (a form of teaching) are rapped out without finding out first whether the subordinate is in the right frame of mind to receive them. Without the active participation of the learner such instructions will be obeyed half-heartedly and in a way which often leads to mistakes and misjudgements. We all know what it feels like to be taught at. And did it do us much good? Did the lessons stick?

Most of us have also had that wonderful experience of really wanting to learn a skill. In some cases the skill to be learnt is one in which we already had some natural ability. Nobody needed to persuade Nigel Kennedy to play the violin, or Sebastian Coe to run. Most of us have natural abilities and there is undoubted joy and fulfilment in the exercise and development of these. So the first clue about wanting to learn is to identify those things which we *can* do. Few people persist with the acquisition of a skill in the absence of any talent. Nevertheless, we have to be given some objective assessment about our ability.

The second clue is that a skill we wish to acquire must be demonstrated to us and be seen as desirable. This is the way we learnt as a child. Probably the most common way in which the seed of desire to do something is sown in all of us by an enthusiastic and successful practitioner – such people are powerful role models and often themselves teachers. It is quite untrue, even malicious, to say that 'those that can, do; those that can't, teach'. If it were, then the skill base of the human race would tend to decline each generation. David Bellamy has done as much to recruit botanists as he may ever have done for the environment. Those that would have us develop skills must first persuade us that a particular activity is enjoyable and worthwhile. If this is lacking, learning will not even start.

Ability, demonstration and positive persuasion must all operate together to make people want to learn how to improve performance. Unless they truly want to gain the skills to do their job better, they never really will. They will adopt another strategy, to do just enough to get paid and not to be dismissed. This can frequently be observed among staff who deal with the public day by day. Good customer relations – as we shall explain later – requires the exercise of a range of specific skills which must be learned and developed. It is clear that many such workers not only do not have such skills; they have no wish to acquire them.

Management in its turn recognises that staff have to want to be be better before improvements can take place. However, there seems to be a school of thought which believes that a desire to do the job better and improved on-the-job performance are the same thing. Thus the latest 'management fix' encompasses a whole range of 'training techniques' which focus on getting staff to feel better about what they do – in effect to try to motivate by persuasion. But wanting to learn is just the first step; such motivation is not the lesson itself.

A large corporation with many of its staff directly in touch with the public – its customers – recently resorted to such an expensive and time-consuming programme to 'improve the quality of customer service'. The programme consisted of a whole series of compulsory mass meetings. The 'training' used the techniques of the demagogue allied to high-tech audio-visuals and a great deal of media persuasion. In effect the idea was to persuade the staff to *want* to perform better by shouting at them. The propaganda was accompanied by a host of trivial slogans and tips many of which, if carried out faithfully, would be more likely to annoy than inspire the customers.

Meanwhile, their customers were told that everything was going to be better. In some cases the extent and cost of this 'training' was gently made public. Similar techniques, glossy and expensive, were used to persuade the customers that the staff would now love them – having been told to – by advertising themselves as 'caring'.

The mass meetings did not work. The staff found them at best a joke; at worst they felt insulted because they thought they were doing a good job already. Nobody they respected had ever told them otherwise. They did not make the connection between the alleged poor performance and their attitude. The propaganda soon wore off, the slogans were forgotten and former habits reappeared. But in fact the situation was even worse.

Unfortunately for such companies, customers are not stupid.

When the promised improvement in performance failed to materialise they got pretty angry and, because the business is a monopoly, they took it out on the staff who then sympathised with the customer. So the actual outcome was low-performance staff, alienated from the business.

To improve poor performance the staff actually have to *behave* differently. To do this they need extensive training to improve skills. Changes in attitude towards customers, for example, result from changes in performance, not the other way round. At events only designed to change attitudes no learning takes place. Everyone may feel better for a while, but with no new skills the old ways will quickly be re-established.

You learn when you see the pay-off

Have you ever been sent on a training session you did not want to go on? Do you remember any of the lessons you were supposed to learn? At worst you probably felt that the whole thing was a waste of time; at best you might have been mildly amused and picked up a few tips. Probably most people's experience lies somewhere between. But it is a fair guess that you did not get as much out of the training course as you might have done because you did not recognise the need.

There is an important lesson about the way managers deal with their own subordinates when they want them to learn something, whether it is a new procedure, how to avoid errors, or even sending them on another training course.

> *Make sure that the individual really understands why it is important for him to learn that particular skill or procedure.*

Almost everybody gets a buzz out of doing his job well. Our personal satisfaction is reinforced by the admiration of our colleagues and the pleasure of our customers. Unfortunately, most training is not represented like this; we are told we have 'needs' and that training will satisfy them. In fact, the simple proposition that we will do our job better would very often persuade us to want the offered opportunity. *So the first task of management is to make sure that the individual understands how whatever is to be learnt fits into his desire to do the job better.*

9

Consider your reaction to the last instruction or even suggestion you received about your work. It may have been an idea at a training course or an exhortation from your manager. It is very unlikely that you thought: 'What a brilliant idea, I must rush out and implement that as soon as possible.' It is much more likely you thought: 'How will that change what I like doing now?', or 'It won't work because . . .' These are natural reactions but not very helpful. As you ponder the suggestion, you ask yourself in practice: 'What's in it for me?' You want to know if it will make your job easier or solve a problem for you. In other words, the acceptance of new ideas and techniques is very personal and really quite self-centred. This book is itself a test of this proposition. It is full of ideas and suggestions. Some you will dismiss as unworkable or inappropriate; others will 'ring a bell'. The latter will be the ones whose validity you can see and test in your own context and according to your own criteria.

Even before we actually start to learn we have to agree the context and accept the content. The two are linked. Far too often top management discusses a change for months and then springs it on subordinates for immediate implementation. They resist. The reason for this disharmony is that the top management team has taken time to understand why the change is necessary, what problem it solves and why it is the best solution. It then assumes that, because it knows the action is sensible, so too does everyone else.

The process of change is a process of learning and everyone involved must have the time to start the process by understanding why the change is necessary and accepting the reason.

A company decided to tackle the problem of its appraisal system. It came to the conclusion that its job descriptions and individual targets concentrated too much on inputs rather than outputs. A meeting was held with the production superintendents to discuss the new ideas.

The initial response was hostile. There was, they said, nothing much wrong with the present system, except the way the personnel department administered it. After a short discussion they agreed the purpose of an appraisal system was to help them, as managers, and not to help the personnel department. They then suggested that three of them should get together to devise a new appraisal form.

Three hours after the meeting one of them who had opposed the new ideas, went to the personnel manager and said: 'I have been thinking about what you said and you are right. Here are our ideas for a new form.'

The outcome was not a perfect new form, but one that worked better because, through the process of understanding, the staff had taken ownership of the system and learnt a lot about how the system worked as well. Discovering 'the point' of learning a new skill actually triggers off the learning process – but still that is not enough.

Learning by doing

This brings us to the third principle. Would anyone try to teach typing from a book without a typewriter? And yet a great deal of training in business still owes more to the traditional school classroom than to the shop-floor. We still try and tell people what to do by standing in front of them and lecturing. In fact, as a teaching method lecturing is about the least efficient. Most people remember a mere 10 per cent of what they are told unless the speaker is exceptional. This is not greatly increased by taking notes while you listen. As for the written word, without practical application it requires great skill and concentration on the part of the reader to actually learn how to do something new.

Learning in business is almost never theoretical. At all levels it needs the individual actively to participate. *You have to do it to learn it.* Unfortunately, across the whole range of business activities there seems to be only a half-hearted commitment to this principle. We must be grateful that no such lack of enthusiasm exists among those who train airline pilots. Management is, above all, a practical skill which centres on the way managers behave. Consequently, learning new skills can only be said to have taken place when it results in recognisable changes of behaviour. Thus, when a manager says: 'It's all right in theory but it won't work in practice', he has learned nothing.

It is not even valid to argue the lesson or skill has worked before. What works for one manager may not work for another in a different situation. So, when you think that you have learned a good idea, you need to try it out to discover whether it works for you. If it does, well and good; if it does not, the act of trying can often lead on to a new and unexpected learning situation.

All this argues for a high degree of on-the-job training. This will be natural for those who work for an enabling manager – one who creates learning situations rather than just issuing orders.

It will also depend on the ability of the business to absorb the inevitable mistakes. Nevertheless, it is clearly impracticable to argue that all business learning, especially amongst managers, must happen in, so to speak, 'real time'. Where complicated and difficult skills are concerned we have to withdraw for training. We shall argue throughout this book that such training must consist primarily of participants undertaking activities which as closely as possible mimic their real life. This principle is particularly valid for management development.

How do you know it worked for you?

'You cannot achieve anything unless you can measure it' is a sound maxim. All of us need to know how we are getting on with our new skills. We call it knowledge of results and many businesses are simply not set up to give individual staff that knowledge. It is not difficult to measure physical changes: better quality control results in lower scrap levels; better supervision in the packing shed means fewer breakages. Intangible changes, however, are more difficult to measure.

We would argue that *businesses must measure what is going on in ways which have real meaning for those who work in them.* This is so important that a whole chapter is devoted to it later in the book. Without such knowledge, not only will real learning not take place but existing performance will also deteriorate. There is evidence that, in the absence of good information about how they are performing, workers will develop their own measures and circulate them through the informal company networks. If there has been a breakdown in accepted goals, as we describe later in the railway case in Chapter 3, these measures will be used to justify the situation.

Learning has to be managed

Learning may be taken to mean the whole process by which a business develops and grows. Learning is not just the acquisition of specific skills, it is the continuing process of change. The manager is both part of that process and the enabler. He is the one who creates the circumstances – the structure – within which others may learn. He does not lay down rules and instructions but rather he specifies objectives and then creates the spaces within which those objectives can be reached.

An American film called *Dead Poets Society* brilliantly illustrates how the process of teaching and learning is transformed by the application of these principles. In the film a class of 17-year-old schoolboys is enthused with a desire to learn, recite and even write poetry.

Their classroom world was burdened by exercises and quizzes based on text books and traditional 'talk and chalk' lessons. Suddenly along comes a teacher who catches their attention, who turns their thoughts into new directions and shows them something exciting in a subject they had imagined to be dull and boring.

First, the personality of the man is attractive. He demonstrates the virtue of what he had learnt as a young man by what he is now. He says things in new and startling ways; he challenges the boys to be different; he encourages them to try out new and unconventional stances. He makes the study of English exciting and he gets the inevitable response – 'Teach us!' But still the boys do not get the point.

'So you want to be like me – then this is what you have to do.' We now see a number of lessons in progress and each time the lesson is linked to outcomes. Reading and understanding plays is the first step to acting. Closing your eyes and speaking your thoughts is the first step to poetry. Expressing oneself in physical movement can lead to better verbal self-expression and that leads to better understanding between friends.

He does not just talk to the boys. We see him encouraging them; even bullying them to do it themselves. They must read poetry for themselves; they must write it. They are encouraged to create their own circle and make their own agenda. Above all he encourages them to experiment by themselves. But all this is not enough. He gives them encouragement – positive and critical – in generous measure. He not only tells them how they are doing, he also shows them how to measure their performance.

However, as the boys quickly become more skilled in one part of their lives the rest is shown up. The headmaster, other teachers and, in one case, a parent are shown as not wanting these boys to learn such lessons. It all becomes too difficult because with skill comes ownership and independence. As always, ignorance hates skill because it seeks to dominate rather than co-operate, and tragedy is followed by the dismissal of the teacher.

The film shows us how much the process of education and learning is of our own making. *Those who would teach and instruct can only be instruments. They can never own the process; only those being taught can.*

A learning environment

Let us now make a very important point. *Improving performance at work involves learning and development over a long period.* Ther are no short cuts. If a company wants to improve its performance significantly, it must become a learning institution from top to bottom. *A learning environment exists when an organisation gains and makes use of new knowledge, values, tools and behaviours at all levels in the organisation, among groups and individuals. People learn as part of their daily activities, particularly as they interact with others, internally and externally. Groups learn as they strive to solve problems and achieve common goals. Learning itself leads to adjustment of goals, criteria for success, procedures, structures and perceptions.*

It requires those in it to be competent in basic inter-personal skills – listening, questioning, summarising, discussing, coping with conflict and so on. Those that manage must acknowledge and share uncertainty, accept errors, share information and respond to the future.

Of itself this is a pretty tall order but it is a goal to aim at. Much of the rest of this book is about helping managers to create such an environment. But the hardest task is to persuade each member of staff to want to perform better. This is not difficult but, as we shall see, it demands resources and commitment.

Motivation

As management advisers and trainers, one of the commonest problems given to us is 'How do we deal with a lack of motivation?' Many times we have been asked how a workforce is to be motivated. It is listed alongside falling demand, rising costs or insufficient capital, as if a quantity of motivation could be added to the business to make it perform better. It is not a quantum but a state. Furthermore, everyone is motivated all the time. They may be motivated to swing the lead or to develop overtime. The problem at work is to get people motivated to perform in ways which benefit the business.

What such companies all too often did not want to consider was the corollary. What can the organisation do for the staff? Motivation is about calculating the pay-off. A highly motivated group of workers has large expectations of a satisfactory return for themselves, and this will be much more than money. A great deal has been written about motivation at work and we shall do no more than summarise. It is quite clear now that work itself is a major motivator. However, this can only be so when the work is fully understood. Just as learning requires that there be a comprehensible point, so work itself has to have an outcome which satisfies an individual's aspirations.

The issue of money

The most obvious pay-off is money, but money is not a good motivator. It is remarkable how often it is still assumed that people work only for money. It seemed pretty obvious when subsistence wages were all workers could look forward to after long hours. Today, however, in a world of wide job choice and an active labour market it should be less obvious. It is also a common experience that, while in the short term more money usually gets a bit more output, in the longer term more money produces less effort as workers discover that they can take some of the benefits as free time. Yet more money may produce even less effort.

Wage payments for work on a large scale are relatively modern. Most payment was for the output of work. People sold things not themselves, and enormous time, energy and inventiveness used to be expended in calculating 'piece rates'. Hour and day rates are much simpler but tend merely to reward attendance. Paying people for the position they hold and the function they perform – paying them a salary – does have great social benefits. The disadvantage is that it uncouples reward and output. Much of the work of modern management, as we shall describe it, consists in establishing a direct link between the successful attainment of objectives by the company as a whole, and the performance of the individual employee.

Because what we do is so central to who we are and what position we hold in society, money rewards are in one sense a concrete manifestation of the value society places on us. Through the labour market, pay levels often reveal truths about our value system that we would rather not know. Unfortunately, money rewards as the pay-off for work also work against individuals. Because certain jobs are much desired and do bring their own rewards, those that can do them will accept lower pay than they otherwise would.

So money is a very unreliable reason for work, and the pursuit of greater income has often proceeded with no regard for the work itself. As Plato observed, the skilled lyre player gained great rewards while the men who took away the night soil were paid a pittance. The former performed beautifully but was of no practical use while without the latter the city would die.

Thanks to work by Maslow and Herzberg[1] we may go further: money is only a one-way motivator; not enough is a substantial demotivator but more than enough produces diminishing returns and eventually there is no reasonable sum that will buy more labour. Job satisfaction operates in one direction too. Insufficient tends to lead to treading water and a survival attitude, while high job satisfaction is a substantial positive motivator leading to high performance.

This short digression on money rewards is meant only to underline the point that *the prospect of doing a job better, and understanding why, is the greatest single motivator*. It is associated positively with other benefits beyond that of simply doing a worthwhile job. There are personal psychic benefits to do with service to others and self-fulfilment. There is promotion and enhanced status. There is the prospect of joining a more highly esteemed group. There is the prospect of power. The key here is that these are very personal motives, and as they are achieved not only the process but the job itself begins to become identified with its holder. Improving performance now becomes part of the job-holder's own drive. All aspects of developing his skills must be seen to yield identifiable pay-offs. Not only this, he will also not be satisfied with simple instructions – he will want to know why.

Learning as the key to motivation

Now we see that our first two answers to the question 'How do people learn?' – when they want to and when they see the point

– not only provide the key to the process of learning but also tell us how people may feel greater motivation at work. The process itself becomes the lesson, and as we learn how to learn so we also learn how to manage.

The most important aspect of developing these twin precepts of learning is that once people want to learn and once they see the point they will want to own the whole process. This is simply the response to improved skills and better performance leading to greater job satisfaction. *The* job becomes *my* job.

Positive motivation to perform well and further the business's objectives means that the staff *want* to perform well. If they gain satisfaction from a job well done, they will want to do a better one. If they understand that it makes sense and benefits them, they will be motivated. The underlying principle here is clear. *People work best when they believe it to be of their own choice.*

Learning outside the organisation

While, we would argue, the whole of a person's career is a learning process, it is when a business decides to change that the need to learn becomes most obvious. But all too often businesses are reorganised, merged or even made to take on completely new tasks with little thought being given to the need for those involved to learn the new skills. Every change in a business requires a major learning input, and this is often the main cost. When we buy new equipment or occupy new premises there is seldom an argument about the need to train; reorganisation is a different matter.

A great deal of management energy in the 1970s went into 're-organisation'. It was widely believed, encouraged by that generation of consultants, that if only a company had the right organisation it would be successful. In many cases such changes were undertaken with no accompanying programme of training and the costs of learning – which took place informally and had to happen anyway – were ignored.

However, this need to learn to manage a new organisation is not ignored by every business, and in recent years many requests for formal training outside the organisation have been occasioned by the need to adapt to a new situation. One such was the original inspiration for this book and much of the work of its authors over the past eight years.

In 1983 British Rail set out to change fundamentally the way it was managed. It reorganised its entire management structure to reflect the various outputs that the customer buys. Business Sectors were created to sell the high-speed Inter-City passenger services, London commuter services, freight, provincial services and so on. These new 'businesses' were to be identifiable and made accountable to the market. An essential element in this change was to be the conversion and development of the management from administrators to businessmen. The aim was to make the managers apply good commercial business practice and manage with reference to budgets and profit.

In mid-1984, one of the authors was asked to develop a course for middle managers in British Rail Midland Region. The participants would be drawn from every discipline in the railway – operations, engineering, marketing, finance, planning – and all the, then new, businesses. All had technical training and were considered, as a result of the appraisal system, to be likely candidates for promotion during the following two to three years. The need was to help them to develop their general management skills in the new management environment.

A series of meetings was held with the client manager, determining in detail what the course objectives were to be and how these objectives would prepare the participants to take their places in the new management organisation. The course would have been of little value if the participants returned from it feeling unable to apply any of the lessons that they had learned.

Four major objectives were identified. The first was to help the participants to be aware of how the decisions they make have an impact on the market for railway passenger service. This meant thinking in terms of the effects of decisions on business results and customer service, as well as on the purely operational aspects of running a railway. This was the most challenging objective because, traditionally, railwaymen have tended to assume that if the operational aspects of the railway are satisfactory, then the customers will turn up to use it. Furthermore, people in posts that do not have direct contact with the public (e.g. engineers) did not readily appreciate the impact of their performance on the market for transport as a whole.

The second objective was to help participants to work more effectively in multi-disciplinary groups where decisions had to be made on the basis of wider considerations than those affecting one department. This related closely to the first objective, in that market considerations often take precedence over narrow departmental objectives.

Thirdly, there was a need to improve the decision-making process. Problems tended to be dealt with on an ad hoc urgency basis without defining and analysing the root causes of a problem before offering a solution. Participants needed to become aware that many problems recurred and were solved in isolation without consideration of why the same problem kept cropping up time and again.

The final major objective was to help participants to answer two fundamental questions:

- What are the real purposes of any work?
- How can I judge my performance?

A number of subsidiary objectives were also identified. These included:

(1) Helping the participants to apply what they had learned through experience, and on previous courses, in the emerging commercial environment.
(2) Demonstrating that real learning takes place through the learner's own efforts and not by just listening to tutors. One desired outcome, therefore, was to help participants to take charge of their own learning when they had returned to their jobs.
(3) Offering personal coaching to those participants who wished for help on any aspect of 'managing' at work.
(4) Dealing with any aspects of managing that course members wished to discuss. For example, most courses raised the problem of managing time.

How we tackled this complicated brief will be revealed in successive chapters. At this stage we shall concentrate on how we intended to ensure that participants were motivated to undertake the planned learning. This had to start within British Rail Midland Region itself. We asked that all those selected for the courses should be interviewed by their immediate bosses and the course objectives explained. This was half the battle, for the participants not only had to know the objectives, they had to accept them and identify with them if our first principle was to be applied.

However, this proved difficult, and we experienced only modest success. Frequently we found that we had to explain why they were there to some course members on the opening evening. We always provided an opportunity for everyone also to say why they were there. As the group introduced itself, each member could say what he or she did and what they expected from the course. Later on we built questions about individual objectives into the review mechanism. No matter how carefully a course has been specified, or the candidates chosen, each must have his or her say. Only thus can they begin to 'own' the process.

Almost invariably there were individuals who did not want to be there – at least at first – and one person even walked off the course. As we have argued, it is not enough to explain the reason for the course or its context. Nor can the trainer become an instant salesman for the course, describing its benefits and the forthcoming enjoyments. The only way to bring the individuals and the training session into harmony is for them to recognise that they want to do their job better and for the training to be shown to be relevant to that.

Of course it is possible that no conjunction exists. On a well-prepared training course this is unlikely. But it may take a while, we have known as long as three days, for an individual to recognise that his career prospects are going to be improved through that training activity. This is probably the most potent motivator of all.

By then our second principle comes into play. Getting a group of managers to see the point of a training exercise is not very complicated. But it is only really possible when the bulk of material used is directly relevant to the experience of the participants. The trainers actually have to know what the participants do and what their working environment is in order to focus every lesson. Above all the process of review has to refer back and underline the relevance of every element.

We determined, in addition, to use the course members themselves as a resource, which would unarguably keep the whole exercise relevant. They had so much to learn from each other that, given the right structure, they could not miss the relevance and application of what they were learning.

Personnel departments spend a lot of time with interviews and questionnaires trying to find out what skill or knowledge gaps exist among individual staff members. If they do not know how to drive or type then the need is pretty obvious. But when it comes to management skill the problem is more complicated. In many cases it is much more a question of the business having a training need. Put another way, it involves a whole level of management – as in the case of British Rail – or a whole management team such as a board of directors. (We shall say more about this in Chapters 3 and 5.)

Summary

Businesses of all kinds exist to fulfil market needs and social purposes. Managing them is the art of making things happen within those businesses through people. But the most interesting aspect of the manager's job is not what he or she does but how. Thus, to make things happen a manager has to deploy skills to enable others to understand group and departmental goals and how they may all work to achieve them.

We have argued therefore that the real job of a manager is to enable those for whom he is responsible to learn and to develop their performance at work; only by so doing will he 'make things happen'. People cannot be forced to learn. They will only learn when they are motivated, they see the point, they do it for themselves and they get a real pay-off. If people at work are encouraged to learn in this way their skills will improve to the benefit of the firm and their own satisfaction will increase – which also improves morale. All this is possible when management creates a learning environment.

There is a wider benefit, too, since that which encourages good learning also heightens motivation at work. In short you cannot motivate people, they can only motivate themselves. *A key to all this is that those who work in a business must understand why they are there.*

While individuals may have training needs, more frequently businesses have learning needs, especially in times of change, which can only be met by specifically designed programmes. In all cases these have to start by there being a clear understanding both by the client management and the participants about the objectives. This will go part way towards motivating the participants but also ensures the immediate relevance of the material which will enable them to 'see the point'.

21

We have described how motivation depends on people feeling that they do a worthwhile job. We must now turn to consider *how* they may know that.

References

1 HERZBERG, F. *Work and the Nature of Man*. Cleveland, World Publishing, 1966.
MASLOW, A. H. *Motivation and Personality*. New York, Harper & Row, 1970.

2

Good Management is Good Economics

The business of business

We all share the experience of disappointment and frustration as consumers. We generally believe not only that better products are possible but that, given a chance, we could probably do better ourselves. The world is full of people with ideas for better products and services, and to bring these about a business has to be created. The whole point about starting a business is to make products for customers. We have heard of individuals who wanted to start a business simply to make money, but the idea that one can decide to go into business without a specific product is absurd.

Before we go any further we have to do some defining. *We define a business as any activity which has as its end result the production and supply of a marketable product even if it is not actually sold for money.* By 'product' we mean any item or service which is amenable to description in such a way that it could be traded. This definition begs many questions. However, it does include all of what the 'private' sector produces and most of what the 'public' sector does too. We should like to go further and include public administration and suggest that its product is fair government.

An ice-cream van is a business and so is a bank. They have products we can recognise which have a price. But what about hospitals and social services? What of street lighting and the fire service? These too have a definable product; the problem is they do not have an easily definable market and customers are difficult to distinguish. Do they serve individuals or the community at large? Nevertheless, they must produce their output to satisfy customers and do so efficiently, which makes them businesses, too. Describing all these different activities as businesses is not to assert that unrestricted markets can provide for a sensible distribution of such goods and services. The point is that all

23

these activities involve the bringing together of men, women and resources to make or do something which brings benefits to consumers. They all require organising and that is the job of managers.

Management is the art of creating output through the combined efforts of the people in the business. It is not a scientific activity, nor is it just a craft. It brings together every facet of human ability and its practice is a skill. It hinges on the existence of constant feedback from its customers. When we refer to market pressures we do not mean some impersonal force, but the combined decisions of many customers.

How consumer choice works

It is often argued that economic activity is in some sense a modern invention. Nothing could be more wrong. From the moment one man could produce more than he needed for his own consumption, he wanted to trade. As soon as trade took place relative values were established and, even though money took a long time to make its appearance, economic man was born. Trade is a natural part of man's social behaviour and, moreover, its main characteristic is that it makes both parties better off.

Observe little boys in the playground. Swapping happens all the time. Peter agrees to give his 'twenty-niner' conker to Paul in exchange for his Superman comic. At that moment each values what the other has as being worth more than what he has himself. The swap takes place and both boys are happy. This is true in every trade. We do not actually have to exchange things – we have money. When we go into a shop we unconsciously start to make calculations. In our mind we have a complete inventory of all the things we have ever wanted to buy and we know their relative value. What is more we continually update this information bank on the basis of our current needs, tastes, inclinations and even whims. So that whenever we are faced with a good and a price, we can instantly decide if it is 'worth it'.

Naturally we mean worth it for us. Every one of us makes this decision for ourselves, but we do so neither independently nor objectively. In coming to our conclusion we can be affected by all kinds of influences. Advertising, hearsay and expectation all

24

play a part, as do looks and presentation. Cheap goods in a tasteful setting may be more highly valued than high quality in the street market. Advice from the Town Hall may be ignored in favour of the well-furnished solicitor's office. In every case we know almost at once what we should like to buy and what we consider to be bad value for money. This means that the actual acquisition of the things we might decide to buy invariably makes us more satisfied – for we value them all at the going price or more.

The next problem is which, out of all the things with prices we find fair, will we actually buy? This is the question 'can I afford it?' Economists call this the income constraint. It means that with finite income there are only so many goods and services we can purchase. The brain swings into action again and now does some amazing calculations. It not only calculates which items are the best buy, but compares completely different products and experiences, pro-rates their relative values and gives a continuous assessment of choices and purchases. It does the whole thing instantaneously, accurately and effortlessly.

In every case you ensure that after each trade you are better off. You virtually never choose items which are only just worth it. There is no need. With limited income you never get that far down the list. You are always choosing trades and purchases which enable you to acquire goods and services, the price for which is below what you would have been prepared to pay. The result is continuous enjoyment. Just look around next time you are shopping – lots of very serious enjoyment. The only dampener is insufficient income and that, for the moment, is not part of this argument.

Market feedback on performance

But what of the people on the other side of the fence? When fixing a price, most traders are aware of what it has cost them to offer the product or service up for trade. Except in the short term, they will always seek to sell for more than that. If there are more customers than goods available, they can increase the price and make short-term profits; generally competition will soon push the price down again. But if there are insufficient customers, then the price must be reduced to encourage enough people to buy. And if this price is lower than the cost of production, the only way to stay in business is to become more efficient. This is the market feedback on management performance.

There is another response, however, which is to offer a better product. Many managements continually seek to improve the quality of their products so that they can ask a higher price. In other cases no actual improvement takes place, but through superior packaging or subtle advertising the product may seem to be better. This is the market feedback on quality.

Yet another response is to change the product altogether or even to invent a different one. Increasingly businesses are having to spend a higher proportion of their costs on research, development and design. Customers' demands for novelty are virtually inexhaustible and products which either are novel or look novel find a ready market. This is the market feedback on technology and design.

In fact, most traders make great efforts to increase the demand for their goods or services so that they can set the price at a point where they can sell all they need to in order to pay all their costs, remunerate their capital and make a profit. In all cases this will be above the minimum that they would have accepted and so they too are happy.

It is axiomatic that at the point of exchange in all trades both parties are better off. This is the animus and flavour of economic activity and it is the only true guide to what people really think about the goods and services they consume: is it worth it, and can I afford it? After the trade things may be very different.

The economics of consumer satisfaction

When making our trade we have made one big assumption, namely that afterwards the object will be as expected. If it is not, disappointment is the very least of what we feel. After that comes irritation, then anger, wrath and finally revenge. Having exercised our brilliant capacity for selecting the best deal and having spent our wealth in the expectation that we would be better off, being let down is a severe psychological blow.

A familiar example of this is the widespread practice of manufacturers to package their products in such a way that the customer thinks that he is getting more than is actually there. A recent purchase of a box of chocolates caused great disappointment to one of the authors because the box could easily have accommodated half as many chocolates again. Of course, the stated contents were correct in number and weight, but the packaging invited the customer to make an incorrect assumption about the contents. This trick is very short-sighted – one successful sale and one ex-customer.

It is not just products which can disappoint us, many suppliers of services perpetrate little tricks which irritate and eventually disappoint.

Airlines have a practice which they call 'protecting the revenue'. When passengers check in, they are not told anything other than that the flight is on time. Never mind that the aircraft concerned may not even have left base or may have its engine in pieces in the hangar, this information is concealed until the passenger is in the departure lounge, baggage taken and committed to that flight. There is then no chance for the passenger to switch to another carrier or an alternative route. The airline has its revenue and the passenger has to suffer – this time!

Not to get what we expect does not just cause us to avoid the shop, or market or airline or whatever, it actually causes us to perform a complete reshuffle of our values and priorities. If there is any doubt about this then just stop here and consider your last expensive disappointment. You probably tried to get your money back and if that failed you, no doubt, swore never to patronise that business again. If your disappointment was in the public sector then that part of your value system will have jolted and you may even have changed your political allegiance.

Successful and continuing trade depends on people believing that it is worth it, knowing that they can afford it and not being disappointed. Together this constitutes market activity and the continual feedback from these is what tells a business how it is doing and where it should go next. All the most expensive market research and the most detailed image-building fails if it fails these simple tests. If a business succeeds it is because it has decided to base its plans on what the market *is* rather than what it thinks it is.

The most striking example of the converse in recent years was the Sinclair C5. The basic analysis of the problem was quite correct. There is almost limitless demand for personal transport. Consumers are prepared to pay for this, even to the detriment of more essential expenditure. The cost to the world's resources is immense and the efficiency of existing vehicles poor.

Clive Sinclair believed that a cheap convenient electric vehicle was the answer. Since electric storage technology still has not produced a cheap battery with a high power to weight ratio, he determined to tackle the other problems associated with electric traction. He developed very sophisticated charging and power control systems. He made the vehicle small and light and, above all, cheap to produce. In many ways he completely solved his own product specification.

Unfortunately, what he produced was not a cheap successor to the motor car in cities, but an expensive successor to the bicycle. Above all, he ignored all the other reasons people buy cars which have little to do with transportation. The market gave its verdict. This was not a product which was wanted in large numbers. Furthermore, since the first buyers were disappointed with poor construction and performance, even the small initial market faded away.

Customer dissatisfaction in the private sector leads to the collapse of markets and the end of businesses. It *is* possible to cut the price down to the point where even the C5 is acceptable. As long as this is above the cost of production, the company survives, but the resultant product may bring no satisfaction to those that produce it.

The public sector has customers too

In the last paragraph the private sector was specified in particular and this distinction must now be elaborated. When the public sector fails to deliver the promised service, strange things happen. In complete contrast to the private sector, where we expect bankruptcy to visit the incompetent and we would not spend a penny to save them, in the public sector there are loud calls for more money to be spent. If the Town Hall does not answer its phone it is assumed that there are not enough clerks; so they need more clerks and the Town Council more money. If there is a waiting list for acute operations in NHS hospitals, they need more doctors and nurses. Why should we assume that such poor performance is simply because of lack of resources? The silent Town Hall phones may simply be because the work of those supposed to answer the phones is badly defined and poorly managed. The hospital waiting list may have much more to do with the behaviour of staff and patients than insufficient money.

The problem in the part of the public sector that does not directly sell its output is that the beneficial market feedbacks do not operate. Disappointed customers cannot 'go somewhere else'. They have no choices. If Social Services perform badly or the Town Hall refuses to satisfy, the only redress is the very remote opportunity to 'throw the rascals out' at the next election which may be many years hence – an extremely blunt instrument of control.

Bad and inefficient service is one problem in the public sector. We would argue that even more damaging is the lack of financial discipline provided by feedback from the market. On the contrary, as we have described, all the pressures are to increase expenditure. Public employees, especially at the higher levels, enjoy an extraordinary degree of job security. Serious misconduct, even gross extravagance may result in dismissal, but mere managerial incompetence is tolerated because there is no easy way to judge such performance. The constant stimulation of the need to sell one's output is entirely absent.

The crux of market behaviour is that consumers have choices which they exercise when faced with priced alternatives. There has to be a choice and there has to be a price for market feedback to work. Most utilities and transport are simply not amenable to the exercise of choice and most public services – health, education, welfare, public order, etc. – are free and those that are not have charges which bear no relation to either the cost of production or the perceived value.

The British National Health Service, in 1993, is Britain's largest employer – vital to all, and the subject of much myth and rumour. Truth suffers in the debate about its performance because it is highly political. Most of that debate is conducted using figures of doubtful validity and the conclusions reached simply do not coincide with the everyday experience of its customers.

At a private seminar in Spring 1990, some consultants were

comparing experiences. They all spent part of their working life in private hospitals and they were all involved in the creation of the new hospital trusts for self-administered hospitals within the NHS. It was their common experience that, in private hospitals when a surgeon is booked for a morning of surgery, all the expected patients are there, ready and prepared as planned. The support functions are reliable and timely. In short, there is discipline.

In contrast, up to a third of any NHS theatre list simply do not turn up. These are patients who may have been waiting for months. In some cases they simply decide to try again later; in others there are confusions of one sort or another. The result reported by the surgeons is underused theatres, surgery lists completely out of balance and delay.

The lesson is that consumers have a very different attitude to goods and services which they perceive to be free at the point of consumption as opposed to those they pay for.

> While visiting a commune outside Shanghai in 1986, one of the authors was surprised to see patients queuing at the clinic to pay for their consultation. The official guide, a Communist Party cadre, said with pride that even the poorest peasant makes a contribution to his own medical treatment and every family contributes to its children's education. When told that in Britain these things are all free, he expressed amazement: 'How can the people value what they have not paid for?'

This is not to argue for 'privatisation'. Many goods and services in the public sector simply cannot be priced for individual consumption and our society deems that a great many services should be supplied solely on the basis of need. However, we must acknowledge this undeniable phenomenon that customers tend to be greedy about goods and services which they perceive to be free. They want no restriction on consumption and they want more money spent even though it will rebound through their taxes. The separation of consumption from payment dulls the economic senses.

The degree to which health, welfare and education are provided free is a political decision. Coping with the problem of satisfying consumer demands in the absence of market feedback is a matter of management. Neither complicated administration nor the construction of surrogate markets will solve this. If we understand that, in a market, demand *and* supply are simultaneously determined by the actions of consumers and producers, then we shall understand the size of the management task in the public sector.

That task is to provide alternative mechanisms for the normal market feedback from the consumer, and specific performance criteria and output priorities for the producer. The first is likely to involve both systems of redress for individuals and more immediate and direct control by the community through democratic procedures. The second will include clear targets, assessment and reward for individual staff, and publicly acknowledged rules for determining priorities.

However, the basic job of management in all business is to produce goods and services which satisfy customers at economic cost and to do so by successfully organising human and material resources. The methods used to achieve this are the same and all depend on a continuous knowledge of customers.

Learning to use the market feedback

Developing a management which acknowledges, understands and makes use of feedback mechanisms requires a continual learning process. There are no blueprints. Every business will find its own answers; every management must have the means to discover its own particular set of skills as well as the opportunity to learn them. This is itself a skill.

We believe that while most learning will take place within the business, more formal training must also reflect this process. It must stimulate imagination and utilise the huge fund of knowledge from within the business while enabling those who participate to learn the many detailed skills and techniques they are going to need. Thus the structure of a development programme must reproduce, as far as possible, the conditions within the business concerned.

Consider what happens on traditional 'management courses'. Perhaps there are twenty people on the course. Each individual has differing needs, experience, expectations and work background. The course syllabus tends to consist of what the tutor thinks the participants ought to learn. Because there has been careful analysis of 'needs' and 'objectives' these aims are credible both to the client

31

company and to the course leader. They also appear credible to the participants when they first look at the timetable.

In practice, however, it all works out rather differently. Each fact, opinion or thought stated by the tutor is received in different ways, and shades of meaning, by the course members. This means that each statement has twenty different interpretations. Each person receives the same message and then applies an acid test. 'Has this message any meaning for me in my work?'

The result is that of the plethora of statements made by a tutor only a small proportion are considered by any one course member to be of practical value to him or her in their work. Yet every statement is based on 'sound' management principles – on what tutors 'know' would be beneficial to the managers. This gap between 'theory' and perceived practical value lies at the heart of the problem of applying what has been learned on a course when people return to work. Traditional courses also contain case studies either used in their own right or turned into exercises and made the subject of skill training using closed circuit television. The problem is that all too often they are designed to make the participants look foolish while the 'expert' explains why everyone is wrong.

Most management-school-style case studies are of very limited use as learning material, however interesting or entertaining they may be. Firstly, in any group of managers it is unlikely that even one member will be familiar with the industry described, let alone the specific case. So everyone has to learn, quite superficially, a lot of stuff he will never use again. Secondly, no case study exactly mimics the real life of the participants because in truth it belongs to someone else – its creator and author. Thirdly, the participants are not asked to make any use of their own personal knowledge and experience outside of the specific issues being discussed. Finally, a great deal of imagination and effort has to be expended relating the lessons of the case to the experience and needs of the participants.

When these objections were first recognised an attempt was made to create 'realistic' cases. These contained a great deal of detailed information about the company or industry concerned. Unfortunately participants were still tempted to play a game which might be called 'beat the case study'. This game involved spotting gaps in the case study and asking for more information. When this was supplied – often it had to be invented – the participants would then seek to discover how the new information was inconsistent with what had already been supplied. The end result was, therefore, that the participants concentrated more on finding gaps and inconsistencies in the case study than on learning lessons from it which could have been useful in their own company situation.

To overcome these objections we have developed courses on which the members are invited to invent their own company and to use it as a basis for learning. Thus the undoubted fund of knowledge brought to a training programme would be harnessed to build up a case which the particpants would find 'realistic' in their own eyes. In other words if they spotted 'gaps' in their own invention, they would be invited to fill them themselves. Neither the game of 'beat the tutor' nor 'beat the case study' could take place.

This was first done over twenty years ago when one of the authors was asked to create a course for the Furniture and Timber Training Board. Over the years a number of other opportunities arose and the technique was refined. We have now developed it as a comprehensive learning opportunity.

Once we had agreed the course objectives with the British Rail Midland Region management, we had to consider how they could be achieved. Our first aim was to structure the course in a way that would be credible and would enable the participants to believe in what they were doing. Credibility implied that, as the course proceeded, each participant would be able to relate directly what was happening to his or her own situation at work. While no actual trading would take place, we wanted to create the circumstances in which we could simulate believable market responses or, at the very least, get the participants to speculate about them under what they would recognise as plausible conditions.

We were, therefore, concerned to structure a course in a way that would facilitate learning, rather than 'teach'. We intended to stress to the participants that the value of the course would only be assessed on the extent to which they actually changed their behaviour when they returned to the workplace. Put simply, we wanted to be able to say: 'If, when you go back next Monday, you do something differently from what you would have done had you not come here for a week, then the course will have been of some value to you.'

We wanted to challenge each participant continuously to

answer the question: 'How can I put this idea, thought or fact to practical use?' It is clear that in the abstract these would be open to many interpretations. A better way would be to encourage participants to think up ideas for themselves, test their validity with their peers and encourage them to consider applying them at their workplace. We believed that knowledge inputs from us should be limited to what the participants requested as a result of their own work. We considered this approach to lie at the heart of encouraging people to take charge of their own learning.

We decided that the basis of the course would be for the members to invent a railway and then to use their invention as a basis for further learning. Clearly participants would only think invention credible if they were asked to invent things which were realistic at their level in the organisation. We, therefore, provided a relevant basic structure of the railway and its geography.

A key part of the course design was that the participants would be asked to plan and launch a 'modernisation' scheme for their imaginary railway. We chose this as the core of the programme because the railway at that time was undertaking a whole range of such projects, and the new style of management, with its emphasis on market orientation, would be appropriate in such circumstances.

Within this framework there was plenty of opportunity to 'invent' detail and to learn lessons about markets and their impact on railway management at their level. (In Appendix I we have produced all the course instructions and briefing material for the later British Rail courses – Documents 3 and 4 are the initial brief and the map of the line.)

In Chapter 1 we declared, in stating our basic principles of learning, that people have to want to learn and they must recognise what is in it for them. Furthermore, we drew the parallel with the process of management and indicated that once these conditions are met, people take ownership of the process. What we discovered, from the many courses we have run using this technique, was that these two principles were quickly satisfied. In such a programme, once the business is invented it is immediately owned by the group. We have many examples of the creation of company logos and histories, and even in one case the printing of company stationery during the course. There are no more arguments about the case; it becomes a useful learning tool. The enthusiasm for an entirely fictitious creation which has been observed speaks volumes for how far a sense of ownership in the real world would foster commitment.

Given the slightest encouragement, the degree to which individuals seek to contribute their own knowledge and expertise is limitless. Perhaps the most surprising feature in all this is that under such conditions knowledge of the business may be applied in quite novel ways. It is amazing to watch, for example, a civil engineer, trained all his life to give conventional answers, break out and propose a brilliantly original solution to a marketing problem. Under these conditions, we have observed, there is no great effort required to relate the learning experience to the real jobs of the pariticipants. But most striking of all, because ownership is given rather than taken, the connection between performance and customer satisfaction is quickly understood, namely that customers enter into trading voluntarily and therefore their custom has to be earned.

Finally, the key point that the process is itself also a lesson is not lost. Under conditions where groups of managers are being invited to make choices about their 'own' company, it is a brave man or woman who denies the importance of market feedback based on customer choice.

Summary

In this chapter we defined businesses as all organisations that produce goods and services for customers whether directly purchased or not. Management is the art of creating these products by combining the talents and efforts of all the people in the business.

Consumer choice works through the operation of markets to provide instant and continuous information about management performance. This enables customers to make choices which tell the business about the quality and quantity of its output. The effect of these choices is felt through the price mechanism which provides management with feedback on performance, quality and design. Thus customers are satisfied and quality controlled automatically. But businesses have to satisfy the expectations on which customers have made their choices; if they do not then customers have the immediate sanction of removing their custom.

In the public sector this is not so. The market mechanism has to be replaced by more direct methods of allowing customers to express their feelings and of controlling costs. These have to go beyond budgets and expressions of public opinion, so that feedback and control become automatic. The public sector management task includes this even though it may not include many tasks familiar in the private sector. The basic skills, however, remain the same.

Management development consists in learning the general skills that enable managers in all kinds of businesses to tackle the specific problems of their own business. There is in every business a reservoir of knowledge and experience within its management. This is an asset that can provide the foundation for management training. By creating a development programme that allows participants not only to participate but also to contribute to the process by 'inventing' a business in order to learn new skills, those participants come to 'own' that process. The courses that we developed had the effect of introducing and enhancing the whole range of management skills appropriate to such an approach.

Having described the principles of a learning organisation and the market feedback mechanism by which businesses are controlled, we now move on to examine what business is about and how staff are motivated.

————3————
What Makes a Business Successful?

Working in a successful business

Do you think that the business you work for is successful? How would you judge your answer? Perhaps you would look at the annual accounts. Maybe you would check the stock market quotation. You might even ask your boss. You might just look around and see the state of the buildings. However you arrive at your answer, it is not very likely to be because you personally identify with the business's success.

Now ask yourself if you like *working* for the company. If you do, ask yourself why. The chances are that it is because of the job itself. On the other hand it may be because of the people you work with, or the people you meet, or the people you are allowed to boss. For a few it will be simply the amount of money they are paid. As we have argued, provided the pay is 'enough', whatever that may mean, this remains the least common reason.

The converse is quite different. Among those who do *not* like the job they are doing, insufficient pay is the most common reason, even though this may on examination not even be the true reason. It is a curious phenomenon, first noted by Herzberg[1], that discontent focuses on pay. Real reasons for dislike will include: the nature of the job, and a feeling of not being fulfilled; disagreeable colleagues, bosses or customers; or the job itself may simply be too difficult, or too easy.

We have noticed that those who are satisfied with their work also tend to feel a strong sense of belonging to their company. This feeling of loyalty is directed at the abstract notion of the company rather than the management who represent it, who are often the subject of fierce criticism. The company is understood not as the legal or administrative entity, but as the community embodied in it. Trade unions have built their strength on the loyalties that build up between workers. People who work together develop great pride in what they do collectively. This may not necessarily be the best way of doing the job from the company's point of view; it may even be unprofitable. When the company tries to change that situation, it runs into enormous opposition and a bemused management cannot understand why the workers apparently do not want the company to be more successful.

> Some years ago a clothing manufacturer decided, after a detailed work study, to alter the layout of the main production department. The changes and the reasons for them were explained in detail to the sewing machinists. There was immense opposition. Only after a strike was it discovered that the changes meant breaking up the informal social groups which had grown up in the shop. Belatedly the company involved the machinists in developing a new layout that would achieve the productivity improvements without upsetting the community. 'Ownership' of the changes had passed to the machinists.

The criteria for company success and those for the individual's contentment are often quite different. Why should workers be ecstatic about improved profits? On the other hand why should shareholders be pleased about the good social atmosphere in the sales department? As long as the aims of the business and those that work for it are distinct and different, management will be a process of compromise, bullying and bribery. Much management training has been concerned with making this process palatable – we believe there is another way.

The most obvious and public manifestation of the success of a business is the esteem in which the public holds its products or services. There is an old Chinese proverb that says: 'What you do shouts so loud that no-one can hear what you say.' We encapsulate this thought in the oft-heard phrase – deeds speak louder than words. In all business this is true. The customer who experiences the product always knows if it is any good. Thus successful companies, without exception, concentrate on their products and the people who consume them.

Customer satisfaction is the end for which we all work. We all know it because we are consumers too. We also know it because it is part and parcel of all those personal motives mentioned above. Notice how often 'contact with the public' is described as a most desirable feature of a job, when what is usually meant is that they like the public's applause. A product successfully delivered or a service well performed gives almost every worker a buzz.

A South London clutch repair specialist has had the premises specially designed so that one part of the workshop can be viewed by customers. It has been carefully decorated and is kept tidy and presentable. Far from making the fitters feel they are 'on show' and want to hide, working in this bay is seen as a privilege.

Being seen to do good work and gaining positive feedback from the customers is, we shall argue, the single most powerful motivator at work. *Workers do not work for managers, and they do not do it for the 'company'. They gain satisfaction from the output itself and that output must be the best. Therefore, when the majority of the workforce seek such satisfaction, the whole company performs well.* Thus we have criteria that not only say why it is a good business but why you like working there. The same criteria. Everybody can understand and share in the same measures of success. If satisfying the consumer – not just today but into the future – is the company objective, it can also be so for every individual member of the workforce.

The consequences of poor market performance

If success for the company is measured by consumer satisfaction, and contented customers give positive feedback to workers, then it follows that unhappy consumers are very bad news for the company and nobody really wants to work for a company that cheats its customers. In the end, people will go on drawing their money, but they will divert their energies to satisfying other goals. The most common of these is to maximise total income – including perks – and minimise actual work. To do this, the workforce has to gain control of the minute-by-minute management of the business. The reader may say such a thing is impossible. But it only requires a management to become preoccupied with fulfilling its own goals for it to neglect its real job. An example will illuminate this argument.

In the transport industry there is immense fun to be had 'playing with the train set'. This means that management time can be whiled away planning timetables and networks, or buying the latest vehicle. Transport is also a very public acitivity and so another group of managers can have great fun simply exercising power. They can decide who or what moves and when. Travellers and shippers are not so much customers as supplicants.

Then again transport is, by its very nature, fascinating to its practitioners. Hundreds of hours can be happily passed simply riding on the system. Transport managers are prodigious travellers and the management is invariably a very large user of the system. Promoting transport and associating with its users is also diverting, not to mention the essential visits to all the places that transport reaches. Finally, transport is very public. It has a political dimension that can provide some of its managers with endless opportunities for personal advancement – up to and including the British cabinet.

But if this is what the managers are doing, what of the workers? They also probably enjoy the business they work in. However, unsupervised and without leadership, they will seek to keep the system going to their advantage. They are generally competent and often share a love of transport with the managers, but they will develop ways of operating the system with the least effort. They will seek to bury problems, only allowing those difficulties to emerge that satisfy either their own or some manager's desire to 'fix' it. By and large the whole system will seek a quiet life. But the cost of this is perpetual demands for more staff and more money.

In the end the staff will effectively be allocating themselves and their equipment to work that they have gradually redesigned for their own convenience, while totally ignoring the plans and rosters created by management, who themselves are not dissatisfied because the plans were an end in themselves and their implementation entirely incidental. And in any case, if the system 'appears' to work reasonably well why disturb things?

Once the staff have gained control they can decide what they do and when they work. Since they are now paid simply for being there, what they do is their own business as long as enough trains keep running – or buses, or planes. By now everyone has forgotten the purpose for which the whole thing started, namely the safe and expeditious transport of people and goods. Customers increasingly become an irritating diversion and the whole organisation becomes defensive trying to maintain the form of a productive enterprise without the substance.

Evidence for this situation is all too clear. The bus driver leaving passengers floundering after him, the guard with better things to do than take out the train and the stewardess more concerned with her expenses allowances than her passengers. When we think about it, our experience of the transport industries is not particularly satisfying. But the situation is unstable. Businesses are simply not able to abuse indefinitely those for whom they exist. The customer always has the last laugh. Out of frustration he can decide to make his own arrangements. Even more likely someone comes along to offer him a real service. He discovers that planes, trains and buses can leave on time, that forwarders can care what happened to his consignment and that value for money is possible.

In the end there has to be radical change. Businesses and adminstrations do fail – the former go broke and the latter get reorganised. Though the symptoms of such neglect may be different, as between the public and the private sector, the disease is always the same. If a business is run for any other reason than the satisfaction of its customers, and especially if it is run for the benefit of its employees, eventually the entire staff will become demotivated and it will fail. Whatever remedies may be proposed – mergers, privatisation, nationalisation or legislation – the solution always lies with the managers.

Why have managers?

Management is about achieving specified business ends through people and the purpose of business is to satisfy consumers. There is so much evidence demonstrating that both workers and management have a completely different attitude to what they do when the purpose is seen to be the approbation of those they serve. The example of the transport industry is not particularly special – many other businesses have similar stories. Just think of those barren shoeshops with disobliging staff, or the appliance that does not work or the furniture 10 weeks late or the sixteenth error on your bank statement or your badly needed operation. Bad treatment for consumers is so common that we take it for granted.

It need not be so. People work best when they are properly managed. And the core of good management is knowing why you are there and using that knowledge to get the best out of the people who must help you to achieve those goals. The only goal that counts is the satisfactory provision of goods and services to the marketplace. If this, the fundamental purpose of business, is not happening, the blame lies solely with the management.

Let us state the problem in terms of the difference between what is happening and what should be. (Later in the book we

shall explain this approach.) If business is not delivering satisfactory output because of the poor performance of managers,
then it must aim at a level of management competence relevant
to the successful operation of the business. The gap is therefore a'
matter of skill, and the solution is the development by the business of any strategy which gets the right result. The process by
which this is to happen has itself to be learned. The emphasis is
now placed on developing each particular management so that it
can achieve the relevant business aims and not just on 'making
the managers better'. As we emphasised at the beginning of the
book, management is a set of general skills which have to be
combined uniquely to run each business.

We have discussed how people come to want to learn such
skills and how to make the process relevant, now we turn to the
core of the process itself. *People learn when they have the opportunity to try out skills and techniques for themselves. In other
words they learn by doing.* This is particularly true, we would
argue, in management but there are problems with such an approach. Mistakes can be very costly – they can even threaten the
business itself – so there have to be limitations on the extent to
which live practice is possible. In many cases it will be appropriate to create learning opportunities such as we describe later.

Since virtually every management job requires its own particular blend of skills, it follows that some are more suited to a particular job than others. The same is true of the training necessary
to acquire such skills. The programme as well as the circumstances under which it is conducted may have to vary with the
aptitudes and personality traits of those concerned. Almost all
management involves co-operative and group activity, and each
group needs a mix of knowledge and behaviour among its members. So before we go on to discuss actual management tasks and
how they may be simulated and developed for learning, we must
consider how to assess managers and how to place them within a
management team.

The personal audit

Managers, like all workers, need to look at why they do their
current job, why they like it – or not – and whether they consider

their company successful. Put another way, they need to know where they currently stand; their knowledge, skills, aptitude and personality. Many businesses do this in great detail through personal assessments and have based continuous performance reviews on them. Adopting a somewhat simpler approach, we believe that every learning process should be preceded by a self-administered assessment, no matter how rudimentary. We call this a 'personal audit'. It is simply a way of helping a manager to express his current position so that he can measure how he changes in the future – learning always implies changed behaviour.

That last sentence contains two important principles.

- The person who knows you best is you; so the most valid assessment of you is one arrived at by you.
- Opinion about subsequent change is not enough; only comparison against acceptable and reasonably objective assessment measures will convince people that change has happened.

It is a frequent failing in management to assume that everyone shares the same basic knowledge of the business. What they do, in fact, share are informal norms and conventional wisdom, often without realising it. Questionnaires developed within the business can be used to test this general knowledge of the business and its goals. Such a test can be extended to cover any area of management.

From this not only do contradictions and discontinuities emerge, but also each individual has a record of his knowledge and opinions about the firm at that point in time. However, where misunderstandings occur they cannot simply be corrected by telling the individual. Learning does not follow from simply being told the answer. To learn, the individual must find out for himself. Thus, many questions will have no 'right' answer. Each individual will need to be able to observe how his knowledge and views change over time.

There are many other tests and exercises that can be used to measure aspects of personality, creativity and intelligence. However, in our experience, those which are most widely accepted by the subject are those in which he or she is invited to participate. Many companies now subject their managers to full-scale Assessment Centres. These usually consist of one or two days of exercises and questionnaires. The exercises may include interviews, problem-solving and group activity. They will be observed and assessed. The questionnaires may range from the apparently straightforward to the ultimately obscure. The whole process is a development of the selection procedures used by the Army and the Church.

After undertaking what can often be a complicated series of tests and activities, some in groups and others in pairs, the purposes of which are always and necessarily hidden, the subject is given feedback on the results in the form of a long interview. While for every test detailed instructions are given, no assistance or explanation is offered and gaps in knowledge and ability have to be coped with by the subjects. All this is understandable in the context of assessment. The idea is for the company to find out about the man or woman in order to plan their future career development.

Although our approach to learning, which we described in Chapter 2, has a superficial similarity, there is a fundamental difference. We do not encourage failure as a way of testing people. In all our exercises and activities everything is open. We explain exactly what is going on and how each task should be tackled. While we sometimes hide information for tactical reasons, there are no tricks, for we believe that learning, like management itself, involves full participation – they are both open processes.

> On the first evening of each British Rail Course, invariably a Sunday, the participants were gathered together for an introductory session. That afternoon they would have travelled from all over Britain and met each other over dinner. Some would be known to each other, all of them would have sized each other up. The usual interpersonal assessments were already taking place.
>
> On most one-week management courses the participants sit at tables in a 'horseshoe' with their names on a card on the table in front of them. They can see the tutors and each other and the whole thing has the atmosphere of a management meeting or conference. At first sight our courses were no exception. The participants took their seats expecting to occupy them for the week and looked forward to what seemed to be a conventional course.

We introduced ourselves and then asked each participant to introduce him or herself saying who they were, what they did and what they expected from the course – all in 30 seconds. Then we handed out two questionnaires. We explained the ground rules very carefully. We knew that managers can feel very threatened by such questionnaires. It was made clear that this material was privileged and would never be shown to their employers. Its sole purpose was to help them to get the most out of the course.

Incidentally we made the same undertaking about the course as a whole. We believe that to create a relaxed and creative learning environment, the participants must feel able to 'let their hair down' and this is only possible if they know that it won't 'get back'. On the other hand, we always made it clear that they ought to themselves report on everything that had happened to their immediate boss because he after all was, in a sense, their on-going tutor.

The first questionnaire was a 'knowledge inventory' – a set of multiple choice questions about themselves and the railway. The same questionnaire would be given again at the end of the course and both sets of answers returned to the participants after analysis. They would thus have a record of any changes in attitude, knowledge or skills over the week. This would not only serve as a record of what had been learned, but could also be referred to later to reveal any long-term alterations in behaviour or opinion.

The second questionnaire was concerned with finding out something about how the individual participants would behave in groups. As we have indicated, our courses are entirely practical. Learning takes place while 'doing', so the entire course was to be a series of exercises and events. These would be almost entirely undertaken in groups. In fact each group was to be a railway company.

It was therefore important that the groups were so constructed that they could begin to function very quickly. We only had a week and there would not be time for randomly selected groups to adjust. Furthermore, we discovered that constructing groups according to a clear set of criteria, based on well-tested principles, itself taught the course members more about selection.

On most of our courses and all the British Rail ones we used the Belbin model of group behaviour. (We shall discuss this at length in Chapter 10, which is about working in groups, and Appendix V, in which we describe the Belbin scheme and other models.)

The Belbin questionnaire satisfies our basic approach in that it is self-defined. It simply offers a choice of behavioural responses to eight different circumstances. These are ranked by the respondent and the consequent scores are matched with the expected behaviour of eight group role models defined by Belbin. From this it is possible to predict which group roles would be likely to be performed by each participant. As we would stress later when the results were revealed, the participants were themselves choosing their own roles.

Once a course member had finished and handed us the paper, he or she received their first full description of the course. This had not been revealed before because we did not want anyone to prepare themselves. Such preparation would simply allow someone to show off and no learning would take place. However, as we have stressed, there should be no surprises, so they went off to bed on the Sunday night with a full description of what was going to happen (Appendix I, Document 1).

We, the course tutors, now had the task of creating the groups for the next morning. The most important role to be identified from the Belbin test was the 'chairman'. We believe, with Belbin, that chairmanship is a function and not a measure of status. It can be performed by the youngest as well as the oldest, so long as the individual has the aptitude and chooses to exercise it. Also it tends *not* to be associated with a high level of contribution to the group. It is the chairman who co-ordinates the activities of the group. This is in marked contrast to the view of chairmanship widespread in business, which sees the chairman almost as the tribal leader who decides for the group.

Having chosen our chairmen we then allocated the rest of the course members according to two criteria – their current job and their preferred group role. Arranging for a mix of professions was often difficult because British Rail has a lot of engineers of all kinds and so our courses reflected that. It was sometimes hard to separate them and balance the groups. We also tried to make sure that each group had at least one member who had some understanding of business aims as described earlier in this chapter.

The Belbin scheme identifies eight group roles and we usually had groups of five – in our experience ideal for management problem-solving. Some role choices appeared relatively infrequently, so constructing the groups was not an exact science. But it proved most effective. By the end of that first

> evening we had four working groups and some knowledge of
> the structure of the course group as a whole – its aspirations
> and the degree to which it recognised the more commercial
> and market orientation of British Rail.

Enabling directors and senior managers to learn requires a
rather different approach. Here the importance of role is not so
marked because the learning group will usually be an existing
management group and roles will be established. The problem of
shared knowledge, outlook and goals is, therefore, far more important. It is our experience that, without some formal method,
such groups seldom reveal to each other what they really think,
then tend to assume that the others in the group agree with them.

So the first thing we do with top managers who come on our
workshops is to give them feedback on a set of questionnaires
that they have completed in advance. We structure these very
carefully in conjunction with the client manager. We may even
have arranged interviews with the participants so that we are
able to at least try to ask the right question. But in every case we
shall be enquiring about the prime objective of the business and
the role of its product and customers in that.

> One division of a major rubber products company produced
> floor covering. It had a substantial turnover and it employed
> some 150 people in a manufacturing, distribution and selling
> operation. It was, and is, a successful business, with a well-
> known brand name. It is undoubtedly a market leader, and
> throughout 1989 and 1990 it was able to increase its market
> share and its turnover in a market which was diminishing. It
> had been well managed over the preceding years, but, like so
> many British businesses, there was no formal long-term
> strategic thinking, though naturally each year sales targets
> were set and achieved.
>
> A new Chief Executive decided that the time had come to
> think about the future of the business in a more structured
> way. He wished to involve his colleagues and subordinates in
> this process because he felt that if they had a sense of 'own-
> ership' of the strategic plan, they would be more likely to
> transform it into a reality.

He asked one of the authors, then working as an independent consultant, to act as a 'facilitator' in a series of workshops, but made it clear that whatever emerged had to be the result of the group's own thinking and not an input from an outsider.

The group consisted of the Chief Executive, the Manufacturing Operations Manager, the Marketing Manager, Senior Sales Executives, the Customer Service Manager, the Cost Analyst, the Technical Manager and the Personnel Manager of the parent company. They went away to a hotel for two days so that they could give undivided and uninterrupted attention to the strategy.

Before the first workshop each member was asked to complete two questionnaires (Appendix III, Documents 1 and 2). These were designed to discover areas of important differences in thinking about the business and the way it operated internally. They were completed anonymously. One was a 'true or false' and the other free format.

Together with the questionnaires, each participant was given a two-page document about the aims of the workshop and how it would be conducted. It stressed that the programme would be 'based on participants working on the problems of the business' and that the role of the facilitator was to help to develop discussions which would lead to specific conclusions and not himself to provide answers. The process would be open and the precise agenda would be for the participants to control.

The first session was a detailed discussion of the issues raised in the questionnaires. Each issue was introduced by telling the group how it had replied to the questionnaire. Often differences were exposed which occasioned some lively discussion. But such differences were not allowed to develop to the point where 'sides' could be taken or the group break into factions. The object in these sessions was to achieve a consensus about where the business is now and an understanding of each other's perceptions.

Two of the 14 important points which emerged from this session were:

- We have created a brand awareness, but not brand identification. Thus we have a similar problem to Hoover and Coca-Cola.
- We tend to seek to compete on price rather than maximising the potential for introducing new and improved products.

Each of these was a statement about the business as it then was, as seen by its own senior managers. These sessions are not exercises in introspection but a necessary first step of understanding. It was followed by a SWOT analysis. Here is a flavour of that exercise:

A STRENGTH – Purchasing power and good relations with suppliers enables us to maintain reasonable price stability.
A WEAKNESS – Lack of market information, other than for conventional market segments, and insufficient resources for new market research.
An OPPORTUNITY – The management weakness of a competitor which could be exploited.
A THREAT – Long-established contacts with some buyers are at risk due to retirements and reorganisation.

Having completed a pretty thorough review of 'where are we now', which, incidentally, gave an excellent opportunity for some of the group to let off steam, voice their grumbles and then start to think, the group now turned to look at the horizon.

This was a classic example of how this approach forces a management to turn to the main issue of producing for the market and we shall see later that they were then able to tackle the strategic issue which had been raised.

Summary

Businesses are successful when their products or services are held in high esteem by their customers. People like to work for successful businesses. The sure way of determining that a business is meeting its objectives is by measuring customer satisfaction. This can be easily observed and understood by every worker and manager. Thus it is the output itself which provides the motivation and, given the opportunity, everyone will strive to make that output the best. When the majority of the workforce seeks such satisfaction, the whole company benefits. Such success is the only real motivating force for managers and workers.

Poor market performance demotivates a company and tends to lead to groups within it seeking their own advantage – often at the expense of the customers, whose response to bad service is to 'go somewhere else'. This will result in poor performance and public dissatisfaction. Eventually the business will fail. If it is a public service there will be pressure for a political solution. But the real solution lies with those who manage and to achieve it they will need the appropriate management skills.

Management is about achieving specific ends through people and the business of business is to satisfy customers. The way this is done in each business is unique; every manager must deploy a specific mix of skills and techniques and the art of developing a good management is to enable these to be learned. The first step in this process is for those concerned to understand something about 'where they are now' so that as they learn new behaviour they can measure the change.

Such a process must belong to those concerned and this is best achieved if it is self-administered and the results fed back to those concerned so that they may use them constructively. Managers need to examine the myths and culture of the organisations they work in and they need to recognise their own inate talents and those of others and understand how they can be mobilised by the business.

Additionally, such assessments also enable successful groups to be created and individuals to perform the roles for which they are best suited.

We now turn to look at the manager's role and how functions and tasks should be defined within a business.

References

1 HERZBERG, F. *Work and the Nature of Man*. Cleveland, World Publishing, 1966.

4

Why Does This Organisation Pay Me?

What is your job?

Try this simple test. Write down on a piece of paper in a couple of sentences what your employer pays you for. That is called the purpose of your job. Now look at your own Job Description, if you have one. If you have none consider all the instructions you have received recently and write them down too. Now compare these with your two sentences. The chances are that they will differ. Your job description probably lists a series of tasks and responsibilities. It probably goes on to say how you are to achieve these. It may say that you are responsible for certain things and it probably lists the people you are to manage.

Typical management job descriptions contain phrases like:

- manage the department efficiently
- carry out laboratory tests
- prepare monthly accounts
- visit customers as agreed with sales manager
- plan the maintenance operation

and perhaps worst of all

- liaise with sales and marketing

Nowadays such generalities are often accompanied by another document – your personal objectives. This will be based on the principle of 'Management by Objectives'. If you have one, take a look at it and tick all those objectives for which you have *sole* personal responsibility. By this we mean the outputs that can, to a great extent, be achieved within your command alone. They do not depend on the co-operation of other managers in other departments. If you have a job which is described in terms of general expectations and objectives which are mostly beyond your power to achieve and which don't have much to do with why *you* think you come to work, do not despair. You are in good company. If the above does not apply to you then bear with us and read on.

Now think about your last performance appraisal interview. How was your performance judged? If your job is described in vague generalities then the chances are you were judged against vague and probably subjective standards. If your objectives required the precise co-operation of other managers and departments, they were probably not achieved. So you had to offer excuses and these were probably along the lines of success being out of your personal control.

We have met young managers who have worked out why they are paid but cannot get anyone to confirm a set of attainable goals. We have seen appraisals, some leading to salary reviews, which contained no objective standards with which the subject could identify. When managers ask their bosses 'How am I doing?', then 'O.K.' is not a legitimate answer; and when they ask 'What do you want me to do?' they cannot be told 'Do better'.

Management is making things happen through people. Business is an activity. It has an end – the successful production and distribution of goods or services. Therefore, every manager has, as his or her reason for being there, a small part of that end. Every manager is there to get something specific done.

The tragedy is that all too often this is never made explicit, which in turn has two inevitable consequences. First, managers themselves fail to make clear to those who must actually do the work precisely what is required. Second, in the absence of a clear purpose, the manager will make one up and the chances are it will suit him and not the business.

A 53-year-old manager sits in the office of the new General Manager with his head in his hands. He has just been relieved of his job. His own office is one of the tidiest in the company. He has perfect records of all his 1,400 staff. He clears his in-tray every day and answers all his mail on time. He visits his staff when they are sick, and he never misses a retirement or funeral. But his department is notorious for poor performance, and actual day-to-day management is dominated by local shop stewards.

He just sits there shaking his head, repeating: 'Nobody told me!' And nobody did. He had made up the job of being a manager so that it best fitted his abilities. Who can blame him? In the end he had to suffer for the incompetence of his former bosses.

The important point is that an organisations's goals are achieved by the combined actions of the people who work for it. The actions that individual managers take are the prime factor. Groups of people have very important functions in business, as we shall see later, but they do not take action. We all recognise that ships, orchestras and brain surgery cannot be conducted by a committee and yet management is often limited by the need to consult and take issues through meetings. This is because all such activities require co-ordination, and that is what managers have to be good at. The key issue is to distinguish between:

- those things that are mine and can be achieved with the resources at my disposal;

and

- those things for which I bear a collective responsibility and can only be achieved with the co-operation of other managers.

The distinction between these two is fundamental. The first set generally defines what I am paid for – why I come to work; the second set tends to define what my boss is paid for. We cannot overstate the point that, although each manager must be responsible for his own objectives, group objectives and co-operation between managers are the responsibility of the boss. So at each level there must be objectives which belong to one man or woman. *The determination of a group of managers to achieve an objective only has any meaning when each individual in the group is willing to shoulder personal responsibility for undertaking actions which will contribute to the achievement of the goal.* For this to happen the group must be managed to the point where each member wants to succeed and can. And that process is precisely at the core of this book and will be tackled shortly.

A job implies a goal

Let us return to the things I can do myself. For this to make any sense, company goals must be broken down and parcelled out for individual action. When it comes to manual labour there is little argument about this; the foreman expects to tell his men what to do. However, when we come to performance or management goals, companies often pay more attention to what it is convenient to measure than to what can be easily understood.

A municipal bus company once had an objective to run its buses so that 98 per cent arrived within five minutes of the scheduled time. This was a severe target since so many of the factors which delay buses are outside the control of the bus company management. However, the target could easily be measured because that company had an entrenched tradition of keeping records and these could be compared with the timetable. This objective was set by the Board, supported by the City Council and handed to the General Manager. He in turn passed it on to the garage managers and they to their superintendents and inspectors. There is no record that this objective was turned into specific instructions for particular individuals which would enable them to contribute directly to the objective.

Performance figures were then produced for each garage and its routes. These were scrutinised after the event and whenever punctuality fell below the standard a 'post mortem' was held. The target itself was too difficult and was seldom met. Nevertheless, great energy was expended on finding out why the buses were late. A driver would say that the bus was late because it had not been prepared properly; an inspector would claim to have misjudged traffic; a fitter had insufficient time; and the Council would be blamed for managing and repairing the roads without regard to the bus service. In every known case it was someone else's fault, and by a well-known management reduction, if something is always someone else's fault it must be nobody's fault. It followed that when the buses ran on time it was pure chance.

The situation remained unresolved because nobody really knew what to do to make the system punctual other than take extensive or expensive action right across the city. Some people did care and developed guilty consciences. Others did not and carried on as usual. For both management and councillors it introduced a whole array of quasi-action, which we shall define as activity associated with a problem that does not solve the problem but makes the participants feel better and passes the time.

If the objective was to make the buses run on time, then it could have been tackled quite differently. First, the timetable had to be 'owned' by those who must operate it. A timetable is a plan and all management requires a plan. It is pointless to publish a timetable which cannot be operated, but it happens. If procedures exist which allow those who must drive the buses to comment on the timetable and to see evidence that what they say is heeded, then they feel committed to make it work.

Second, the goal of punctuality has to be embraced as part of the 'product' of the company. Customers do not wish to consume just any bus journey put on at the convenience of the bus company. They want and expect it to take place at a particular time. In fact, the timetable is not just a piece of optional information, it is a description of the goods for sale. It is actually part of the 'contract' – even if all transport undertakings do include punctuality disclaimers in their terms of business.

Third, each worker must know what he or she must *do* to make the buses run on time. Every action must be entirely within his or her capability. Thus, drivers should concentrate on developing tactics for dealing with congested traffic. Garage staff must be able to relate vehicle availability to levels of punctuality. Inspectors must be supported in making on-line decisions. In addition the co-operation of those Council staff responsible for the city streets has to be sought and bus service criteria given to them too.

Fourth, and most important, whatever action is required of each worker, it must be amenable to direct measurement and targets of success based upon it. For example, individual bus performance can be observed and compared with a norm; or, vehicle reliability can be related directly to punctuality. Everyone concerned both inside the bus company and outside must have measures of work related to timekeeping.

This problem is not unique to bus companies. It is common to all transport operators because punctuality is the most widely recognised performance criterion. It is also the most difficult to get right and the most frequently neglected. Transport managers will claim that they do their best but poor punctuality is in the nature of the operation. But if they continue to attempt to achieve global targets, they are unlikely to make things better. If they really want the buses to run on time then they must become committed to solving the problem, recognising that there will have to be changes in what people are doing, understanding how to get commitment to such change and finding ways of judging success. Our example may be fanciful but those involved will know how to do it properly because that is what it is to be a transport manager.

Incidentally, the achievement of performance targets has a great deal to do with company culture as well. The behaviour of the whole business has to be consistent with the need to produce quality output. (In Chapter 9 we describe how this was brought home to the British Rail Midland Region Course.)

The manager's role

Because a manager is a functionary, an enabler who makes the conditions for others to work, the job cannot be described in terms of what is to be done. A manager performs a role in his company just as surely as an actor in a play. We have already made the point that the role is to organise the business and that it involves taking responsibility for a specific part of the organising activity. The definition of that responsibility is called a role description. Every manager needs to know:

- Why am I here?
- What am I being paid to achieve?

Take for example, an actual job in a factory where each major department had an engineer whose role was:

> To ensure that the Operations Manager is provided with an engineering service which enables him to meet both the short- and long-term targets. This service to be provided within standard plant operational parameters as laid down by the Engineering Manager and within the departmental budget.

This may be translated as: 'Keeping the machines in good order and doing it at the lowest cost'. Just as lawyers and accountants and other professions find it necessary to use special language to describe their activities which the rest of us may sometimes find incomprehensible, so managers may have to use their own terms in order to be precise (remembering always to ensure that those concerned understand what they mean).

In fact, this is quite a good role description. It does say what this manager is to do, for whom, to what end and at what cost. It will not change much from year to year and it therefore enables the man to say quite clearly why he is there. Above all, it is uniquely his; he can own it. What will change from year to year, perhaps more often, is what he is specifically to achieve. This will depend on goals derived from those of his boss, in this case the Operations Manager. The standard of his performance will, however, be dependent on both the operating standards and the allowable costs; and these two are also dependent on each other.

We are now at the heart of describing what managers do. Unlike almost any other profession they are occupied every day in the trade off between production standards and costs. No management task can ever be specified without also considering what it costs. The fundamental difference between bureaucracy and management is that the bureaucrat gets things done by sending messages – signing pieces of paper – while the manager must decide every action as if he had to pay to make it happen with actual pound notes. This is why every task and every action must be tested against the criteria of cost and quality and a relationship which we have seen is revealed by the market. Thus every action can be traced back to the purpose of business, namely the effective production of marketable goods.

The manager's key tasks

Every manager needs to know his key tasks which are statements of:

- The main results expected of him;
- The activities which will occupy most of his time.

We now come to one of the great problems in management and that, put simply, is communication. The reader may groan and every book on management has at least one chapter on communication, every management training programme tackles the issue and every speech by a senior manager contains a homily about it. We would argue that, in spite of all that, managers still get it wrong. There is much to be said about comunication because that is how managers convert intentions into actions. They have to talk or write to someone.

Since communication is at the heart of the management activity, we cannot ignore it. On the other hand, we do not propose to write yet another chapter about it. Just as in every company or department, improving communications has to be worked on all the time, so we shall return to the subject again and again throughout the book.

The point in this instance is that the language used to describe what a manager should do has a great influence on his perception of his role and tasks. We would argue that detailed descriptions of activities will not work. If we tell our staff what to do on a 'blow-by-blow' basis, we shall either get unthinking performing monkeys or the instructions will be ignored altogether. The same certainly goes for managers. It is much more effective to describe a job in terms of what is to be achieved, since this invites the individual to contribute and gain ownership of the job. In effect, the person will invent the job once given the objective.

Since each manager has to do his work to further the company or departmental objectives, his tasks must be described in terms of his contribution to those objectives. In essence these are a sub-set of those larger company or departmental tasks in which each key task is framed to indicate exactly what is to be achieved.

There is a well-known chain of fast food roadside cafés in Britain. The buildings and plant have all been put together to a single pattern. The external image is familiar and consistent, and the 'brand' well established. The idea is to convey to the potential customer that an entirely reliable and consistent 'product' is available inside. This is reinforced by a standard menu in words and pictures. The same food and the same service is available from Brighton to Berwick. In order to achieve this, the staff are trained to follow a comprehensive manual which describes every activity from the preparation of the food to the payment of the bill. Complete obedience to this manual is obligatory and the result consistent and inevitable.

At least that is the theory. If a standard series of instructions is given and a standard set of inputs provided, the result should be guaranteed outputs and happy customers. Unfortunately, this is not achieved, and the result is often ludicrous as well as disappointing. See the puzzled expression of a family waiting patiently to be shown to a seat in an empty restaurant! Watch the food wasted by customers who do not want the full portion but only part! Experience the frustration of an understaffed café whose waitresses have no idea how to cover for each other.

The problem is that, with the best of intentions, this management has got things half right. They have potentially a good product and the right objectives. Unfortunately, because the tasks do not reflect actual circumstances most of the time, the staff are confused and the gap between the idealised instructions and the reality of customer service yawns wide. The manual should have said things like: 'Ensure every customer is spoken to by someone within one minute of entering the café', or, 'Never leave a customer more than five minutes without attention', above all, 'Provide a service with a smile which encourages the customer to come back next time'. The whole thing preceded by a clear and comprehensive statement of the intended objective. Beyond this, the specific processes should have been left to those who do the work and those who manage them, with performance being judged only against the final outcome – satisfied customers.

Although this example refers to those who actually do a productive job, the lessons are even more appropriate for managers. They are:

- Tasks must be defined in terms of outputs. (What will happen? What will be achieved?)
- Tasks must be done by the individual concerned. (Does he have the authority, equipment, scope to do them?)
- Tasks must be achievable. (Can this be done this week, this month, when?)

The problem in management is that there are very few tasks which would fulfil these conditions in their complete purity. It simply is not possible to circumscribe the activities of a manager to such an extent that his work is separate and independent. Management is a collaborative activity and therefore that very act of collaboration has to be part of the tasks. This means that instead of simply stating that liaison and co-operation will take place, key tasks have to be specified stating exactly what must be done and with whom to achieve the desired end. This means that the willingness to co-operate must be assured; the senior manager himself must clear the necessary lines to make this manifest. So, providing the resources for our subordinates, including creating the right environment, is itself a key task.

Let us go back to the Area Engineering Manager. In order to fulfil his role, one of his key tasks will be to ensure the level of spares in his department is consistent with planned maintenance requirements. The final decisions on this do not rest solely with him, so the necessary collaboration needs to be built into the key task:

– To ensure that on 95 per cent of occasions the spares required for maintenance are available within 10 minutes of request.

To achieve this he will recommend a spares holding, justify it and negotiate its acceptance by the Operations Manager. In case of disagreement he will inform the Plant Engineer.

This is a clear statement of a desired outcome which can be unambiguously measured. It contains a number of important points.

(a) It recognises that it is impossible to have all spares available all the time. However the target of 95 per cent implies that the Area Engineer will assess the priorities and create a spares requirement to meet the target. It also implies the setting up of a replacement and reordering system.

(b) The 10-minute time limit implies that there will be a stocking system which enables any spare held to be located rapidly, whether this is held in the 'area' or 'centrally'.

(c) The cost of holding spares is a matter for the Operations Manager and the Plant Engineer; therefore, in determining how to meet the agreed standard, the Area Engineer must make a sound case, possess the skills to persuade, and know when to seek help from the Plant Engineer.

All these actions are within his control.

This is an interesting case, but not unique. This key task clearly indicated, when it was first given, that some new action was required. Its implementation required initiating activity on the part of the Area Engineer. But the same task after the first year would require monitoring and supervision and only need positive action if the circumstances changed. It has become routine. This illustrates how stressing outcomes rather than activities enables the manager to use appropriate behaviour, and bosses to apply consistent criteria whether the outcomes required are novel or continuing.

Listing these outcomes is as important as thinking out each year what the crucial things are which have to be changed if the dynamic business objectives are to be achieved. Not all tasks require the manager to be an initiator. In many cases we inherit our jobs and our key tasks are routine.

Creating a role description

In Appendix VI we show some other examples of role descriptions. They have the following points in common:

- A clear statement of why the job exists in terms of expected outcomes;
- A series of statements of what will be happening when the role is being filled;
- A list of key tasks necessary to achieve the outcomes.

A role description is more than a job description. Not only does the different name imply that the individual plays an integral part in the production of the final output of the business, it also contrasts sharply with the notion that what we do can be broken down into a sequence of discrete steps. Such analysis, beloved of those who believe in evaluated pay systems, would tend to depersonalise work and sterilise management, if it were taken seriously. On the other hand, developing a role description is worthwhile, because at the end of the process the job holder has a clear insight into what he or she is expected to achieve – personally. This idea of personal responsibility lies at the heart of good management. There should be no escape and no alibis. Either the required outcome is achieved or it is not.

The language of the description has to be clear and unambiguous and the analysis thorough. Phrases such as 'to work in a team', or, 'to support company policy' are useless because no personal responsibility for action is required; but also useless are impossible targets like 'achieving a given rate of return on capital'.

The process of creating a working role description is lengthy and itself requires considerable skill. It will probably take hours of detailed discussion between the job holder and his boss. The first time this happens, some outside assistance may be necessary. Talking the role through step by step and relating it to the company's objectives and the boss's role may, in our experience, be helped by a third party who does not know the job well. There is an advantage to having someone who can ask the 'idiot' questions that often lead to a blinding insight of clarification. When an 'outsider' really understands what a job is about, then there is a good chance that the core of the job has been properly described.

Tasks and roles as part of a training course

Learning to understand what we do and how to structure our work is perhaps the single most important skill a manager must acquire. Because it is to all intents and purposes invisible, we tend not to recognise it. However, the disorganised manager is all too common and all too obvious. In all our work with managers and directors we have not only sought to emphasise this skill but have so structured the courses and seminars as to make the lesson manifest – to create the opportunities for participants to learn the lesson.

On the Monday morning of the British Rail Midland Course, members came into the room to find that their seating positions had been moved and they were now sitting in four groups with chairmen in the middle of each one. The choice of chairman often elicited surprise but we promised to tell them why later. In fact we kept the whole basis for the creation of the groups on these courses secret because we did not want to create self-fulfilling prophecies. We wanted the members to behave as they thought appropriate and then help them to see how far that matched our expectations. We also wanted to demonstrate how groups function.

The reader will recall that one of the objectives of the course was to enhance the participants' skills in working in interdisciplinary groups. The composition of the four syndicates, who were to invent and manage their own railways, had to reflect a spread of experience and technical background. In the event, many of the participants found that they were working with colleagues from other disciplines for the very first time.

In line with our approach of working always for success, the morning would start with one of the only two talking sessions. One of the authors would explain the basis on which the course was founded – roughly the contents of Chapter 1 of this book – and then explain how it should be tackled. While course members might not take too much in, certain ground rules were spelt out and some clear advice given – all, of course, backed up with summarised written material.

The first rule was that any data, once invented, could not be 'uninvented' later. The whole course was divided into fourteen stages – basically a sequence of tasks – and once a stage was finished whatever had transpired was history. Thus, all their decisions had to stand and all other events they described would hold, unless the tutors specifically allowed otherwise. They had to live with their own history – just as in real life.

The second rule was that since they were to create a real part of the railway, they were not to indulge in idealisation or fantasy. They were to use their own knowledge and assume the world as it is, applying the real circumstances of their normal jobs to the fictitious railway. We wanted each group to believe in what it was doing.

Each stage was to consist of very specific objectives either in the form of a clear requirement or a question. How these were to be tackled would be up to the groups. But everything would be subject to time constraints. We had structured the stages very carefully so that there was always somewhat more work than they might expect to fit into the time available. This meant there was always pressure, just as there is in running any railway. However, we did build in some 'buffers' to allow any slow group to catch up. They were encouraged to organise themselves from the very beginning. It was stressed that they could only achieve what we set them if they worked methodically and assigned tasks among the group.

We told them to distinguish between roles defined in management terms (e.g. accounting or marketing) and those in group or task terms. We warned them that someone would have to take notes for the group from the beginning. Since time was of the essence, someone had to watch that. And they needed to be reminded constantly to 'keep to the point'. Later on, in Stage 11, we did ask them to assign specific roles to each other.

We introduced the idea of constant summarising as a valuable activity by the individual group members as well as the chairman on behalf of the whole group. This simple technique together with questioning was stressed as the core of all interpersonal activity, and we shall return to this later in the book. They were also encouraged to do SWOT summaries of the newly invented business and other incidents and problems as the week progressed.

While only one major presentation was planned during the week, the groups were warned that they might be asked to make mini-presentations in order to report on their work so far. Again, this reflected a very important principle – that it is an important part of understanding and checking one's work to be able to describe it to other people.

At the end of the introductory session the groups were turned loose on the first stage (Appendix I, Document 3). This required them to undertake the basic invention subject to a framework of data and a map (Documents 4, 5 and 6). We observed that in spite of our careful guidance, most groups set off headlong to complete the given tasks without any regard to organising and planning their activities. They thus immediately revealed one of the major shortcomings of the management culture of which they were a part. It was a response to a corporate attitude which encouraged managers to 'get on with doing and never mind what' that tends to be typical of production-oriented businesses.

Some groups did take a more measured approach and spent time understanding what had to be achieved and planned how it was to be done and by whom. This lesson of the need to define tasks and plan how to tackle them was eventually absorbed by all participants as we shall see. The pressure of the course on which they were embarked made that inevitable.

By lunch-time on the Monday, each group had created and introduced their own railway. They now had to invent some operating and financial data, and that was always when the fun really began.

Summary

All too often managers are still expected to assume their responsibilities from vague and general job descriptions. Frequently these are beyond the power of the individual to achieve by himself. But management is a collaborative activity with its purpose being the successful production and supply of goods and services. For this to happen, everyone must know his or her role. They must recognise their part in the achievement of company goals. They must also understand exactly how success and failure are going to be measured for them.

Every manager therefore should seek to work towards specific ends. The successful achievement of those ends requires that progress is known and the desired end is recognised when it is reached. This can only occur when there are clearly understood criteria which have direct meaning for those who are to do the job, so that they can actually do something about them. Distant global targets do not encourage positive action.

A manager is a facilitator who creates the conditions for others to achieve. At all times he must ask himself what he is being paid to do and how his activities will further that end. Once that is determined, the specific tasks that must be undertaken to get there will be identified and these will inevitably involve other people. Just as a manager will understand his job in terms of a role directed at successful outcomes, so he too has to create work for his subordinates in the same terms. He is not there just to issue instructions, but rather to help staff to understand the whole group activity and determine their roles within it.

So: Tasks must be defined in terms of outputs.
    Tasks must be specific to individuals.
    Tasks must be achievable.

The manager is not just another worker. He performs a very specific role – that of enabling others to achieve. In doing so, he assumes responsibility, takes decisions and accounts for his actions. All this has to be contained within his role description, which should be a living, working document that the job holder has developed with his boss. This process is lengthy and is often helped by the intervention of a third party as facilitator. Learning to understand what we do and how to structure our work is perhaps the single most important skill a manager must acquire.

This whole discussion of management roles has centred on the achievement of company goals. We now turn to the question of how such goals are decided and how the strategy to attain them is created and by whom.

5

Do-it-yourself Strategy

What directors do

However successful we may be, we all have dreams about our future and the business of which we are a part. At our Board Member Seminars we usually ask the participants to tell us about their dreams for the future and the answers are often long and detailed. Significantly, the contents of those dreams are predominantly about developing better products and increased customer satisfaction. We seldom hear about personal ambition for its own sake.

The old conventional picture of a top businessman 'as shown on TV' is of a rude, ruthless, pushy individual whose main preoccupation is with money. The unflattering image of Galsworthy's Forsytes has proved very long-lasting in English language literature. This is probably because few writers have ever run a business. On the other hand, the public sector manager shows up even worse. He is portrayed as incompetent and lazy, up to his neck in paperwork, totally rulebound and motivated solely by the prospect of promotion or his pension. Once more let us remember that few writers have experience of being administrative civil servants.

Although they can contain an element of truth, these stereotypes are generally extremely wide of the mark. Yet they are so ingrained that it is often hard for managers themselves to escape them. Young managers do not expect to take control of staff and organise action. Imagination and creativity are not the attributes they expect to find in a board room. As for ideals and ethics these are believed to be unheard of in business.

Our experience is quite different. Firstly, few top managers and directors would describe their dreams in terms of money and if they did it would only be to describe the size of the business or market. Secondly, they all recognise that their success depends on the willing co-operation of others and that bad behaviour is simply bad business. For most really successful men and women the real buzz comes simply from doing business, whatever it is.

Even if you ask them what they would do in the face of unexpected bankruptcy or redundancy, they will usually answer that they would do it all over again.

Most people remain unaware of how the huge array of goods and services now available to them come to be there. They just take it for granted that shops are stocked, utilities function and entertainment is available; that is until, for some reason, they do not. But managers know that the processes by which the many things we consume come to be there are very complicated. They require the co-ordination of many skilled activities and that needs all the many facets of management. But no product or service will even exist unless one day one person decides that he or she will cause it to be made. That requires vision; the ability to look ahead and imagine that something quite new and different could exist.

In the business world, the people whose eyes are focused on the distant horizon are typically called directors. Elliot Jaques[1] has described the different levels of business responsibility in terms of the time horizon of thought and attention. Supervisors are concerned about the next shift, junior managers about the next month and middle management live by budgets which tend to run for a year. General managers have to plan next year and, perhaps, look forward one more. It is the directors alone who are responsible for where the company will be in 10 years' time. In Europe we have a tradition of rewarding along the same lines. The farther the horizon the higher the salary. But this is not the whole story. *Directors actually exercise different skills from managers.* We would argue that it is by no means self-evident that someone who has been a good manager can become a good director.

Another way of looking at this distinction is to consider the car and its owner as a system. This is a man-machine system which has internal inputs and outputs between the man and his machine, and external inputs and outputs to the outside world. For example the car gives visual information (instruments), aural information (engine tone), and sensual information (orientation), and the man manipulates the controls. The car is subject to road conditions and needs fuel and oil, the man receives inputs from the world outside to determine his actions and the car outputs noise and gas.

Now, in all this process, control is being exercised on a variety of levels. The actual activity of driving once learned, quickly sinks to the level of the subconscious. The driver steers and brakes without having to consider his actions. At a higher level he is constantly responding to the world outside. He has to pay attention. He has to decide what to do next, where to drive and how. At a yet higher level he needs to decide when to fill up with petrol, check the tyres and service the car.

All these activities, undertaken at various levels, lack one thing, a larger purpose. The car has to be going somewhere – unless this is a joyride. Someone has to determine the purpose of the journey and its destination.

A business is exactly like this. It too is a man-machine system with thousands of inputs, outputs and internal feedback mechanisms. It is dependent on many inputs from the world outside and it exists, as we have said, to provide something worthwhile for its customers – its output.

Supervisors, foremen and managers control all the many interfaces within the firm. Many managers must deal with the world outside: buying supplies, dispensing the company's legal and social obligations and above all selling the output. But every company must be directed; someone has to say where it is going and how. This usually falls to those we call directors, but in some circumstances, as we shall see, senior managers must do this as well.

Strategy in business

There is a direct parallel with the Army here. It is the generals who decide the objectives and the principal moves to get there. They do this not only on the basis of information and intelligence but also because they have been given a political goal and a vision of victory. This they call strategy.

Business has adopted this term to describe the principal activity of directors. Their function is to determine the feasible futures for the business and choose the most appropriate ways of getting there. This is not a science; it is the art of creating a consensus within a group. For the resultant strategy to have any chance of success, no matter how it is derived, it must be accepted by all those involved. In the Army, strategy has been defined as 'the opinion of the senior officer present'. In business this would be a recipe for failure. The key is to develop strategy in a way which allows those who must take responsibility for its execution to gain ownership of it – they must have a personal stake in its success.

We would go so far as to state that strategy is an essential part of all business activity and none can operate without it. If it has not been developed and stated explicitly, then it exists implicitly either in the mind of the leader or, in the absence of a clear lead, in the collective wishes and aspirations of those who work in the company or department. When we discussed how management can be 'taken over' by staff in Chapter 3, we were showing how, in the absence of a clear strategy, one had been invented by those doing the job, tacitly agreed and actively pursued. Since the process of management is a sequence of decisions which cannot be made independently and are never autonomous, it follows that every decision must reflect the overall policy – often confused with strategy – of the business.

If there is no policy, then those that make the decisions either assume one or they make it up. *By policy we mean a body of consistent guidelines that determine how those who run the organisation are to behave.* For such a policy to be coherent and sensible it must have a purpose and *that* is strategy.

In areas of the public sector we call this process politics. Our representatives are elected because of their declared support for a general direction of affairs. This, in well-run councils, they refine into a strategy, and that forms the basis for their policies. In recent years this level of political activity has tended to become debased so that, for example, reducing local taxes by 10 per cent is called a policy. In this case the policy is lower taxes and the objective is a reduction of 10 per cent.

A board of directors must follow a similar process. At some point the members must make clear to themselves and one another where they want the company to go. Then they must determine how this is to be achieved. The process requires commitment, imagination and great perseverance.

The mission statement

The starting point is a clear and, often, public declaration of the purposes and objectives of the business. Such documents have come to be known as 'mission statements'. Many major businesses now have them and they are also appearing in the public sector. While we recognise that the writing of mission statements has become rather fashionable, there seems to be little consistency about what they are for and what they should contain. We would argue that such a statement is a necessary part of every strategic debate and should have the following characteristics.

- It describes for everyone exactly what the business of the organisation is.
- It enables those who lead the organisation to declare clear objectives for it.
- It tells all who work for the organisation what it is going to do and thereby enables them to recognise what contributions they can make and how.
- It tells the organisation's customers why it exists and the nature of the products and services it intends to put on the market.
- It tells the world at large what the organisation aims to achieve and how.

Thus a mission statement is at one and the same time *an article of belief, a description of behaviour and a menu for action*. It should be a public statement because that way it requires the commitment of everyone concerned since they have to act on it.

But a mission statement has another, different, but equally important purpose. The very activity of creating such a statement makes those involved feel quite differently about their organisation. It forces them to review their own thoughts and feelings; it reveals to those concerned their strengths and weaknesses and it often illuminates new opportunities for action. It can be a very unifying process. We shall return to this below.

While the main responsibility for creating such a statement must rest with the directors, or their equivalents in the public sector, in order to gain the commitment of those who must implement it, they should ensure that the process includes some form of wider consultation. Some of the more enlightened boards of directors have opened up the process and arranged for there to be consultation at every level. This carries with it the obvious consequence that the results, even when not to the taste of the directors, may nevertheless have to be incorporated in order to avoid some very destructive disappointment.

Because of this, some boards, having decided to devise a strategy, have nevertheless tried to keep the process secret. In our experience this does not work. That the business mission is being discussed will always become known, so frustration is inevitable. It is not possible to feign participation; such a charade is quickly recognised for what it is. Since the implementation of a strategy requires the wholesale co-operation of management and staff, their dissatisfaction will defeat the whole process anyway. If boards want to retain all policy in their hands and run the business as an authoritarian organisation – a perfectly legitimate principle – then the processes we describe here are wholly inappropriate. There is, however, plenty of evidence that such businesses are less likely to be successful.

To be useful, a mission statement must be understood. It must not require lengthy explanations. It must be immediately clear and unambiguous to all those to whom it is directed. Management jargon is wholly inappropriate. While the writers may not aspire to Churchillian English, it should at least be comparable to the best commercial copy. The problem is really one of style. There is usually a strong desire to keep such statements short. But sometimes this can result in something so compressed as to be unintelligible. On the other hand, some managements try to get in every idea they have ever had, no matter how trivial. This merely bewilders the audience.

Each section should encompass a recognisable and discrete set of ideas. It should lead the reader from aspiration, through behaviour to action. In other words it should say: 'This is what we are, therefore we shall do the following.' While the process of arriving at the mission statement almost inevitably produces a sort of verbal camel, i.e. designed by a committee, those concerned should try to have the courage to commission good communicators to make it generally intelligible.

Whatever emerges from the process, it will be a statement of mission and that means the business is going somewhere. It must be dynamic. The test is to be able to ask: 'From this statement can we tell where the business will be in five years' time – what will have been achieved?' If that cannot be answered, it is not a mission statement.

Finally, a mission statement will not only be read by the sympathetic audience of those inside the business. It will pass into the public domain. Those concerned have to be aware that statements understood within the context of a business's domestic affairs may have a quite different interpretation when more widely disseminated. So care has to be taken to see it from outside as well.

Creating a strategy

It is our experience that the actual process of creating a strategy can seldom be done in the first instance without the help of some outside intervention. This may be an external consultant or someone within the company who has the confidence of the board. Such a facilitator is not there to contribute technical expertise on strategic planning, though he might do so, rather he is there to ensure that the built-in assumptions, prejudices and habits of the board members do not 'get in the way'. His role is to ask the awkward questions, or test well-tried assumptions, or tackle behaviour that may inhibit the group. Such an important enabling function cannot be done inside the board, but without it important issues may never be tackled nor creative solutions aired.

We have worked with a number of boards and senior management groups while they developed their strategic thinking and once the 'ground clearing' described in Chapter 3 has taken place, the key questions concerning goals can be posed. Inevitably this will be a bringing together of business goals and those of the individual directors or managers.

Having analysed their present position at the start of their first 'workshop' (described in Chapter 3), the Management Group of the rubber products company next considered the future. Each member was asked about his own personal 'dreams' for the business. Out of the following discussion four key words emerged to describe the future to which they could subscribe:

- *dominance* – the intention to dominate the market;
- *aggression* – towards competitors at home and abroad;
- *Europe* – the single market in 1993;
- *contracts* – a major opportunity.

From this debate a first draft mission statement was formulated:

> We aim to increase our share of the quality West European domestic and (industrial) contract market, while maintaining profitability. To achieve this we will invest in technical innovation, additional production capacity, strive to improve trade and consumer perception of our products and provide well-researched and reputable new products.
>
> We aim to be a professional, aggressive, innovative team which will enable our share of the domestic UK market to grow by 2 per cent each year for five years; to penetrate the UK contract market so that we hold 10 per cent of market share by 1994, and to identify, educate and develop the West European market.

The next step was to identify the key areas for action in the realisation of this mission statement. In other words what had to be done and by whom:

- Increase production capability;
- Launch new products;
- Formulate three market plans: domestic, Europe, contract;
- Improve warehousing and distribution;
- Enhance the company information systems;
- Find and provide the people resources.

The group was then split into two smaller working parties to consider these tasks in detail. For each one, criteria were identified by which it could be said the objective had been achieved, i.e. 'What will be happening when . . .' Then the series of sequential actions and events were outlined which would have to take place to meet the criteria.

If we look at the first task, two of the criteria suggested were:

- Standard lines will be available 'off the shelf';
- New custom lines will be available three months from order.

In this case the actions required would be complicated and numerous. The key objective was to improve warehousing and distribution, the criterion was a guaranteed 24-hour delivery, and the actions started with a study of how to do it.

Once each working party had reported back and the objectives, criteria and action had been agreed, one member of each group was made responsible for ensuring that each action took place by a specified date. This individual was not necessarily the particular functional head, though he had to have the relevant authority. The idea was, when practicable, to give responsibility for progressing action as a way of developing and broadening experience and skill. True management development in action.

The written summary of the first workshop is worth recording:

> The clear conclusion was that implementation of the strategy will involve people in doing additional and different things. This implies that everyone will need to consider the use of their time and to stop doing things which do not directly relate to the strategy. This will put a high premium on everyone knowing what they have to do and how.

Not only did the group and its Chief Executive develop a strategic plan, they also enjoyed the process. They all left with a clear understanding of what they had to do and just to ensure that the whole process was not simply an amusing game, it was agreed that there would be a follow-up workshop in six months' time.

These workshops did not involve a group of directors seeking a winning strategy for a large business. Nor was it about how the public sector decides how to manage its scarce resources to meet popular aspirations. It was a group of subsidiary managers who took time off from their day-to-day work to consider the wider implications of what they were doing and to take their future into their own hands. This was by no means the end of the story, as we shall see in Chapter 12.

The conditions for good strategy

The rubber company had an enlightened and skilled Chief Executive who recognised the importance to himself of the process he set in train. But he realised that his own position and personality would inhibit the very process he sought. So he delegated in the most sophisticated way, to his own and his company's benefit, the leadership of the exercise to someone interested but uninvolved. He had to trust his colleagues not to take advantage but to co-operate in the process. This ability to trust one's colleagues is basic to this approach, and is, we shall argue in Chapter 11, a crucial characteristic of good leadership.

So the seminars were led by an outside facilitator. Without him they would simply have been just another management meeting, or, worse still, a complicated game by which the participants tried to rearrange the company pecking order. An important task of such an outsider is to keep the show on the road. There has to be a structure. Even though the participants may think they are making it up as they go along, to produce useful outcomes the whole event must be disciplined.

Then again, without an outsider the official hierarchy will prevail, people will defer and things will be left unsaid. In such circumstances it is unlikely that the conclusions will belong to the group but rather to the boss or the dominant participant. The facilitator can break up the internal pecking order by assuming his own delegated authority and ignoring it. He can then ask awkward questions of anyone and arbitrate in arguments. Above all, the facilitator enables the group to look at its own deliberations through his eyes. He it is who summarises, who moves the debates forward, highlights the questions and lists the conclusions. He is concerned with the process so that the participants can give all their energies to the content. Finally he reports on the whole process as objectively as an outsider.

We can draw a number of lessons from this case. First, any business, or part of it, will benefit from considering its strategic aims. Inevitably these will focus on the market for its products and beyond that to its customers. Whatever future is desired, it will depend on satisfying those customers – who through their purchases create business prosperity. It is our experience that every such group needs little encouragement to put this at the centre of their deliberations.

Secondly, and this follows from the above, such a group needs to include a proportion of members who have a direct, first-hand knowledge of customers and their requirements. A successful strategy is fashioned by forging a partnership between those who produce and those who must sell. Surely, we in Britain have enough bitter experience of producers making what they want, from Concorde to the C5, and expecting it to be sold, to know that is wrong. In recent times we have also seen the rise and fall of companies dedicated to 'selling at all costs and never mind the producer' even if he is driven out of business. Only a balance works.

Thirdly, such an activity must itself have a measurable output. There must be action and it must be the responsibility of individuals. Standing up in front of your peers and saying that you accept the responsibility of doing a specific task bestows a high degree of ownership. Under these circumstances, action – successful action – is likely. What is more, by accepting the criteria for achievement there is considerable peer pressure for success.

Fourthly, as individual tasks are owned, so the whole strategy becomes the property of those who developed it. Its success requires the combined efforts of the whole group. We have noticed how through such exercises one manager will become aware of another's responsibilities for the first time. New collaborations have been forged under such circumstances.

Fifthly, nothing is set in stone. Mission statements, action plans and criteria for success evolve as the business progresses. This is a continuous process of feedback, review, diagnosis, planning and action. Strategic planning is an activity not a state of grace. Every business must listen to the market, interpret the message and act. The process described here is one way of doing this.

But perhaps the greatest lesson is that the workshops are fun. They give great satisfaction because the people involved understand that they are at the heart of decision-making. This fact has led to an interesting sequel in the company concerned. Junior members of the sales staff noticed that there was a greater sense of purpose in the business. They asked if they could hold workshops of their own so that they, too, could have an input into how their activities might enhance their contribution to the strategy.

Everybody needs a strategy

It is not just at the levels discussed above that we need to understand the importance of business strategy. Unless there is a clear sense of direction, there is no context for decisions within a business. We are all too familiar with the sight of some of the largest businesses in Britain, both public and private, lurching from decision to decision without any clear direction. We also have the opposite example of some of our most successful businesses. If line managers are to understand this fully they need to be exposed to the processes by which strategy is converted into working plans.

Late on the Monday afternoon of the British Rail Midland Course, the groups were asked to express in one sentence the strategic objective of modernising their particular railway. Remember, they had been asked to invent an existing railway. The second exercise was to create a financial and operating structure for it and we shall return to that in Chapter 9. Now they were told that the line was to be modernised but not why. They were asked to say in one sentence what such a modernisation was to achieve.

It might be thought that with all the constraints placed on these invented railways and the assumption that a political decision had been taken to modernise, such a request would produce a virtually uniform response. Far from it. We seldom had two that were even similar on the same course. Some groups saw it in social terms, others as a purely transport investment, yet others as commercial and yet more in a railway context. Each group expressed their own aspirations. But the lesson was not lost that any one of these objectives could be the result of a much wider consensus.

They were told that having thus expressed an aim they should consider the wider implications and its timing because all their subsequent work and decisions should reflect this statement. In fact, it was quickly seen that to have recognised an overall objective, individual decisions had to have a context and a meaning. On this basis they could move on to consider the new product that the proposed investment would make possible.

Summary

There is a clear distinction between the role of a director and that of a manager. A director has to be concerned with the longer-term aims and objectives of the company. A board of directors has as its prime task the development of these and the duty to inform the whole business about them. That statement of what the business is and where it is going has come to be called a mission statement. It is an article of belief, a description of behaviour and a menu for action. It contains the main strategic thinking of the directors and will be the basis of all decision-making in the business.

Most strategic planning is not dependent on a great deal of detailed information. The activity of strategic planning should involve everyone and should be as open as possible. The knowledge and experience embodied in those who work in the business should be mobilised. In the final stages, we suggest that the process needs the intervention of a facilitator who will help directors to test their assumptions, question their prejudices and realise their dreams.

While formal seminars and workshops are not always possible, the process should enable directors to: take a hard look at where the business now is; decide where it is to go; devise objectives; specify the criteria for success; define key tasks; and review the process. The resultant strategy will enable directors to provide an environment in which managers can manage effectively and successfully. It is always about presenting the products of the business to its customers and the key to that process is marketing. It is to this we turn in the next chapter.

References

1 JAQUES, E. *Measurement of Responsibility*. London, Heinemann, 1972.

6

Market Research for Mortals

Innovation is not enough

'Make a better mousetrap and men will beat a path to your door.'
But the markets are full of gadgets that nobody wants. The belief
that you only have to make an interesting or different product
and people will want to buy it is deep-rooted in Britain and
widespread in many other countries. It is not the way of the successful enterprise. There is a basic distinction between invention
and innovation. Invention is the act of making one device, one
tool, one machine which does something never before seen and
which works. Innovation can be distinguished as manufacturing,
producing or supplying a good or service which is new and
which is seen to produce a surplus over the cost of its production
and can therefore be successfully sold again and again.

To be successful a new product must answer a clearly articulated need at a price the customers can afford. No matter how
clever the inventor or how convinced he is that 'everyone' wants
his new gadget, an assertion of need or usefulness remains just
that. Since innovation requires a positive market response, we
have to try to predict that response before we innovate. That is
what market research should be; not the attempt to confirm the
inventor's prejudices nor the producer trying to persuade reluctant buyers. Rather it is the constant feedback from the market
which informs the producer.

However, businesses are not just concerned with new products. The great majority exist to make possible the repetitive and
reliable supply of existing goods and services to satisfied customers. All too often managers assume that they have to keep
changing things to ensure commercial success or even business
survival. The evidence is to the contrary. For every novel product which successfully enters everyday life there are thousands
which continue to be completely satisfactory. Here, again, the same
rule applies. The customer knows what he wants and resents

being told what to buy by businessmen. 'If it works don't change it' is not a bad precept. If one looks around at the most success-ful commercial enterprises, they are characterised by great conti-nuity of product which engenders deep customer loyalty. This is true of consumer goods like the Volkswagen or the Aga, food-stuffs like cornflakes and services like McDonalds or Marks & Spencer. With such products the problem is to maintain markets and reinforce the loyalty of customers and that also involves constant attention to feedback from the market.

All this is not to argue against change and innovation, but rather to emphasise that it is a characteristic of successful companies that they institutionalise the process of development. Every manager becomes involved to the point where it becomes a crucial part of his job to scrutinise all aspects of production in the light of the market. We would argue that this is not only a crucial part of the manager's job, but without it everyday performance will decline. The real art is to balance innovation and continuity for the benefit of the customer and the advantage of the business.

The question then arises: 'How does a manager judge the fu-ture potential of his product, and how does he know which inno-vations to back?' The answer is simple; the means difficult. *The only reliable measure of current product performance and future potential is the market; by this we mean the real decisions of consumers when faced with choices about purchasing actual products at actual prices.*

The market made easy

The most reliable measures of market performance are the actual sales figures. These tell us exactly what happened. They are like the weather outside. If it is raining we know we will get wet; if the sales figures are bad we are going to get our financial feet wet. However, like the weather they do not tell us why, and as a method of prediction they are as useful as yesterday's rainfall figures. Management action based upon such past data tends to be a process of trial and error.

As managers, we are interested in what is going to happen. So we turn to traditional market research, which has tended to focus on asking questions through surveys of one form or another.

Often these are very sophisticated and involve meetings and interviews, complicated questionnaires and even simulations. The resulting reports tend to have great apparent authenticity. But there is a problem. These methods, though useful, all suffer from the drawback that answering questions is easy, but the only consumer behaviour that really counts is when the customer uses his *own* money to make a purchase decision.

> A recent bankruptcy concerned a company which was launched a couple of years ago to market a hot water bottle with no water. Instead it was filled with an inert gel and was permanently sealed. This was a good idea which was thoroughly researched in the conventional way. A market research firm found a substantial demand at a small premium over the conventional item. The product was put into production, whereupon it was found to cost more to make and distribute than the predicted selling price. There followed a number of price rises and the market disappeared. The Managing Director complained that the banks were impatient, the manufacturers inefficient, and the distributors greedy; and in any case it was a great idea which the public were eager to buy.[1]

The point here is that all market research has to include a price. That is why 'test marketing' is particularly popular with the soap and sweet manufacturers. Unfortunately, many product and service innovations cannot be test marketed because in order to produce the new product, the old one has to be abandoned. While test marketing of a completely new product may be feasible, even a modest launch may mean a large unrecoverable capital investment.

There is a third approach and that is to look at the potential market as it now is. No innovation is so far out that it will not in some way displace some current consumption, because any consumer purchasing the product must forego something else in order to afford it. A great deal of data always exists about any market. We can find out how many potential purchasers there would be, what their incomes are and what their current tastes and purchasing patterns are . All this 'desk research' using public and private statistical sources can be used to build up a pretty comprehensive picture of the potential market. From this we may begin to deduce how the market will react.

No matter how it is done, market research must lead to some

sort of prediction and that requires a great deal of interpretation. One of the most serious problems in recent years is that, like 'planning', market research has been carried out by specialists who operate independently of line management and who often have no responsibility for the end result. Even worse has been the tendency of top management to use and even misuse the results of market research because it has provided easily documented and numerical answers to difficult problems about which no consensus exists.

In 1977 a large European airline was facing strong competition on a number of its long-haul routes. The company had new but inexperienced management who were keen to tackle the problem. One route was the ultra-long stretch to Australia where the major player had succeeded in creating a very strong 'identity' around some neat product improvements. A great deal of this was cosmetic, but it had been accompanied by substantial improvements in punctuality and reliability. A research team was set the task of finding out what would appeal to the predominantly Australian and migrant traffic and recommending a product development.

Meanwhile on other Far East routes there had developed a great deal of what the airlines call 'fare discounting'. What this actually means is that very cheap fares are made available in certain markets by selling agents with the collusion of the airlines. The consequence is that passengers sitting next to each other on any particular aircraft may have paid very different prices for the journey. This gave rise to much unhappiness among passengers who saw that superficially they were all getting the same service but paying vastly different fares. The truth was that the cheap fares had conditions attached to them and were only narrowly available and that was why they were cheap. Once again market researchers were asked to look at the problem and recommend a solution.

The first group reported that the airline should 'brand' its product to Australia. A name would be given to the whole service, cabins re-decorated to match, aircraft named and special menus introduced. There would be substantial promotion and advertising. Most importantly, the basic service had to improve to reinforce the brand image. All this to be done at no extra cost to the airline.

The second report was more radical. It proposed the creation of a third class to come between first and economy. It proposed that the airline make a virtue out of a multiple fare structure by having three differentiated categories of service. In this new 'middle' class passengers would have more space, better seats, nicer meals, free drinks and so on. Meanwhile to make it quite clear that economy

82

passengers were on cheap fares, that product was to be made more spartan. To give the new class the aura appropriate to the predominantly business market it, too, was to be 'branded' with a name appropriate to its status.

Now it must be said that the idea of differential pricing on the same plane with recognisably different on-board service had been around for some time. It had very sound economic and commercial justification. It had been resisted because it meant quite considerable redesign of the aircraft cabin – a big investment – and some very sophisticated seat-booking programmes in the airline's computers – also a big investment.

These two market reports were both presented to the Marketing Director in early 1978. At that time he had another, much bigger problem on his mind. The airline was suffering severe loss of market share on the North Atlantic routes. The problem concerned both the poor performance and some very aggressive behaviour by competitors. He had a problem and some solutions. He put them together and announced the launch of three-class operations with a special name for the new class and an overall branded product for the Atlantic services to be introduced the following autumn. The fact that the solutions belonged to different problems and that the Atlantic problem had not in fact even been analysed was lost in the enthusiasm of innovative action.

This announcement was received with consternation by those responsible for actually running the airline. The engineers simply had not designed either a 'middle' class cabin or the flexible cabin that such differential pricing required. Cabin services management had never been consulted about dividing cabin crews into three. Ground services had no idea how to manage three classes on the ground, and so on.

Meanwhile the 'branded' product was going to cost the caterers, the engineers, the crews and everyone additional expense and managerial resources at the same time. Unfortunately, all protestations about implementing such a major change in six months were treated as disloyalty and prevarication. Even with the greatest effort possible, some of the features of the new products given huge publicity in America, such as wider seats, were simply not going to be available. Others could only be achieved by compromising normal performance.

But much more seriously, these great product changes were going to worsen the real problem which was one of unsatisfactory operational performance. Punctuality was very poor, the serviceability and cleanliness of the aircraft was bad, the performance of all the operational staff, riven with industrial disputes and inappropriate work practices, was deplorable. This was why the airline was

losing its markets. The line managers, in daily touch with the customers, knew this and what to do about it. The new class and its
brand did indeed make matters worse and in November 1978 the
airline reached the depths of poor performance.

The effect of all this was not just to make a bad situation worse,
but to alienate the airline's most important customers – the regular
business travellers. They were made extravagant promises in the
name of brand promotion, which then could not be kept. What they
wanted was a punctual, courteous and clean airline that did not lose
their baggage. What they got was a pretentious charade as the airline tried to cover up its undoubted deficiencies with a marketing
smoke-screen.

It took three years to recover from this, during which time the
three-class cabin proved to be a sensible innovation and brand
names passed into history. At the same time the operating managers
regained control of the product and the airline learned to keep its
promises.

There are two powerful lessons to be drawn from this story.
First, market research is a continuing conversation between a
management and its customers. Sales figures alone tell us
whether we are successful; complaints tell us of our failures.
Market research helps us to understand why something has happened and what we might do in the future. Management must
make use of all the different approaches and not react on the
basis of just one. The Far East research studies might have been
applicable to the North Atlantic, but to apply them in the face of
other evidence was foolish.

Secondly, because market information is gathered at the point of
sale and remedial action will always require line management resources, it is line management that must take the central responsibility for marketing. Marketing and production are part of the same
thing. No business can survive unfulfilled promises, for what is
said to customers about a product or service becomes an integral
part of that product or service. Thus all promises have to be costed
and planned for by those who must deliver them; they in turn must
make provisions to judge and monitor such performance.

Marketing as a way of life

None of this is to imply that marketing specialists do not have an important part to play. Detailed studies of the market together with the day-to-day experience of managers explains why a product is successful and how it may be developed. Observing the market, looking at the product through customers' eyes, has to be a way of life for a manager wherever he finds himself in a business.

Perhaps we should pause a moment to define some terms. By 'market research' we mean the systematic collection and presentation of data about the market for a particular product or service. 'Market information' is any one set of data which forms part of such research. 'Marketing' itself is the business end of such activities and consists in the development, production, promotion and sale of goods and services designed to fulfil particular market needs.

It is clear that because, as we have argued, these are the central management activities, all managers have to be involved. All too often marketing has been what other people did. Specialists there must be, but the example above serves as a grim warning of what happens when it gets away from the managers. To be of use to a management, marketeers must use terms which ordinary managers see as relevant. Managers want to be told not only what the figures are but what they mean and, above all, what can be done about them.

At an early stage in his career, one of the authors was a commercial manager in charge of a section of a service business. Each Monday morning the General Manager would have his departmental meeting. This would always begin with a discussion of the sales figures for the previous week. This 'discussion' would start with everyone 'looking at the figures' – which in many cases they were seeing for the first time. There would then follow a series of comments such as 'Scotland did rather well' or 'Pity about Newcastle'. The group indulged in a sort of group chunter about the numbers in which those 'responsible' for the good figures felt better and those with bad figures felt impotent.

At no time in the meeting was there any attempt actually to *do* something about the bad results or capitalise on the good. That was all supposed to be something for the marketing division, but if there was any responsibility it belonged to those around that table.

Market research and market information matter, but they have to lead to action. For this to be relevant, management has to take the lead. The problem being addressed has to be specified within the overall aim of the business. A great deal of information about the market will already exist among the managers themselves. The problem is that they tend not to realise how much they know. It is possible, and from our experience even probable, that you, the reader, who may be a manager responsible for production, technical matters, engineering or any aspect of a business not directly concerned with marketing or selling, remain unconvinced that you have a real, positive contribution to make to your company's marketing decisions. When you read about the experience of the BR managers on page 90 later in this chapter, you may yet change your mind.

The elements of marketing

If we start from a product, new or existing, there are four questions which a manager must ask. They are in fact the most fundamental questions. The dreadful truth is that they are frequently not asked. All too often management starts by asking who will buy what it has already decided to make. The crucial questions are:

(1) Who are we selling to?
(2) What do they want?
(3) What should we produce?
(4) Is the price right?

Define the size of the potential market

Market research tends to be expensive. So a product manager will make use of as much free or cheap information as necessary. Public libraries not only contain government statistics but also a host of privately collected ones such as annual reports, newspapers and journals and reference books. Often describing the market is a lot easier than managers think. There is, however, one very common error. Because so much market information is given in terms of sales, it ignores multiple purchases. What is particularly important in forecasting demand is the number of customers. For example, we often hear that London transport carries a million commuters each day – but this is less than a half a million customers.

Describe the needs of potential customers

The obvious way to find out what people want is to ask them. As we have already noted, this suffers from being divorced from the actual expenditure of money. Managers tend to have much more immediate sources. Salesmen provide constant feedback on what customers want and the customers themselves complain and congratulate. With new products and, to a certain extent, old ones this information has to be structured and it should emphasise ends and not means. The questions should ask what the customer expects to have happened in order to be satisfied.

One of the most striking developments recently has been the growing importance attached to 'customer service'. This is not just because businesses believe this to be in some way good for trade, but rather because customers now see it as part of the product. In other words, it is not enough just to sell the goods; the *way* they are sold matters too. An active management will be constantly defining and redefining its products in the light of such feedback from the marketplace. At times of major change in the product this should not be ignored in favour of some 'one-off' research. The two have to be put together.

Specify the product in the greatest detail

Successful managers know that the whole of the relationship of a business with its consumers constitutes the 'product' in the widest sense. However, if the customer wants a mousetrap do not try to sell him a shotgun, no matter how nice you are about it. All product definitions should have two parts – necessary and discretionary. A lawn mower is supposed to cut the grass. This is a necessary characteristic. Its colour, packaging, delivery, after-sales service and so on, are discretionary. This is not to say these latter characteristics are unimportant – they may well be what sells the lawn mower in the end.

The importance of defining products this way is that it helps prevent what happened to the airline in our example. In their case they forgot that air transport from A to B at a certain time with a certain reliability was a necessary part of an airline product. Every manager must remind himself about these necessary characteristics – for that is why the business is there. So all the time managers must ask: 'Does it do the job?' Only after that can we begin to review and develop all the other aspects of the product.

Ensure that costs of production will allow for an appropriate selling price

This is the part of market research which all too often goes wrong. If the most beautifully produced product is put on the market at too high a price, there will be no buyers. Many product features wished for by customers fail when subjected to the market. On the other hand, as we have seen in the food industry, nowadays consumers will pay very substantial premiums for product enhancements which they find useful.

> Recent years have seen a very large increase in sales of chilled, frozen or sterilised prepared meals. This is the same food we always bought only now it is virtually ready to eat and its preparation has added value which is recoverable in the market.

Every change in sales, every swing in customer opinion and every piece of market research has to be tied to price. All too often price is expressed as a product feature. We have even seen market research which included low price among product features ranked by potential customers in a survey. Naturally they chose it; we are all in favour of low prices just as we are against sin. The point is that price is a *consequence* of a product definition. If the customer demands something then it must be costed and offered back to see if he will indeed buy it. A water-free hot water bottle may be demanded – but not at twice the price of the conventional article. Thus the circle is closed; a product with a sale price allows us to ask who are we selling to and at how much they will buy.

A market-oriented management

Until the last ten years, British management, whether in the private sector or the public, tended to concentrate either on producing the goods and services, or on the financial affairs of business. Both of these are important, but we do observe that other countries have somewhat different priorities. In other countries, perhaps most notably Sweden, the product itself has been the great preoccupation of business. Good design, quality in production and pride in services well performed has been the rule. While in America, as always, the customer has been king. All business there is oriented to meeting customer demand at the keenest price, for if your business does not, someone else's will.

In Britain we seem to have come late to the benefits of a market-oriented business. As we have argued here, the satisfaction of providing customers with good products at sensible prices can become the unifying motivation for the whole business. In such a case, market information becomes part of the everyday conversation of management. To work in such a firm is to hear about sales, customers, competitors and the products all the time. In a market-oriented management, directors and managers spend time out in the market-place, be it the shops, the streets or whatever. They go to trade fairs not to lurk on their own stands, but to visit others. They are always testing their own products against the competition. Above all they *want* to speak to customers to hear what they think.

Thus a manager widely removed from the point of sale nevertheless spends time getting to know what customers think about the product. As part of his everyday activity he will consider how far his own activities either help or hinder the making of the best product possible.

The British motor industry learned almost too late the truth of this. Not only did production workers show little interest in the customer, but toolmakers and maintenance engineers behaved as though he did not exist at all. Meanwhile in Japan, through such techniques as quality circles, every worker was given company time to consider the product and the customer. They were encouraged to discover how work could be developed to improve the product, which developments were to be tested in the market. Staff at all levels were expected to contribute their own knowledge of the market and even conduct modest market research themselves. So toolmakers and maintenance engineers came to learn that the *way* a car is made actually determines what sort of car is built and that customers know it.

Creative marketing

Once managers have been encouraged to participate in the marketing of the firm's output, we have found that not only has the company tapped a rich source of information, but there is also a new-found enthusiasm for producing the right products. Developing the right mechanisms to bring this about requires both training and organisational innovation. It also requires the commitment of senior management. Being market oriented is not an optional extra – it is the one sure way to engender motivation among staff based on selling a good product to satisfied customers.

Having been told that their railway was to be modernised but not exactly how, the groups on the British Rail Midland Course were next asked to invent some market information. Almost all the groups were appalled by the task. In most cases they said they knew nothing about market research. So we suggested that they forget about the jargon and discuss what they knew about their passengers.

Pretty soon everyone realised that they did know a lot about their customers – in fact they and their families were customers themselves. One group, we remember in particular, had by chance rather too many engineers in it. At first they were nonplussed, but they soon began to pool their knowledge and they realised that they might not be marketing geniuses, but they were all mathematicians. When we visited the group a little later we discovered they had worked out how to describe the market characteristics 'from first principles'.

As we show in Appendix I, we provided a worksheet which at least gave the groups a framework. In most cases, they went much further and later described in great detail the demands of the community which their railway was to serve. They worked out that it was necessary to understand the structure of the community if one was to provide the right kind of service.

We then rounded off the first day of the course with an exercise designed to loosen up the members' thinking about their product. We wanted them to recognise that there are many more eventualities than are normally allowed for in a large business. It is possible to invent many new ways of satisfying customer demands – even in a traditional business

---

like the railway. In most of their lives managers are not called upon to be creative. We believe that a 'learning culture' is one which seeks to capitalise on the creativity of its members. So we set the groups the task of thinking up as many product features as they could for their renovated railway. And the technique we introduced was 'brainstorming'.

The key to this is that it formalises and structures what might otherwise be a rambling and ill-directed activity. The most important feature of most brainstorming techniques is that everyone gets a chance to contribute without their suggestions being questioned, scrutinised or challenged. As a result many novel proposals survive to be tested against the market information.

We found that every course produced at least one entirely new way of constructing or marketing the railway product. It was in this activity that the multi-disciplinary composition of the courses came into its own. For while many bright ideas fell by the wayside, many others could be inspected by an informed group with knowledge unrestrained by prejudice. The lesson was not lost on the participants. The most important conclusion to this first day was the realisation that the customer and his needs were inescapable, no matter where a manager might find himself in the business.

Our experience with courses inventing their own businesses has been echoed in our senior management seminars. We have found that there is almost a fear of marketing among top managers, which can be dispelled by getting them to just think about their customers. That is really what marketing is, only put into a structure which brings together knowledge and action.

Summary

A successful product must answer a clearly articulated need at a price that consumers can afford. This is the test of all new products and the criterion against which the continued success of established products is measured. While every management can respond to historic sales data – the only completely reliable measure of market response – this is not enough.

To plan and develop intelligently, managers need to know how the market will behave in the future. While market research by experts is important, many managements forget that among themselves there is a wealth of knowledge about the market and that with care and time this can be extracted. All too often they fail to make use of their own resources. Above all, managers alone know how to produce the product and what it will cost, so they are well positioned to make business judgements using market information.

A market-oriented management is one in which every manager considers himself to be part of the marketing effort. His knowledge and information about customers will be placed at the company's disposal. He will seek to inform himself about the market and recognise the potential for new products. At every level managers will be monitoring market performance and suggesting action to maximise sales. They will constantly be posing these questions:

- What can I find out about customer reaction to the product?
- How do my actions affect our customers?
- What can I do to maintain and improve the product?

Marketing issues must be presented in easily understood form and always compared with the operational logic of the business. Carefully structured group creativity can then be used to reinforce this process and ensure useful and productive outputs which will tend to underpin management motivation. The managers will not only identify with the resulting market strategy, they will own it. We now turn to the question of how the business responds to the market and plans its production.

References

1 *Financial Times.* 17 February 1993. Page 26.

7

Data-free Planning
or
'Maybe We Know More Than the Computer'

An everyday task

Every day we undertake a myriad of activities for which we plan in the utmost detail. No matter whether it is a journey or a social occasion or any other of a multitude of activities and pastimes, we plan. But in all this domestic and social planning, how often do we stop and ask for a 'special feasibility study'? Do we halt the proceedings of the Church Concert Committee to ask for additional data? No, we use the available information and we assume that those involved can contribute, or they know someone who can. Just occasionally, we may have to seek out specialist advice and appropriate data, but even then we tend to let circumstances determine what we seek. Contrast this with much of business planning.

Before we go any further, let us agree that to build a bridge or run a railway the most careful plan must be created using properly validated data. The reason for this is that such undertakings require the co-ordinated activities in time and space of many disparate contributors. We understand that a great many production processes require detailed quantitative planning. It would be silly to deny the need for expert planners in such cases. However, we question the assumption that business planning is entirely of this highly structured and quantified kind.

All data-driven planning depends on sets of assumptions. Thus the numbers are always dependent on circumstances. Planners like us to believe that the results are precise; the truth is that every plan is subject to the assumptions made. But such is the power of numbers that business plans presented as sets of numbers tend to have great face validity. In short, they are believed because they suggest certainty, which for managers has a particular attraction. Management is a skill, an art and a specifically social activity. It is subject to ever-changing circumstances. Thus planning a business must take account of those uncertainties, just as we all do in other parts of our lives. It has to start from shared objectives, as we pointed out in Chapter 5. There must be a concerted policy and an agreed strategy. Therefore such planning has to start from a process not unlike the social arrangements mentioned above.

In the early 1970s, Corporate Planning enjoyed a considerable vogue throughout both the private and public sectors of British industry. The development of huge conglomerate businesses meant that detailed financial and operational plans were required of the constituent companies. Government, too, with nearly a third of the economy in the public sector, decided that this was the way to exercise control. The plans were extremely detailed and usually predicted how the business would develop over the next five years. They were, without exception, written by experts and, with hindsight, we know them to have been almost universally wrong.

This approach to planning was the logical extension of the highly analytical and numerate style of management and marketing which had developed in the sixties. The whole movement was based on the belief that every decision – investment, location, resourcing – could be specified as a sort of equation. Provided the right data could be obtained, a correct answer would result. Thus decisions to site steel mills, build atomic power stations and develop aircraft were taken and, conversely, railways were closed and shipyards abandoned. At the time, the predictions were taken uncritically as fact. It was no accident that this coincided with the rise of the computer. Never before had so much data been made available to decision-makers at every level. Managers were in awe of the planners and accepted futures which even contradicted their own experience.

Two classic examples from that time were the Advanced Gas Cooled Reactor Programme and the 1973 Channel Tunnel Proposal. The former depended on a technology yet to be invented and a demand that was difficult to predict – and was bought. The latter relied on Victorian technology and an entirely predictable demand and was not bought. In both cases the figures produced at that time supported the decision even though subsequent history has shown them both to be wrong.

However, the failure of this approach was not entirely the fault of the planners themselves. At first their efforts were put forward largely as written. But increasingly the application of the then current policies to the available data gave some pretty gloomy predictions. Leaders of industry could not accept this and demanded silver linings. These were duly delivered by the planners who merely altered the assumptions. Thus by the mid-1970s almost all public sector corporate plans predicted satisfactory profitability by the third year – whatever current results showed. The first oil crisis destroyed that rosy picture.

The lesson here is that data must support the planning process, it cannot *be* that process. Managers want to plan things that will actually happen. All too often planners have planned things which can never happen.

Personal planning

For the manager, planning has to start with the job itself. He or she has to decide what to do next. A great deal is written about time management. Most of it is probably sensible but tends to remain unused. Our approach is minimalist and consists of a few simple suggestions.

The key to all planning is the use of limited resources to achieve specified ends. The same is true of time. We all have specific tasks, as we discussed in Chapter 4, and limited time in which to perform them. The question we should ask ourselves when approaching every task is: *'Does this further my role? Does it contribute to what I am paid to achieve?'* The degree to which this is true defines the *importance* of the task. However, a manager's life can often be one crisis after another. Problems and demands come flooding through the door and often there is hardly time to assimilate them all, let alone deal with them. Every task faced by a manager has a time limit, either real or implicit, and this defines its *urgency*.

It is often the case that priorities based on these twin imperatives of importance and urgency emanate from our bosses. It is they who set our agenda, just as we set it for our subordinates. We must be part of their planning process, which starts, as we have said, with the setting of objectives and targets. Many tasks are urgent but unimportant; these must be dealt with quickly or not at all – delegation, to be discussed later in Chapter 11, is often the way here. A few key tasks are very important but not urgent and time must be found for them. *It is never true to say that we 'have no time' – what we actually mean is we choose to do something different.* If we choose to do unimportant tasks, however urgent, we fail to further the activity for which we are being paid. How then can we expect our subordinates to perform well at what we pay them for?

But there are occasions when even the best-organised manager begins to be swamped with tasks that are both important *and* urgent. When this happens the tasks invariably present themselves as an endless stream of problems. In this case some drastic sorting out is needed. We suggest the following simple exercise.

Keep a notebook readily available. When a problem is brought to you write it down under a general classification and put a 'tick' after it. When the same type of problem occurs again, put another tick after that category. When a new type of problem comes up start a new category. After a month or two review what has happened. If the same type of problem has occurred, say, 10 times, the chances are you do not have 10 problems but one. Find out what that is and solve it. Then there are those problems which are not really yours. Those kinds of problems need to be re-routed in future. What will be left are some small urgent problems, which you and your staff need to know how to deal with quickly, and a few important problems to which you should devote the majority of your time, because that is why you are there.

From time to time there will be big once-in-a-lifetime problems. Being able to spot these early and tackle them properly is an acquired skill. If there is some similarity with another problem, it may be possible to re-use the experience gained on that. If, as is usually the case, the whole thing is unexpected, then the little scheme described above of systematically sorting out the special and important problems and subjecting them to serious problem-solving will stand that management in good stead. But even big problems must not entirely blot out routine.

A great deal of what we do at work is someone else's agenda, usually our boss's. However, if you spend all your time on tasks that have been set by someone else, you will fail to do other than mark time. Every management job should carry both the business and the job holder forward. To make this possible there must be time to think. Often, imagining what might be is an important first step in planning. Into every manager's time plan must go time to consider and think about what he is doing.

In 1960 Dr Richard Beeching was appointed Chairman of British Railways. He was paid a very large salary since he had been enticed from the ICI Board. Journalists were scandalised to discover that he spent a part of every morning 'just thinking'. It did not square with the, then, conventional wisdom that managers always had to be busy. The result of those thoughts may have been controversial, but without them there would have been no new strategy for the railways.

Departmental planning

This is the level at which the details of what people actually do is worked out. Since all the really important information on which the plan is to be based will be known to the group concerned, and they will have to make the plan work, it has to be a management-led task. The first and most obvious point is that there must be time. Every management team must make time to plan. It is our experience that whenever there are pressures on management time, planning suffers. Of course, the opposite should happen.

The second key element in planning is the involvement of all the relevant people. In this case, relevance has more than one context. It may mean relevant knowledge, but it may also mean relevant authority. Often the two go hand in hand. The point is that those who are responsible for carrying out the plan must play a full part in its creation. Once again, it is the need to have ownership; to understand the point of it all. It is too easy to make planning an important but exclusive activity. Modern quantitative techniques can bestow an entirely spurious mystique on the process, making its participants special and its conclusions 'the word of God'. This can be just as true of forecasting and production planning as of the more precise arts of timetabling and scheduling.

In 1970, British European Airways was heavily committed to improving its operational productivity. It had spent a great deal of resources during the 1960s developing computer-based scheduling techniques. Not only could the aircraft fleet be timetabled and the aircraft and crews allocated, the whole thing could be simulated and shown to be the optimal use of both machines and people. Unfortunately, the planners were never really given a chance to prove themselves because as soon as the plan was sent to the operational staff they re-worked it for reasons which seemed right from their own standpoints. They had not been involved with creating the plans and they felt no obligation to abide by them.

There grew up a serious rift between those who planned, and had the ear of top management, and those who actually ran the airline. The planners argued that if only flight operations would 'fly the plan' the airline would be much better off. In the end the planners gained the ascendancy and the operating managers were ordered to obey. Unfortunately, this coincided with a planners' brain-wave for improving productivity.

It was always accepted that it took 40 minutes to turn an aircraft at London Airport – refuelling and reprovisioning. A planner calculated that if this was cut to 25 minutes then three aircraft and 20 crews would be 'saved'. Furthermore, the planners had studied the aircraft turn-round using work study techniques, and the 25 minutes was possible. The Chief Executive approved the plan and the budget based on it.

It did not work. The staff and equipment were not available for the faster turn-round, the management on the tarmac was inadequate and, above all, nobody had told the passengers they had to disembark more quickly. Every day aircraft were late and off-schedule from morning onwards. Extra staff and aircraft were needed to fill the gaps. Not only were there no savings, but expenditure was increased because often the extra aircraft had to be chartered. After a disastrous summer the airline reverted to 40-minute turn-rounds and everyone sighed with relief. The credibility of the planners was destroyed and for many more years 'hand to mouth' operations continued.

The tragedy was that the planners were right. The airline could have been more efficient as it was to become under other management 10 years later. Had the planning process included all those who would have to implement it and had the process started with shared objectives and acknowledged criteria, it might have succeeded.

The key point is that even the most sophisticated, objective, and quantified planning has to start with a debate about ends and this must be free of the constraints of data. The basis of planning is imagination and knowledge. Once we have decided how to judge the plan – how we shall know when the objective has been reached – and what must have happened to get there, then we can subject these conclusions to analysis. Data becomes the servant of planning and planning itself becomes a continuing activity. Managers function in real time so all plans are provisional, to be modified as time passes. For that to be possible those involved, managers and planners must work together.

A good example of this was provided by a company selling household furnishings. Traditionally they marketed their products through wholesalers, who in turn sold to retail outlets. The company became aware that three of their major wholesalers, who accounted for 40 per cent of their sales, were likely to undergo major restructuring or, in one case, be taken over. One of the authors was invited to facilitate a seminar over a long weekend to plan how they might meet this threat.

They started by working in three groups – each one examining the unique features of their relationship with one of the problem wholesalers. They had to come up with suggestions either to protect the existing relationship or to redirect that volume of sales into an alternative market sector. When the groups reported back, it emerged that working entirely independently the three groups had developed a common approach and similar recommendations for action, and in every case they had realised that, in fact, the problem did not revolve around the wholesalers.

Each group had recognised that the ultimate buying decision was made by consumers and it was their choices which stimulated the retail trade, which in turn influenced the wholesalers. The wholesalers were simply reacting to retail demand, while it was the retailers who could actually influence consumer choice. Therefore they needed to take steps to protect their retailer base. To do this they planned the following:

(1) Action to establish that their products were seen as being 'different' by retailers;
(2) Action to satisfy retailer needs for high availability and customer service;
(3) Action to ensure that the company was seen as 'approachable'.

From this they derived criteria to judge these actions on the basis of 'what would be happening if':

(A) New and improved products were available to retailers;
(B) Retailers were helped to give the product a high profile and good after sales service;
(C) The company's image was enhanced in the eyes of retailers.

The next step was to examine inhibitors. What was preventing the company from:

- Being a dominant name in the industry;
- being seen as technically expert;
- being perceived as professional but approachable;
- being recognised as 'caring' for the retailers.

The resulting plans were directed to specific goals, had criteria for success and addressed problem areas. A series of initiatives were put into effect as a result of these deliberations and they worked. All those who took part realised that they had the material to develop a workable plan once the process had been structured and the objectives made clear. Only after the basic plan had been worked out was detailed analysis undertaken in order to refine the actual application.

Despite the onset of a severe recession, this company increased its market share and maintained profitability. When things got better it was well placed to expand sales.

There is a serious drawback to the manager as sole planner. He may become so committed and enthusiastic that he fails to notice the build-up of bad news. Such a circumstance can result in an Edsel or a Concorde. The only protection is to include outsiders in the planning process and to listen to what they say. In effect neither manager nor professional planner can work independently. Much business planning happens implicitly when managers meet together, agree ends and accept tasks to achieve those ends. Just as we pointed out in Chapter 6 that marketing is a continuous management preoccupation, so planning may be understood to consist of converting market information into action on a continuous basis. However, business plans need to be formalised so that they have structure and consistency and can therefore be a basis for action.

Directors as planners

We have discussed how directors should work together to develop a strategy for the business. But they cannot stop there. When we work with boards of directors we always end with Action Planning, which simply means deciding what has to be done, by whom, and when. At this level, planning has its own set of pitfalls. Those concerned know that how something is to be done, and by whom, can actually modify the what. Thus the process can become political as the participants seek to control future action and exercise personal power through the planning process. It needs a shrewd Chief Executive to prevent this and often the intervention of an outsider.

While data continues to be important to validate plans and actions, it must be freely available. We have seen directors using their access to, or control of, data to influence decisions and plans. It is even more dangerous when data are misused by ignoring the assumptions on which they are based.

> The future success of a large chain of department stores had been predicated on the retention by the many constituent stores of their traditional clientele. The group had been put together in the 1970s from a number of metropolitan and provincial stores, most of them household names in their locality and all of them somewhat 'up-market'. The very thing which made them special was their individuality, much of which reflected the communities they served. In most cases the merchandise was a little idiosyncratic and diverse. Customers were used to a wide range of lines and a distinctive quality image. While none of the stores were startlingly successful, all were profitable. What made them particularly attractive to their new owners was that most operated from freehold premises.
>
> When the new group had been assembled, the directors put in hand an ambitious plan. By using the latest marketing and buying techniques, high-quality goods would be put into every store where they would be professionally and consistently merchandised. While turnover might not increase, costs would fall dramatically and profits would rise.
>
> Unfortunately, the strategy succeeded in destroying the very thing which gave the stores their revenue base – namely their individuality. They became bland clones of the London 'flagship' stores which in their turn became cool and characterless. Initial failures were followed by further cost-cutting and the inevitable plunge down-market in pursuit of revenue. Such stores are ill placed to attract on the basis of price and they now stand half empty of merchandise waiting for customers who do not come. The end is surely in sight.
>
> This is an example of how not to do top-down planning. The plan, though supported by data, missed out essential elements known to the group's more junior managers. These junior managers were not only ignored, they were replaced – so ensuring that when things got difficult there would be little experienced management to cope.

101

When we refer to 'data-free planning', we do not mean 'information-free planning'. It is vital that those committed to the task of planning the future of a company make use of all the facts, no matter how unpalatable. This is where an outside facilitator can be useful. In the power interplay of a board discussion, inconvenient facts get left out because they might predispose the group against an idea preferred by one particular director. If, on the other hand, such facts are elicited and displayed by a disinterested outsider, they can freely enter the discussion.

Just as facts, however inconvenient, must be part of the planning process, so must consequences. Among the more cynical observers of the British political scene there has developed a belief in the 'theory of reverse consequences', which states that every political action has the opposite effect to the one intended. It springs from the tendency for planning discussions in both politics and business, to be about solutions and not problems. So, frequently, good ideas for action are paraded as solutions but in fact have quite other consequences, (like the case of BEA, above). We shall look at this in detail in Chapter 10, but in the meantime let us remember that correctly specifying a problem is the beginning of all planning and an objective assessment of the consequences of proposed action often requires the observation of an independent pair of eyes.

Planning as part of training

Of all the skills of management, planning is perhaps the one which can most appropriately be learnt by doing, and perfected by practice. We have indicated some of the basic approaches here and there are many systems and techniques, such as Critical Path Analysis, which can be applied to business situations. But in the end planning requires the use of creative imagination and that is a knack which can only be developed through actual experience.

A business plan is not just words and numbers written on paper; it is the culmination of a great deal of discussion and thinking by the managers or directors concerned. There has to be a very detailed review of 'where we are now' as well as consideration of 'where we want to be'. Only when the group is clear about these two states can it contemplate the detailed steps required to get from one to the other. We would argue that, at the primary stage in this process, the emphasis has to be on handling facts and their interpretation and not on being tied down by masses of data.

It is difficult to reproduce this in a learning situation – and impossible to do if the group cannot identify with the circumstances and has no personal grasp of the facts, as is the situation with most traditional case studies. Planning the future of a company which they have invented at least has the virtue that it belongs to the participants and its circumstances are the result of their combined knowledge.

On the second day of the British Rail Midland Region Course the participants were asked to plan the modernisation of their newly invented lines. They had been given a comprehensive 'shopping list' of all the available railway capital goods (see Appendix I, Document 10); they had also invented a market and speculated about the kind of railway product features to be incorporated in the new service.

We next asked them to specify the new product, bearing in mind the constraints of available capital and potential revenue, not to mention the overall transport environment (see Appendix I, Document 15). Later they would be asked to develop this into a marketing plan and it will be seen from the instruction (Appendix I, Document 20) that we were insistent that they had to specify their targets and how they were to be exploited.

On many of the courses it was at this point that the groups began to get fired up. In many cases nobody had ever even asked the participating managers to speculate about what the railway *might* be. In general, it was always accepted to be what it is. We encouraged them to use their combined knowledge to look at new ways of both producing and selling their services.

A couple of examples will demonstrate what we mean. One group decided that the railway stations themselves should become an integral part of the community. In many cases they observed – or maybe had invented it so – that a station was situated close to shops and entertainment, while in other cases it was more remote. They argued that by making it a place to which people went for reasons other than travel it would become familiar and friendly, enhancing its position in the community and attracting people if remote. This way they would gradually switch to rail because it had become the 'convenient' mode.

So they planned to rent space for shops, restaurants and other places of entertainment and incorporate them into the station buildings and platforms. Furthermore, the whole marketing effort would be built around this idea of 'friendly stations'. The stations would not only look and feel more comfortable, they would also experience less vandalism and be better maintained. An added bonus was that all these new businesses would provide rental income as additional revenue.

On another course a group had begun to look at the attitudes of the staff towards the passengers. Traditionally, train crews and other operational staff are rostered quite indifferently so that all the good and bad work shifts are shared out reasonably evenly. This means that every driver or guard eventually ends up on every service. It also means that nobody feels any sense of 'ownership' or responsibility for a particular service and the customers tend to know this – they feel that nobody cares.

This group had among their number an operating manager who had observed that a high proportion of passengers on such lines tend to travel regularly on the same train. So they decided to assign particular services to teams of operating staff, so that the trains became identified by the users with particular staff. The teams would take responsibility for their own rostering and routine management and would thus feel a sense of commitment. The result would be a relationship between staff and customers which could be exploited to market the service. It should be added that such an approach to staff allocation and rostering went against all conventional wisdom at that time, and the idea that such matters might form part of a marketing plan would have been thought absurd.

There were many other examples over the years of groups using their own knowledge and experience to turn ideas into workable marketing plans. The next stage was to see if the plans worked operationally. The groups were asked to create a complete operating plan. They were given some guidance in the shape of a series of specific questions, (see Appendix I, Document 17) but in the main they had to discover how to apply all the information about the proposed investment to their plans. They had about three hours – they often took half the night.

It was quite remarkable how, in the course of the day and a half which had passed, the groups had learnt to work together and pool their resources of knowledge and expertise. We observed, on almost every course, a level of application and ingenuity which, when questioned afterwards, most participants simply did not think they possessed. Under these conditions managers from many different areas of expertise were able to work and experiment in an entirely unthreatening situation, and this released both energy and creativity.

We also encouraged individuals to take responsibility for aspects of the plans. Already at this stage the groups were asked to assign functional management among themselves and begin to create action lists. While we did not allow 'flights of fancy', we watched dozens of entirely plausible and workable plans emerge unrestricted by the constraints which might be imposed by quantifying each proposal too early – but plans which the group members could argue for because they had thought them through.

Summary

Planning means deciding how to make things actually happen. It is a common activity in which we all participate but which seldom includes detailed numerical analysis. Rather we think about what we seek to achieve and try to fit together the essential stages. The reason for the failure of much quantitative planning is that the underlying assumptions about management policy and behaviour are ignored when the plan is put into practice. Planning is not forecasting, it is about deciding the action needed to achieve agreed ends and then deciding who does what, how and by when.

Personal planning depends on understanding the difference between what is urgent and what is important and recognising that our use of time is always subject to priorities. Those tasks and problems which further the goals for which the company pays us are important and should take priority, while the many tasks which are urgent but not material to our goals should be disposed of quickly or ignored. Personal time management consists entirely of recognising what sort of problem or task we are dealing with and acting accordingly.

Business planning must involve all those who will be responsible for carrying out the plan. If they remain outside the process they will feel no commitment to success and doom the whole thing. At the core of our work with top management groups has been this belief that all those charged with responsibility for achieving business aims must together work out solutions to their problems and then take charge of the agreed action. We also argue that this process can benefit by being directed by an outside facilitator because such groups sometimes become blinded by their own plans. Planning is an essential group activity. It forms one of the most crucial learning and development activities and when so used tends to produce workable plans which improve performance.

The role of the professional planner must be as supporter and quantifier of the process. Data must serve the planning process: quantification may modify plans, it may even render them unworkable, but it must never drive the planning process. Eventually, however, all plans have to be subjected to quantified analysis in order to test their ultimate feasibility and to provide the criteria for success. It is to this that we now turn.

8

Keeping the Score

The language of numbers

One of the earliest numbers that really means something to us is
body temperature. Parents often describe an ill child as 'running
a temperature'. What they mean is, of course, an abnormally
high one – greater than 98.4°F. 'Being ill' is recognised as a temperature of more than 100, and 'fever' is 101 or 102. It is strange
how we still know exactly what they feel like. Although 39°C
also describes an ill person, for those of us who grew up with
Fahrenheit it has far less meaning.

The numbers we grow up with have real meaning, they convey a state, a reality. One could use many words to describe a
fever, but one number says it all. That is exactly what a statistic
is: a number which describes a situation or a state – a number
which encapsulates many other numbers and tells us about them.
But to understand it we have to know the language, just as we
did with Fahrenheit body temperature. Changing the basis of the
number, say to Centigrade, is like changing the language and it
can leave people just as confused.

Today a great deal of the public debate in business and politics
is carried on using numbers. The problem is that very often they
are misused and frequently abused. The plain fact is that very
many people do not understand figures. They do not even recognise the different kinds of figures: which are estimates, which are
aggregates and which are statistics. Numbers are an essential
way of describing what is happening in a business. The problem
is that, just as with language, communication can be fouled up
because the speaker and the listener think the figures mean
something different.

The worst aspect of using numbers to communicate springs
from their seeming lack of subtlety. Whereas a word like
'mountain' can have many meanings and conjure up many im-
ages and feelings, there is apparently not much argument about
the number '5'. It stands there sharp and distinct defying us not
to believe it. With words we are taught, either explicitly or by

bitter experience, to sort out the meaning by placing the word in context. If that does not work we can ask questions and be given explanations. With numbers, most people ignore the context – and explanations, far from being requested, are actively discouraged. A really eccentric figure is seldom challenged because nobody wants to admit that they do not understand what it means. But for us to manage effectively everyone has to know what we mean.

Measuring performance

For management to be purposeful, a business has to 'keep the score': it must know exactly what it is doing, what it costs, what the revenue is, how many workers, how big the market, and so on and so on. Some people believe that management is *only* about numbers. Our view is that all commercial activities are amenable to measurement, and only by expressing what we do in numbers can we unambiguously set standards and judge whether we fail or not.

> In his first day in the job the General Manager sought out his management team. As each was phoned by the secretary they were found to be either at a meeting, going to a meeting or between meetings. He felt rather like the rich man in the Bible who gave a feast and nobody came.
>
> When eventually all his subordinates were gathered he enquired what the meetings were about. Each seemed to be very important and essential. He then asked them in turn how many meetings they went to each week. He was told 10 or more. How long were these meetings? Well, not longer than half a day usually, came the reply. But if they were spending all this time at meetings when were they doing their work? It transpired that they were either working late, or giving all the 'routine' to their subordinates, or simply not doing the work they were paid for.
>
> The situation was clearly unacceptable, but it was obvious that exhortation would not be enough. So he got his managers to agree some rules. In future no meetings were to last more than 60 minutes (a reasonable span of attention) and no manager to spend more than 12 hours a week in meetings (roughly a third of his usable time). Each manager was to monitor his own performance, but with a measurable target to work to it was relatively easy. Suddenly everyone had more time.

The effort to quantify has an important benefit. It enables us to inspect our activities critically, which helps in deploying management effort where it does most good. When we understand what is really going on we can perhaps do something about it.

In most offices there is a great deal of paper. In many cases there is far too much. Perhaps the worst department in business for creating paperwork is the personnel function. There seems to be an in-built tendency to require multiple copies of everything.

A large personnel office in a major corporation came under the scrutiny of internal consultants. The manager had requested larger premises because of overcrowding and these had to be justified. The main problem was the space occupied by filing cabinets. The first thing the consultants noticed was the amount of paperwork in circulation. They realised that it would not be sufficient simply to question the need for the paper; they had to analyse the problem in ways that demonstrated possible solutions to those involved. So they decided to quantify it, and since they were not sure what the problem was they enlisted everyone's co-operation.

They got every worker to count the papers that crossed their desk each day. These were categorised as originals or copies. If they were originals, did they require action; if they were copies, then how many were in circulation; which ones were needed and which were merely interesting? The consultants tracked the destination and origin of each piece of paper: who read it, who wrote on it, and who filed it. Slowly it emerged that the same pieces of information were being stored by two or three different people. A classic was sickness records, which were required for at least four different purposes and each function kept a copy. A number of forms were criss-crossing the office two or three times. They investigated the amount of paper in store, how long it had been there and how frequently it was accessed. Soon they had enlisted the entire office in the game of adding up.

By now the problem was obvious – too much unnecessary paperwork. The department did not need a new building, it needed to eliminate the paper. And since those concerned had been involved in the enumeration, they were the first to propose solutions.

We would argue that one way or another everything can be measured. The trick is to find a valid and useful way. Often great ingenuity is required to find the right method. We cannot just count things up. We have to use a variety of different kinds of numbers.

The syntax of numeracy

Let us start by looking at the three great classes of numbers used to describe the world we live in. An *aggregate* is simply the number you get by adding everything up. It is the number we first come across as children. We learn that there are 25 bricks in our box; later there are 36 children in the class; still later that there are 107 naturally occurring elements. In all these cases we can count the objects or people or whatever. This number tells us nothing about the contents except how many there are. It is the start of all numeracy.

Measurements are the numerical description of the physical world. In every case they are comparative and compare what we are measuring with some known standard. In many ways they are dependent upon an early grasp of what the various units or measures feel like: 25°C is a hot day, a 6'6" man is a tall man, and so on. As we grow older we add many more examples and experiences, which allow us to make mental calibrations that rival the official ones. We learn to visualise objects and situations on the basis of numerical measurements. Whenever we learn a new skill and its environment we have to learn its measuring system. Learn to sail and soon you will know what Beaufort Force 5 is without looking at any instruments.

But though we could describe the whole world in terms of quantity and size, the result is pretty unsubtle. The third class of number, *statistics*, allows us to go behind the data. That there are 36 children in a class tells us a little; if we measure their individual height we can say much more. The trouble is that it will take a long time and by the time we have called out the last height we shall have forgotten the first 30. So we use one number to impart this information and we say the average height is 1.40 metres. Now we can actually envisage this class, and given that number we could guess at others. We might guess its average age, for example, since we know something of the relationship of age to height. Often a few statistics allow us to build up a picture of the people we are discussing. However, all statistics depend on the formula used, how they have been computed and the assumptions on which they have been based – even the 'average' can be calculated in at least five different ways. And like any language, the listener is supposed to understand what they mean. Many people today do not even properly understand percentages even though they are widely used by journalists and politicians.

In 1975 when the Labour Government, faced with near record increases in the cost of living, were preparing the 'Fight Against Inflation', they decided to discover how much the British public understood of the problem.

Inflation is a uniquely numerate problem. It actually changes one of our most crucial measures – the relative value of money – but it can only be described satisfactorily in numbers though we all experience its effects. So a survey was carried out to find out how far the British public understood inflation. It showed that a significant majority did not actually understand what inflation meant. It was widely believed that rising prices really proved that someone was getting bigger profits. What was worse, although inflation is expressed as a percentage, only a small minority understood what a percentage was. Many did not know the difference between a 10 per cent and a £10 pay increase.

It was realised that no campaign to change the behaviour that caused inflation could succeed if it did not also explain the phenomenon. And that formed the basis of the subsequent propaganda, which formed part of the only attempt in Britain so far to counter inflation by social rather than fiscal or monetary means.

Each of these three types of number serves its purpose in enabling us to describe and measure business activity. But there are many pitfalls in the interpretation of data as well as its collection because numbers have a superficial simplicity. Here are some of the fallacies and beliefs which have grown up with our increasing use of them.

The myth of numerical truth

The biggest problem with numbers is that, since we all start by counting the bricks in the box where the answer is clear and demonstrable, we tend to be very trusting of all such figures. If it can be counted we assume someone has done so, checked the answer and that is it. Unfortunately, nothing could be further from the truth. Most of the aggregates we use are based on some form of estimation. We cannot reach or see every unit so we count what we can and estimate the rest.

Most people believe that the world is facing serious over-population. Almost all the debate on this subject concerns solutions to this perceived problem. To our knowledge, little thought is given to the basis of this belief.

The taking of a census is a very modern activity not to be confused with poll tax gathering in earlier times. It depends on being able to count all the people at one point in time, in essence they have to be asked to 'stand still while they are counted'. In most advanced countries, this is done with the co-operation of all the householders who are asked to count the people sleeping in each particular house on one specific night. Essentially the 'standing still' is imaginary but since almost everyone co-operates it works pretty well.

But this method depends on there being a society of identifiable households, reasonably literate householders, trustworthy enumerators to gather the data, and a tradition of objectivity and honesty in the collation of such data. Above all there must be almost universal co-operation and the expectation that the outcome is neutral for the population – in other words no incentive to falsify the figures.

In very few countries across the world do these conditions exist. No less an authority than the United Nations clearly indicates that accurate census-taking is rare. In its annual *Yearbook of Statistics* it lists the population figures submitted by the member states, with annotated qualifications alongside. The subsequent notes tactfully describe the degree of reliability which can be ascribed to the figures. Only 29 countries have none – all the most densely populated are heavily qualified. The United Nations itself is carefully sceptical of the figures shown but can do no more than publish.

The truth is that we do not actually know what the population of the globe is. Everything is an estimate. It has been suggested that the figures are likely to be an exaggeration. In the absence of reliable systems of census-taking governments had to estimate, and because population size is a very important status symbol for nation states, especially new ones, the temptation to increase the estimates has been irresistible.

So the first rule of interpretation is to find out who collected the figures, how that was done and to what extent estimation has been used.

Because numbers tend to be easily believed, managers who want to win an argument always call for some numbers to back them up. If the correct aggregate or estimate is available, all well and good, but if we become too fixed on the numbers themselves then the less scrupulous will simply say to their staff: 'Never mind the evidence. This is my decision, so go away and find me some numbers.' There was a time, during the British Government's preoccupation with corporate planning for the nationalised industries, when the Treasury was consistently lied to. It demanded figures but had no way of knowing the truth.

The cricket score fallacy

In the game of cricket, as in most games, the score measures the activity directly. It is possible, with effort and skill, to increase the score. Many businessmen seem to believe that it is possible to manage business affairs in a similar way. If they do not like the numbers then they seek to increase the score directly.

> The transport industry has always recognised that the fuller their vehicles, the more profitable their businesses. The measure they use to express this is called the load factor. It is a simple calculation of the amount of output actually used, expressed as a percentage of the available output. Typically in air transport this is 60 per cent and for railways 25 per cent. Every transport manager knows that a higher load factor is nearly always associated with greater profit. So great efforts are expended on increasing this number directly.
>
> The most obvious way to raise the load factor is to cut output, for it is reasoned that fewer trains or planes will mean more seats occupied. Unfortunately, this does not work because the number of passengers wanting to travel on a particular service depends on the frequency of the service. Fewer trains or planes means fewer passengers and so we are back where we started.
>
> Another approach is to reduce the size of the vehicle. This is popular with the railway because it can detach carriages. But the number of passengers presenting themselves for each train is not constant. There are peaks, and if these are consistently left uncatered for because there is no room, then the passengers go elsewhere and we are back again where we started.
>
> The point is that while load factor is a good measure of the efficient utilisation of transport resources *after* the event, its determinants and therefore the ways of improving it lie not in the operation of the service but in the way the service is marketed. The load factor measures performance much as a car's speedometer does, and trying to manage this number directly is like trying to make the car go faster by twisting the pointer on the dial.

Numbers measure what they measure and nothing more. While

they give us insights into relationships, we often have to look much further to find causes. As we shall see, this is particularly true of profits, which are determined by a whole host of managerial decisions and outside influences. However, managements, when faced with a stock exchange which bases all its judgements on profit, find themselves almost obliged to 'manipulate' that figure, without actually doing anything to the business.

The curse of spurious accuracy

We have pointed out the tendency for numbers to be believed even to the point of denying experience. Even worse is the insistence on expressing them to the furthest place of decimals. This is supposed to bestow added credibility.

> There was once a curator of a museum who was asked how old his huge fossilised dinosaur was. He replied that it was 3,000,011 years old. The enquirer was astonished and impressed: 'And how do you know with such accuracy?' 'Oh!' the curator replied, 'When I came here I was told it was three million years old and I have been here 11 years.'

The lesson is clear but frequently ignored. Any number can only be as accurate as the weakest estimate used in making it. While this is obvious of aggregates and measures, it is equally true of statistics. It is no use dividing two estimates by each other and then expressing the result to three places of decimals. (Unfortunately, a great many government statistics are like that.) Most of the, so-called, key indicators vary month by month by less than their potential errors; only long-term trends tell us anything useful.

Perhaps the worst aspect of this fallacy is manifest in forecasting. The important lesson for all managers is that a forecast is just that; it is not a prediction. Business and economic forecasting is a very inexact science which has a somewhat worse record for accuracy than weather forecasting. And yet many companies express such forecasts using decimal places and single-figure percentages when the basis is often no more than a guess.

Most forecasts depend not only on assumptions about the behaviour of the business in question, which at least can be controlled if the managers choose, but they also depend on assumptions about the market, business in general and the government, which can never be more than informed guesses. So every forecast can only express a range of probabilities based upon a set of assumptions. None of this is to deny the usefulness of forecasts, only to remind us to be wary in their interpretation and sceptical of great accuracy. History tells us that most forecasts are wrong.

Over-interpretation, or 'Do numbers have feelings?'

There is a growing tendency to ascribe feelings and motives to institutions, societies and even populations on the basis of numerical data. The clearest example of this is by-election results. We listen to a victorious candidate declare that 'the people of Barchester (or wherever) have sent a message to the government', and so on, as a result of what is described as a crushing defeat.

All that has happened is that three or four electors out of every hundred have changed their votes since the last election and a few more have stayed at home. In most cases the reasons, when they are discovered, turn out to be quite other than those ascribed. Even worse, a few seats change hands in an election, general or local, and our politicians assume a mandate to reverse all the policies of the previous administration. Again the cause may be a few changed minds. Even a 2 per cent swing in a general election, sufficient to change the government, could be the result of only half a million people changing their minds.

This attitude has now started to appear in business. These days, every morning by nine o'clock we are told the mood of the stock exchange based on movements in a complicated index. All that has actually happened is that a few market makers have altered prices in the expectation of deals to come and one or two deals have actually happened.

Much of this behaviour springs from the widespread use and misuse of sample surveys to try to understand popular opinion and consumer preferences. As we said in Chapter 6, a great deal of care has to be taken in interpreting survey data but at least it is designed to yield an interpretation. Simple statistics and aggregates are purely descriptive, in general they tell us what has happened. They are not able to tell us anything about why things happen nor can we assume feelings and motives.

Micawber's discontinuity

This is the belief that the difference between success and failure is just a hair's breadth. So often even the numbers themselves have a margin of error which exceeds this apparent failure watershed. This is most telling in the consideration of profit. Too often it is forgotten that profits are always the difference between two very much larger sums. Quite small shifts in either revenue or expenditure can change the results from profit to loss. This does not mean that an otherwise satisfactory business is suddenly a failure. Equally profits 'created' out of the balance sheet do not make an unviable business successful. This discontinuity is also felt when matching performance to targets. Falling a little short does not signify abject failure – though the opposite view is particularly widespread in sales organisations where salesmen are fired for missing their quota by a tiny percentage.

The truth is that success has to be measured by much more, and managers must make use of a wide range of figures to judge their performance. In fact a great deal of business activity is mediocre – neither success nor failure. It is in this area that the interpretation of figures is so important, for it sheds light on relative success. In fact the lack of a discontinuity enables many managers to survive and prosper, not by waiting for something to turn up but by making things happen through careful analysis.

Information overload

Most of us make up our minds on the basis of a fairly small parcel of information. It is said that, in general, individuals can hold and consider six pieces of information at a time; give them more and they will simply ignore one of the facts and decide on the basis of the revised set. What is worse, they will make their own choice about which pieces of information to reject.

Being able to handle more information simultaneously is a skill. Those who can do it – judges, professors, scientists and so on – have spent many years perfecting their skills. But most of us have no capacity for taking complicated decisions on the basis of a mass of information acquired over many days. Nevertheless, there are managers who never use one number when a thousand will do. There are directors who measure the output of their planning departments by the weight of the reports produced.

The Roskill Commission on London's Third Airport, which reported in 1971, wrote an 800-page report with an eight-volume appendix of data and over five hundredweight of evidence. Even the report itself had many pages of tables and diagrams. The Minister for whom this work was done never read the report and neither did any of his colleagues. Instead they relied on their officials to produce digests, summaries and recommendations – and none but the lowliest official read the report.

In the light of public opposition to building the third airport at Stansted, the Commission was asked where and when the airport should be built. It undertook the most comprehensive cost-benefit study done up to that time and its methodology has stood the test of time and become quite conventional. But such a study inevitably produces a huge amount of material and requires the most careful interpretation. It is necessarily based on many assumptions and because this was part of the Commission's work, its members insisted on specifying many of those assumptions. As a result, the study was flawed and subsequent events proved it to be over-optimistic.

The Commission itself was a failure. It fell between its attempt to create a logical and rigorously researched decision and its perception of what was 'politically possible'. The assumptions it made were not supported by the politicians, it included options which the study showed to be impossibly expensive and it excluded more reasonable alternatives. Nevertheless, it did recommend what to this day was probably the best site and it conclusively dismissed the most popular site, which was at Maplin Sands. This conclusion was supported not only by the enormous study but by both written and oral evidence taken over 72 days of public hearings.

In the event, the report was 'accepted' and then ignored. Ministers and their officials could not cope with the information provided which in any case went against popular opinion. They decided for Maplin. But three years later that had to be abandoned because the huge costs forecast by the Commission were proving correct. The best site was put in the 'too difficult' category and the third airport was built at Stansted after all.

This cautionary tale must stand as a lesson to all decision-makers. *When you need to monitor business activities with a view to making decisions about them, choose a small number (less than four) of numerical measures which can be accurately measured and easily understood.* This is no less true of routine management. We have to select key numbers which will enable us to control the processes for which we are responsible.

> When the new General Manager took over, about the first thing he noticed was that his in-tray was filled each day with sheets of numbers. There were market analyses, staff rosters, absence figures, performance data and so on. Each set of data was many pages of closely printed figures, or extremely complicated graphs. These had been produced by many departments in the company and clearly were meant to demonstrate the diligence of those who collected the data.
>
> He enquired about this and was told that all his managers and most superintendents were getting the same information. He asked what they did with it and whether they read it. Many simply did not understand what the numbers meant. Others simply selected a few figures which seemed to mean something. They all felt very guilty about not reading this mass of data.
>
> So the General Manager stopped the flow and appointed an information officer one of whose jobs was to take all this numerical data and turn it into a few simple tables, each with less than 20 numbers and each informing managers about their actual responsibilities. The result was put together in a weekly information bulletin, which all the managers not only received but were required to carry with them when they went to meet their staff. In their turn, the managers were shown what the tables meant and were coached in how to use them.
>
> An interesting postscript is that those who had supplied the original data became so angry that it was to be simplified and demystified that a number threatened to stop supplying it.

Accounts and accounting

There is one group of numbers which, above all others, managers use to do their work – financial data. We do not intend to attempt to write in detail about accountancy as such nor did we ever encourage our course members to try to learn accounting on our courses. Our approach is much the same as we described in relation to marketing or planning. We believe that all managers must understand what management accounts mean and how to use them to do a better job. So we emphasise two simple propositions about accounts. The first is that all regular accounts measure, in one way or another, the flows of income and expenditure through a business and the difference is either profit or loss. These accounts are expressed over a period of time – week, month, year – and they tell us how we are doing. The second proposition is that the balance sheet tells us what the business is worth, or it does if everything of value owned by the business is included. Taken together these two sets of accounts always balance because profits or surplus always mean an increase in either cash or assets, be they property, equipment, or stock. And, because the balance sheet expresses quantities of value or cash, it is always expressed as at a single point in time.

Perhaps the best illustration of this is the water mill. The stream is the profit and loss account and the mill pond the asset statement or balance sheet. If more water runs in than out – positive profits – then the pond fills up; if more water flows out – losses – the pond drains a little. So accounts are the key method of keeping the score. They fall four-square into the category of enumerated figures which can seldom be affected directly but are the result of everything that the management does. They are also subject to convention and assumption and, while they can be described as accurate, they are not exact.

There are two kinds of accounting generally in use in business. These may be described as 'budget accounting' and 'cash accounting'. In *budget accounting*, the paper transactions of the business are totalled month by month, to which are added conventional estimates of internal costs such as depreciation and stock movements. This gives a comparison between invoiced sales and the cost of supplies required to make those sales, and the difference is profit or loss, which is what such accounts are also called.

Management accounts are based on these and the budgets to which managers must work refer to them. What they purport to show is the month-by-month activity of the business and the cost of that activity. What they actually show is the sales revenue and its cost. Even this is a conventional rather than a real set of figures because it depends on rules which provide estimates of the use of capital and the movement of stock.

In businesses where there are great lags between actual activity and the remuneration of that activity, things begin to get very complicated. If a manager wants to know how his unit is progressing month by month, all these paper transactions have to be allocated to a particular period and that means more rules and

119

conventions. As if this was not bad enough, there is the problem of departments and functions. Final output may be as the result of the efforts of many contributing departments. They will all want to know how they are performing. Again there have to be allocations and these are *all* arrived at by agreed assumptions and conventions.

But departmental accounts do not tell the whole story. Most businesses include activities which do not actually contribute to output but must nevertheless be done, such as accounting itself. Every productive activity has to take its share of these costs, or in the more usual jargon, they must make a contribution to business overheads. The problem is that all these estimates are then made to add up to the real totals in the profit and loss account which gives all the sub-totals a validity that they do not deserve.

Without the most detailed and continuous research, it is impossible to price the activities of each department and function in a business. Monthly management accounts are very comforting, especially if they are well presented and profitable. But managers can easily be taken in by them and come to believe that they are the only true numerical description of the business, when in fact they may depend on a whole host of subjective and arbitrary assumptions.

> Perhaps the worst example of bad accounting data being used for crucial management decisions concerns British Railways. In 1962, the Beeching Report was published on the future of Britain's railways. The apparent problem was that they were losing a great deal of money and delivering a poor service. The cause was said to be that the system was much too large for the available traffic and therefore too sparsely used. The solution adopted was to close nearly 40 per cent of the track miles.
>
> The evidence claimed for this was a series of accounting studies, all of which included conventional cost allocations. However, even at the time, both internal and external evidence showed that those figures did not support the policy. The real waste was elsewhere and could even be identified.
>
> Without going into details (better done elsewhere[1]), let it be said that hindsight has demonstrated that the figures on which the policy was based were almost entirely wrong. Virtually no savings were actually made and a great national asset was destroyed.

Businesses, especially small businesses, have always been run with a close attention to the cash flow. Today *cash accounting* is being used much more widely – as it always has been in the public sector. The problem here is that a strict monitoring of cash into and out of the business tends to make for a very 'short-term' approach. It necessarily treats long-term expenses as immediate and, in the case of capital, such expenses can always be postponed. However, while cash accounting may be useful for a whole business, it is virtually useless for individual units or departments. Where it has been attempted, only costs could be controlled and that subtle and necessary connection between revenue and output was broken. As a result management either blindly cut costs or they became wildly extravagant.

We take the view that traditional accounting methods are certainly appropriate for ensuring the probity and honesty of those who run a business. They are also useful in assessing its worth and in a great deal of planning. Cash accounting, on the other hand, does focus on the immediate needs of a business and helps to remind us that revenue has to be collected and expenditure controlled. What precise mix of these two approaches will be appropriate for a particular business is for those involved to decide. Both accounting approaches are necessary and, in addition, specific measures of output and performance have to be developed for every activity. But *the most important point about accounting is that it must produce figures which are relevant, intelligible and accurate so that a useful picture of the day-to-day activity can be seen.*

However, accounts above all other numerical descriptions of a business can be dangerous, since they suffer from all the numerical fallacies put together. They combine totally accurate figures with conventional estimates, the numbers have very wide levels of accuracy, the results are expressed as narrow differences and most of the statistical derivatives are dependent on estimated aggregates. There are no absolutes in accounts – in a sense they are what we say they are. Nevertheless, they are usually all we have and we therefore have to become knowledgeable about them within our businesses.

Communicating with numbers

It is not enough simply to keep the score. Managers must all know what that score is. Management information systems often break down at this point. Good communication depends on one overriding principle and a small number of basic rules. The single principle is that *the leaders of any management team must be committed to communicating with their subordinates right down the line on every subject, every day.* There are no exceptions, for although self-evidently some information is sometimes confidential, there is always something to be said, some data which can be revealed about every situation.

It is our experience that staff always know when their management wants to be open and nothing ruins a business culture more quickly than secrecy. On the other hand, the more junior staff tend to find it difficult to cope with bad news, not to mention the effect on those with whom the company does business. So a management must tread a fine line between frankness and frightening its staff. There are a few basic rules which we find to be useful:

- Be positive. All communication must be in the context of answers not problems – this does not mean behaving like 'Topsy' telling only good news, but it does mean being sensitive to the effect of what is being transmitted.
- It must be regular. An information flow develops expectations and any pause raises doubts – 'What are they hiding?'
- It must have apparent validity. This means that those receiving it should be able to test it against their current experience – 'How can we be doing so well if they just sold the company cars?'
- The numbers must mean something to the recipients. It is no use communicating information that can only elicit a shrug of the shoulders; it must refer to the actual experience of those concerned.
- Everybody ought to be able to relate their performance to the information. We all need to know 'how we are doing' and this is the way we find out.

There are, in addition, a number of presentational rules as well, such as clear tables and diagrams, easy accessibility and appropriate language, but these are common to all presentation and communication and are dealt with in a large number of books on the subject. The most important feature of 'keeping the score' is that it provides the basis of management feedback systems and the material on which performance can be reviewed. This we return to in Chapter 12.

Learning about numbers

We have found that this basic introduction to management information and accounting has proved sufficient to enable managers in a learning situation to tackle quite complicated issues. They realise quickly that they do indeed know a good deal about it already. Nevertheless, these matters were the most frequent subject of our interventions and mini-lectures to groups on our courses.

> The participants on the British Rail Midland Region Course came face to face with management accounts very quickly. Halfway through the first day they were asked to invent a cost:revenue account for the existing lines. We did not ask for a balance sheet but we did ask them to estimate the capital value of the assets.
>
> When we created the course we realised not only that there would be wide disparities in the levels of numeracy, but that some of the managers were almost too numerate. These were the engineers, for whom every number was precise and carefully qualified. The world of management numeracy would be irksome because they would find it a fraud. For them the invented railway was ideal. They not only had to make up the numbers but their whole training meant that they would want to justify them. For the others it proved a very useful way to appreciate the ways in which the parts fitted together.
>
> At first, when faced with the challenge of having to invent a cost:revenue account, many of the participants shied away leaving it to the minority who knew about such things. In the event they could not escape because the success or failure of their proposals was going to be measured in money. Most of the participants found they knew enough to create a sensible financial description of their company.
>
> As can be seen from Document 7 in Appendix I, we provided each group with a worksheet which had some of the figures already on it. This was because it would have been too time-consuming and of little application for every group to have started from scratch. An interesting by-product of this

was that for over half of these mid-career managers – often with over 15 years in the railway industry – this was the first time they had seen estimates of the actual cost of operating such a line.

It was when they came to evaluate their modernisation plans that matters really became interesting. Instead of it being just a matter of providing the best product or operating the best service, now they had to ask: 'Can we afford it?' Once again they had a fair amount of basic data given. What they had to do was to demonstrate in financial terms whether or not their particular scheme worked. Most of them had spent a lifetime of management working in a bureaucracy where everything happens as a result of sending a piece of paper. Now they had to consider what would happen if everything had to be paid for and justified in terms of the revenue it would earn.

On course after course it was at this point that the lesson about financial results being the result of management action, and not the other way round, really sank in. We can remember many hotly contested arguments as the groups faced the fact that managers must operate in a world of finite resources and can only do what the market is prepared to pay for. Nevertheless, by most Tuesday evenings each invented railway had a product, a plan and a financial justification all of which had to be assembled into a presentation for Wednesday morning.

We made each group prepare a full presentation using conventional visual aids such as overhead and slide projectors, and flipcharts. We asked them to imagine that we and their fellow course members were the public authority providing the funds and they had to make the case for their particular plan.

Once again, we experienced the enthusiasm and originality of managers released from the constraints of their organisational culture and able to communicate their own ideas and vision. For many participants this was a high point of the course. It also placed a considerable responsibility on us to give positive and constructive feedback so that lessons could be learned which would be appropriate after their return to work the following week.

Summary

Numbers are a language that has to be learned by managers. The only way we can chart our progress is by measuring it, and the actual process of measuring tends to help us to understand our work better. One way or another, everything can be measured. Numbers have their own syntax – there are aggregates, measurements and statistics – and of these statistics are the most useful because they are descriptive. However, there are important fallacies associated with using numbers, such as the assumption of truth, the importance of the score, spurious accuracy, over-interpretation, Micawber's discontinuity, and information overload.

The most important numbers in business are management accounts. These should not be mysterious but are there to help us to understand both the daily processes of the business and its long-term value. Above all, they are the prime way in which we 'keep the score'. But they, too, suffer from all the fallacies mentioned and have to be treated with knowledge and caution. To communicate with numbers we have to recognise the basic skills of communication as well as the language of numbers. We have to be positive, truthful and intelligible.

Starting from the proposition that businesses exist to provide goods and services for their customers, we have argued that it is the satisfactory nature of that provision which is the main motivation both for management and staff. Every business needs to know its markets, plan its activities and monitor its performance. Above all, it needs to relate to its customers, and it is to them that we now turn.

References

1 HENSHAW, D. *The Great Railway Conspiracy*. Hawes, North Yorks, Leading Edge Press, 1991.

Customer Care is More than a Slogan

What is a customer?

A new definition of an old word has entered the English language. Whereas in the old days we were passengers on trains and buses, clients at the solicitors, citizens who were provided with services from local authorities or just plain consumers, now we are all called customers. This word 'customer' is supposed to suggest 'familiarity and regularity, a one-to-one relationship'.[1] In this book this is precisely the sense in which we have used it. In contrast, a 'consumer', is much more remote and takes his place in a global market. For us, a consumer is any person or body who consumes the final output of a business.

This cosmetic change of title was an attempt to change attitudes but its use in circumstances where there is no readily identified familiarity is out of place unless some effort is made by all the staff to establish a genuine customer–supplier relationship. The use of the word 'customer' has beneficial consequences in the long run, for it acts as a reminder of a key element in the relationship between consumer and supplier – namely that the product or service should match what the customer might reasonably have expected. However, the other crucial element is choice. A customer in the private sector can choose what product or service he buys: a consumer of monopoly or public services cannot.

In this last case, we believe there is some confusion about who exactly is the customer. If there is one, it is the whole community, for the level of service, once set, is bound to be maintained for everyone. Furthermore, the relationship is made more complicated by the fact that as a body of voters this 'super-customer' constitutes the authority by which councillors make decisions about expenditure and levels of service. In essence those officials who want to treat us as customers are in fact our employees.

Nevertheless, realising that customers do have power, even

with respect to monopolies or the government itself, some large businesses have recently commissioned expensive customer care programmes for their staff. These will have little effect unless accompanied by other far-reaching changes which may not be on the management agenda; for example the buses and planes do actually have to run on time and patients do have to receive the correct treatment. The staff know this all too well. Often such customer care programmes have no real effect or are treated with cynicism because they seek to *cover up deficiencies with 'caring behaviour'*. It is quite common for this to have the opposite effect from that intended. In the end we all tire of endless apologies, no matter how well meant. Eventually customers simply lose patience and the disillusioned staff sympathise with them and join in blaming the management.

In the market relationship, the way in which customers express their satisfaction with the product or service is by choosing to repeat the experience. This is why many well-run businesses will go to enormous lengths to re-establish the customer relationship if things have gone wrong. If the service was bad or the product unsatisfactory, it is not considered enough simply to apologise. The customer will be compensated to such an extent that his satisfaction is restored and he is once again predisposed to choose that product. Herein lies the clue to the sort of behaviour, at the point of contact with the consumer, which might provide the motivating force relating production and consumption when the market does not or cannot function. *Every person selling or providing a good or service should behave in such a way that the consumer will be predisposed to come back again next time.*

In many cases things have gone much further. It is now recognised that the way the consumer is treated has become an integral part of the product itself. It is no longer enough to know how popular a product is or how strongly it is demanded; businesses now need to know the reasons why, and the answer usually depends on this relationship. Frequently the product is entirely similar to others; what makes the difference is the way it is sold. We would go farther and state that *every product and service bought or supplied to the public is now perceived to include the whole experience of the consumer in receiving it.*

Customer care is a far wider matter than training staff to behave well to customers. The relationship between the 'customer' and the business is crucial to the whole approach discussed here. It is at the point where the customer receives the goods or services that all the aspects of management are brought together. The delivery of the product is the end to which all management is directed and the reaction by the customer provides the feedback to the business which fuels its motivation. So in developing this approach to management and its training we must focus very particularly on this.

Customer satisfaction

In the case of commodities and products, the existence of customer satisfaction and its measurement are generally self-evident. Every salesman will be carrying the message back to the business even before the actual sales figures are available. What is less obvious is why customers express particular preferences. We now know that the factors which influence the purchase choice are much more complicated than a simple desire to consume or own the product.

One of the earliest findings about the television advertising of soap powder was that, while such adverts actually engendered hostility among those not using the brand, they tended to please and encourage those who were already using the brand. This phenomenon is now widely exploited through, so-called, 'designer' labelling. Consumers choose particular brands with which they identify and which they believe will enhance their image, and they want those brands clearly identified. In some cases the brand has become the product.

Another element in the purchasing decision is the way in which that purchase is made and the attitude of the seller or supplier to the customer after the purchase. This is customer service. It involves not just being nice to the customer but actually seeking to influence future behaviour by providing support at and beyond the point of purchase.

A good example of this is the supply of domestic electronic appliances. There are a number of large multiple chain stores in the UK which seek to sell televisions, video recorders, sound systems and so on solely on the basis of price. The goods are stacked high and garishly displayed with the whole emphasis on cheapness. In order to maintain such prices, costs have been held to an absolute minimum. Unskilled staff are hired and given no training, and the level of customer care is consequently very low. As for after-sales service, this is almost non-existent since any faulty appliance is simply replaced provided the customer brings it back.

Contrast this with a growing number of small businesses in the same field, particularly those specialising in car radios. Here, while prices may not be so low, the appliances will be installed and tested, the customer will be shown how it works and any snags will be dealt with at once.

These latter businesses recognise that their service is part of the product. Customer satisfaction is not just being nice to the customer, it may mean committing real expenditure in order to enhance the customer experience and so influence future behaviour. It is notable that businesses which concentrate solely on making the sale at all costs, and often with reduced profit, tend not to be well managed. They seem to sacrifice the pursuit of quality for the pursuit of turnover. Those that have investigated successful companies[2] have identified a concentration on customer satisfaction as being a key factor in good management.

Those of us who buy office equipment have watched a dramatic change in that business over the past 10 years. Formerly, salesmen would do almost anything to get a sale. They were known even to place the photocopier in an office and providing free trials, while lying about payment terms implied in a typical lease purchase agreement, or to arrange the bogus 'repurchasing of obsolete equipment' – leaving behind an expensive machine which nobody wanted to service.

Now, thanks to market pressures and government regulation, the emphasis is on after-sales support and cultivating the long-term relationship with the customer. No longer is every effort bent towards getting a signature on the agreement. Now one is almost embarrassed by the courtesy and attention one receives. The result is that such salesmen now boast not about one sale but the prospects for their future order book.

For the service industries customer care assumes a very significant importance. It is a large part of the product on sale. No longer can a hotel merely rent a bed, or a bus operator sell a journey. Now it is recognised that the whole experience is what the customer buys. Unfortunately, in much of the service sector the customer is faced with a monopoly. The response of government has been to regulate the price and quality of the product and to try to structure the businesses so that they at least resemble competitive commercial enterprises and even experience some of the market forces. Which brings us back to the public sector. If calling people 'customers' who attend job centres, or hospital clinics or local council offices helps to focus on the need to give a satisfactory service, then it is useful. However, it cannot hide the fact that such 'customers' have no choice and so management has to invent procedures and sanctions which can substitute for the commercial pressures of an open market.

Managing the customer relationship

We return to our principle that a business must be dedicated to its policies as a whole. If customers are to be made 'kings', then everyone in the business must subscribe to that view. Every pronouncement, plan and objective must reiterate the policy and put the customer first. Staff should not even joke about customers being a nuisance. From top to bottom everyone has to be aware that they *are* the wages.

True customer care involves every aspect of the organisation's operations and starts at board level. If the board consistently thinks about what the customer wants, if they treat their own employees well, then those employees are more likely to behave well to customers. One of the keys which unlocks positive customer-oriented thinking is for board members to experience first hand what it is like to be a customer for their own product. They need to travel on their own trains, stay at their own hotels, shop in their own shops, buy their own furniture, wear their own shoes. And they should do it incognito so that it does not degenerate into just another 'photo opportunity'. Furthermore, the Board needs to ensure that everyone in the company recognises that their job has an impact on customer behaviour – even when they themselves never have direct contact with a customer. This applies as much to a floor sweeper in a food factory as it does to a national grid linesman.

We have said that a great deal of management is concerned with problem-solving. In business almost every problem involves the customer. But all too often problems are perceived to be internal, or 'operational', and in the solving nobody gives a thought for the customer. In fact we have observed situations where the business was effectively brought to a standstill so that the 'problem' could be solved, while the poor customers had to cope as best they could. How often have we fumed on empty railway stations or in blacked out hotels where nobody will explain what has happened or when it will be put right? And let us not assume that such behaviour is limited to the service industry. The manufacturing sector of the building industry has a trick or two as well.

A builder once went to a factory that made doors and windows to order some special non-standard doors. The architect had specified one-metre glass doors to open on to a terrace. At that time all production doors were 72 cm. The factory manager first explained that they only produced 'standard' doors. When pressed he admitted that wider ones could be produced but they would be expensive. When that was accepted he said he could not deliver at once but it would take eight weeks.

It turned out that to keep his factory working steadily and his life easy the manager wanted to build standard doors off a substantial waiting list. He would not even break this policy for money. The builder needed the doors that week so he went elsewhere.

This illustrates the widespread malaise of believing that the product, or the operation, or the goods are the only reason for running the business. In the UK we agonise about hospital waiting lists. But there are waiting lists everywhere. Try buying anything for which an order is necessary and be told that it 'takes eight weeks'.

A customer-oriented business is one in which the needs of the customer are treated as paramount in all decisions. No matter at what point in the production and delivery system, every member of staff is aware of his or her contribution to customer satisfaction, and the first consideration in every problem is 'how will this affect the customers?'

A Swedish furniture retail business has recently entered the United Kingdom market with spectacular success. This has been achieved by making the principle of customer satisfaction manifest. It has always been the way of the British furniture trade that the customer has to wait. Whether at the top or the bottom end of the market, shops and showrooms were simply places where you placed an order and then waited days or weeks for the goods. This company realised that furniture constitutes one of the most expensive and significant purchases made by a family. A great deal of time and care goes into decisions which are then followed by the great anti-climax of having to wait.

The solution has been to sell furniture which can be carried away from huge but very user friendly warehouses – there are even car roof racks for hire. And when the item is too big, it is the customer who arranges delivery by van – usually the next day. The company is now capitalising on the recognition that the activity called shop-ping, which involves both buying and taking the purchase home, is almost as important as the product itself.

Customers want answers not sympathy

The essence of customer care is to recognise that customers want answers not just sympathy. This implies that systems must be in place which enable customers' problems to be dealt with in a reasonable time span. How often have you telephoned an organi-sation and been told that the person who would deal with your problem is unavailable or sick? Procedures should be available that enable the customer to be given an answer at once. It is per-fectly satisfactory to say: 'Please give me the details and I'll phone you back.' It is unsatisfactory to say: 'I'm sorry, the per-son who deals with this won't be available till next week.' The procedures, therefore, need to establish how the staff in contact with customers are to get the necessary information. Setting up these procedures is time consuming and not easy, but is essential for any organisation which takes customer care seriously.

Everyone accepts that not all manufactured items are perfect. Over the years consumer rights and producers' liability have had to be created through legislation. Now, however, many sellers of products are prepared to offer much more than the legal mini-mum because the forces of competition have elevated customer service so that it is an important component of the product.

It is not just that Marks & Spencer have good clothes at reasonable prices – they also operate customer policies which give great reas-surance. All goods can be returned or exchanged and liabilities are accepted without question. And the whole policy is conducted in a courteous and civilised fashion, so that the customer does not feel obligated. He is not 'being done a favour'.

Nowhere is customer satisfaction so keenly a part of the product than in transport. After all the aim of passenger transport is to move the customer's own body from one place to another. It is impossible for him not to be involved in a very personal way. Yet we have found in our dealings with a number of the main transport undertakings that what actually happens to the passenger is seen as somehow less essential than the operation of the transport system itself. It is an attitude that can lead to a preoccupation with the details of the operation on the grounds that it does not really matter what state the passenger is in when he arrives as long as he does arrive.

We have been surprised to discover that, in the planning and operation of services, passenger comfort and care are often treated as an extra after considering the vehicles, their path and signalling whereas the passenger himself has a very clear idea of what he wants and expects and is usually prepared to make his purchase of transport services with that in mind. The key is to know what the customer really wants.

In the public sector and in monopoly businesses, if customers are disappointed they generally cannot change to another supplier – they just get angry. It is these customers' reactions which have to be harnessed by the management to replace the simple feedback mechanisms of an open market. This requires some subtle techniques. Customers have to be able to complain, the businesses have to build in procedures to placate and compensate customers which often go far beyond what would be the case in other businesses, and the staff concerned have to be informed about those customer reactions.

One afternoon the Inter-City express from the West Country bound for Paddington failed to stop at Westbury. Three very irate travellers, needing to be in London for appointments, could not afford the time to wait for the next train which stopped – two or three hours. They would have to go to Swindon by taxi. The Station Superintendent heard about their problem and not only arranged for the taxi, but arranged for British Rail to pay – all done promptly and with no argument. This may not seem remarkable now – 10 years ago it was.

When we first introduced the idea that customer care extends to *everyone* in the organisation to our course participants, they tended not to grasp the point. It simply did not occur to them that customers could be a priority at every level in a business. We had to ask each one to think about all the links between his job and the individual customer and then to consider how the performance of his particular unit could improve or detract from the final product.

It is a peculiar characteristic of almost all public businesses that the way jobs are described is almost entirely task directed. Manuals for civil servants in contact with the public describe, in the most minute detail, what the official may do and how the administrative systems work, but they seldom describe how to satisfy an individual member of the public. Ticket clerks on the London Underground, one set of employees to whom virtually everyone talks, were for years given no instructions, let alone any training, about how to deal with customers. Telephone engineers are given the most detailed training in their arts but are left to cope with their customers as they choose. If management is ever to provide the techniques to enable all these and more, to provide a complete service, they must themselves be sure what the customers want.

There is an important proviso to all this. Customers may want things which the organisation is incapable of providing or unwilling to provide. Each organisation must list all the things which customers want and then determine those items which it is both willing to provide and capable of providing. Two key phrases are: 'Never make promises which you cannot keep' and 'It is better to say "sorry!" than "yes!" and then not deliver what was promised'.

Defining customer needs

The answer to the question 'What do customers want?' lies at the heart of true customer care. Too often this question is answered by senior management who think they know what would be 'good' for customers. So they have a bright, and often expensive, idea which may enhance the product but does not meet real customer needs. (We described one in Chapter 6.) A sounder way to explore customer needs is to ask the staff who deal with customers. Because such staff are junior in the organisation their first-hand experience is often ignored. Almost all businesses now find some way of asking their customers what they want. The problem is that they do not know what to do with the answers which are often expensive and confusing because the context is unclear.

When the first combined British Airways cabin crew was being created in 1978, it was decided to take a thorough look at what the actual job of air stewards and stewardesses should be. They all have to perform a safety function, but there are many more on each aircraft than would be required by a strict application of safety requirements. The airline was quite clear that they were there for customer care. The manual that described their job did so in the minutest of detail, telling them where to stand or sit, what to do in every eventuality, how to serve meals, how to do first aid and so on. What it did not do was to describe how to care for passengers. In fact the word passenger did not appear once.

The management decided to change this. The first thing was to agree an objective and the one chosen was similar to the one we suggested above, namely that: 'Cabin crew should provide that level of customer service such that every passenger would wish to travel with British Airways again.'

Some recent surveys of customer comment and opinion were researched and the cabin crew were consulted to create a list of what passengers should expect to happen on a well-ordered flight. What emerged was the '39 Steps'. This was a list written from the *customer's point of view* of all the things which he or she might reasonably expect. It included such things as: 'To be greeted with a smile', 'To be helped with luggage', 'To have the call button answered in reasonable time', 'To visit clean lavatories', and so on. This list was then turned into a new-style cabin crew manual which described how to achieve these results.

Publishing all this was not the end (though it often is with some managements). The management and supervisory staff were then consulted about how to make this happen. Clearly, there had to be a change in training. But cabin crew, on average, visited the training centre every five years, apart from safety checks. So on-the-job training was introduced using the senior cabin crew. There was also a series of briefings from the management given while actually travelling with the crews. But most important there was a change in the way cabin crew work was inspected.

In the past the travelling inspectorate had concentrated on safety, aircraft operations and catering. Now they were required to look critically at customer care, using the 39 Steps, and coach the crews in how to achieve better performance. The scheme worked well apparently. There was a good deal of enthusiasm and much management effort. The next problem was how to measure the effectiveness of the changes. (Remember this was a quasi-monopoly situation and the market cues would be far too difficult to interpret, even if they could be satisfactorily detected.)

As a matter of routine the airline's marketing department was polling passengers in the baggage halls after their flights. (They usually have time and can be quizzed without being delayed.) This seemed an ideal opportunity to ask them a few more questions about the care they had received on the flight so recently ended. A very high response rate produced excellent data.

The questions were all in the form: 'Were you helped with your luggage?', 'Were you greeted with a smile?' and, of course, 'Was the call button answered promptly?' They were then processed and expressed as percentages satisfied or not. The data were collected on a monthly basis and the results given to the cabin crew management.

They could then plot progress, decide future action and from time to time tell the crews. In fact in due course the General Manager made the attainment of targets based on these data part of their role descriptions and performance reviews.

There was a measurable improvement in customer satisfaction over the following year.

In this example we see work being set out in terms of ends and in response to a known objective. We see those involved being included in the development of the action and gaining ownership. We see the results being quantified and published, so that those concerned had knowledge of results. Finally, we see management being set known and attainable goals and being judged on the results. Above all, the customer benefited and everyone concerned knew and was encouraged. Without an obvious market feedback mechanism, management had succeeded in developing a way of achieving similar ends using the basic principles we have described here.

Organise to reflect customer behaviour

Too often, either in the search for greater efficiency, or because change appears to be desirable for 'political' or other reasons, enterprises reorganise without taking the consequences to the customer into consideration. In Chapter 7 we cited the case of a department store chain which ignored their customers' wish for merchandise which was 'different'. In the early 1980s the United Kingdom government decided to deregulate and privatise the bus industry which resulted in a very much poorer service. A few years later the same government decided to break up the public house cartel with the result that there are now fewer and more expensive pubs.

The moral of these stories is that reorganisations almost never benefit the customer. What he or she wants requires the painstaking application of straightforward management skills. All we can hope for is that some careful thought might minimise the bad effects of reorganisation on customers. What can happen and did in the case of the British Rail reorganisation (described in Chapter 1), is that it provides the opportunity to change and develop the management of the business in the customers' favour.

When we began to plan the courses it was made clear to us that it was British Rail policy to be market oriented and that meant highly responsive to the customers – the passengers. It was also pointed out that we would have managers from all parts of the Midland Region and that many of them did not see a live passenger from one year to the next. It was clearly no use our exhorting the course members to be kind to the customers, not could we persuade them that each of their contributions affected travellers. They all believed in a vague philosophy of serving the 'travelling public' but they thought it could be satisfied by trying to make the trains run on time if possible.

We had to get them to demonstrate the importance of customer care to themselves. The first thing was to encourage them to define the market in very personal terms. We discouraged forecasts in 'passengers' and got them to discuss customers. The point here is that the whole transport industry counts every passenger as if he or she made one journey. The reality is that each makes at least two – there and back – and most make many each year. There is indeed a continuing personal relationship between the traveller and the railway – he is truly a customer.

When we asked them to brainstorm their product it was to be from the customers' point of view. We made them put themselves in the customers' shoes. They soon discovered that the possibilities for satisfying the customer were finite but involved everyone. They wanted to create a railway product with all the features they had long desired but never seen in practice. Perhaps the most dramatic was punctuality. But as soon as this was discussed it became clear that almost everyone had a hand in it. Every aspect of the railway business comes back one way or another to the timetable and its operation.

We used a very simple device to bring this home to the courses. While there was an agenda for the course, we always made it clear that the actual timetable would be flexible to allow for the inevitable varieties of pace and knowledge. At the start of the course we stated a simple rule: *at the beginning of each stage we would tell them by when it should end, and at every break in the course we would state the exact time of the next meeting.* We even warned them to be punctual. We then kept a record of what happened.

Almost without exception we were never able to start an activity on time because someone was late – sometimes a couple of minutes, frequently more. Invariably one group would be late back from its work to report. There was no real commitment to keeping to the simple timekeeping rules we had laid down.

After two and a half days we would bring this to the participants' attention. We would ask them if their own management meetings took place as scheduled; if they made appointments on time; if their activities were completed in the time specified. In many cases they admitted that this was not the case. In fact we knew that time management and punctuality were poor. 'How then,' we asked, 'can your railway ever run on time and your staff be punctual and timely, if they have before them the example of a perpetually late management?' The lesson never failed.

But the point at which most course members realised how they could affect customer care invariably occurred in the problem-solving exercise. We carefully constructed problems which nearly always described how the railway was or was about to disappoint its customers. This was after three days when every opportunity had been taken to emphasise the issue.

Almost every group at first would set out to solve the problem in its own terms. The tunnel collapsed so dig it out and divert the trains; there is a competitive attack, so cut prices and go for competitive timings; and so on. But gradually it dawned that, whatever the problem, the customers had to be cared for even to the point of putting them in buses if need be while the line was repaired at the company's expense.

It was quite remarkable how, given the chance to take their

own decisions and not being constrained by departmental taboos, the participants began to offer quite radical solutions often at the expense of their own department or discipline. As they tackled problems within commercial criteria, they found that satisfying customers was no longer an optional extra – it was the whole job.

Summary

Customer care is much more than telling staff how to be nice to customers. The reality of good customer care depends on the systems and procedures that management installs to enable their staff to satisfy customer needs. Every person selling or providing a service should do so in such a way that the customer will want to come back again next time. Products and services should be designed with the customer in mind, as should the operational systems to deliver them. If management plays its part, it will discover that the vast majority of its staff have a propensity to behave well to customers. Staff training does not need to be about being 'nice' – it does need to be about how to get information and how to operate the procedures.

Customers are satisfied if they receive what they thought they had paid for. If they are disappointed then this will have an immediate commercial impact. In large monopolies, or near monopolies, this simple feedback does not function. Management must therefore invent other ways of allowing customers to express their feelings and comment on what they have received. This information should then form part of the system of management and supervision enabling staff to discover the satisfaction of doing their jobs well.

A customer-oriented business is one in which the needs of the customer are treated as paramount. Every job in a business has some effect on its customers. Each manager should try to plot the connections between his responsibilities and the final product so that he can understand how his own performance will improve it. Training for this must at first concentrate on behaviour, for it is essential that the management as a whole concerns itself with customer care in everything it does. Every problem and policy should be tackled with the customer in mind.

We have emphasised that a preoccupation with customers should be part of an entire business culture and it should enter into the work of management groups, now we turn to consider how these groups are constructed and how they function.

References

1 BAYLEY, S. *Taste: The secret meaning of things*. London, Faber and Faber, 1991.
2 PETERS, T. J. and WATERMAN, R. H. *In Search of Excellence*. New York, Harper & Row, 1982.

10

Work is a Group Activity

The group at work

It was Adam Smith who first appreciated the importance of the division of labour. He observed that by dividing a productive task up into its components and then allocating each to a different individual, those workers could specialise, improve their skills and so raise overall output. He recognised that work is a group activity. What Adam Smith saw was nothing new. Men and women had been co-operating in work since the dawn of mankind and the creation of the first societies. There are indeed many activities which can only be performed by a group, but modern man often goes out of his way to make work a group activity.

The most interesting questions about working groups, some of which were addressed by Smith, concern not so much the consequences, higher output and better quality, but why this happens. The plain fact, with which we are all familiar, is that any group is more productive than the same individuals working alone, and the difference cannot just be accounted for by division of labour and specialisation.

There is a completely different feel to work done under such conditions. Firstly, a group has endurance. Even the most dedicated and professional craftsman working by himself has trouble keeping going. There is always the temptation to take a break or go a little slower. Secondly, the group gives encouragement to its members. We all thrive when our efforts are appreciated by others. In fact some people need such feedback all the time. We have already characterised this as the need to have knowledge of results. In group working it is more than that, it is the repeated acknowledgement of a contribution to the group activity. Thirdly, the group provides examples. One aspect of the process of improving performance which is not within our four principles of learning (described in Chapter 1) is the importance of example. All of us learn by watching others and the group at work provides continuing opportunities for this.

Clearly, much more is happening in a group than the simple division of labour. The members are doing things for one another which enable each individual contribution to be increased. This is the dynamic of the group and is itself the subject of an extensive literature. Such a group is a social organism; it is not only externally productive but internally satisfying; it gives strength and support to its members. Furthermore, it is a common experience that simply being part of a group fulfils some very deep needs for individual members. Thus most work takes place within groups, either formal or informal, and for most people this is a very important part of their life at work. It is therefore a central part of the management of work to create and organise working groups. But management itself is a group activity. This is not only because it needs many 'hands' to do the various tasks which must be done simultaneously, but also because no one manager can have all the knowledge and skills to do the work.

Management is a group activity

It has been our experience that well-constructed groups are able to tackle management tasks very effectively. In Chapter 3 we discussed the way in which Belbin's Self-Perception Analysis could be used to construct the groups on our training courses and how these groups rapidly learned to work together effectively. It proved a very useful way of creating an ad hoc group which would be able to move easily into the tasks and exercises quickly without spending a great deal of time getting established.

Ideally, of course, one would wish to construct real life working groups in the same way. In practice this is unlikely to happen because groups at work tend to be based on the functions performed by people, rather than their preferences as to the role performed in a group. It is important to remember, however, that to be effective a group must 'perform' all the roles described by Belbin. Someone needs to ensure that group tasks are completed; someone needs to generate new ideas; someone must explore the ideas and turn them into concrete plans and so on. An important lesson from the training courses was that most people can perform far more roles than their one or two preferred ones. The needs of the group can, on occasions, propel individuals into taking roles they never imagined for themselves and the group will then provide the strength and encouragement for this to be a success.

The lesson, therefore, for managers is that they should be aware of the various roles which must be performed in the group of which they are a part, and, if a role is not being performed, to perform it themselves. Because a significant amount of managers' time is spent working in groups – most of which are called meetings! – the rest of this chapter is devoted to examining how managers can make best use of the time they devote to group activity and how we have enabled, managers to learn this.

Maximising group resources

The first thing to be said is that meetings are about ends not means. The outputs of meetings, that is decisions leading to actions, are the raison d'etre of having a meeting. Agreeing about actions which members of the group really believe in is a question of technique. In other words, however well a meeting is conducted, and a feeling of well-being engendered in the participants, the meeting is of little value unless it leads to action. It is because so many meetings tend to be 'talking shops' that they have earned themselves a bad name.

The most important feature of a group is that its output is likely to be much greater than the sum of the individual outputs of the participants. When we work together we encourage one another and build on each other's work, utilising our strengths and compensating for weaknesses. In short, *a group does best when it makes the maximum use of each individual's contribution.* But a group will not just be successful because it is a group. It will need to be disciplined, and to follow some simple guidelines in order to make the most of the contributions of its members. It will do this most effectively when leadership is shared. This does not mean that there should not be one member of the group who organises its activities and takes the chair. What it does mean is that this is not a position of power or status, but rather a way of enabling the group to function better. Thus, at different times in the group's activities different members will be taking the lead and moving the work along. This allows everyone to make a contribution. Furthermore, it also allows everybody to adopt an appropriate role.

Let us first look at three techniques which we all need in order to contribute actively to successful group activity. These skills are not only essential for working in a group but should in fact be part of our everyday social equipment. They are 'questioning', 'summarising' and 'effective listening'.

Questioning is the oldest form of learning known to man. It is the way children learn every day. They ask about the things they see and feel; they ask 'what', 'how' and 'why' all the time. Everything they hear is immediately relevant because they have chosen it to be so. Socrates used questions to develop the thoughts of his pupils and Christians learn their faith through the catechism. Questions are the fundamental building blocks of the learning process. This is because learning requires the transmission of knowledge and skills from one human to another and questions require both parties to be active. Making speeches needs only one participant to be active, the other can be asleep. Remember our precepts for learning in Chapter 1: it happens when we want it to and when we see the point. Only in a questioning environment can those two be continually reinforced.

In order to do its work a group must always start by learning about the topic. Every subject at every meeting involves a learning process – however short. It is our observation that groups that use questioning learn fast and tackle problems better. But questioning not only gets all the information on the table it helps to structure the work too. In conversation, questions enable us to keep the discussion 'on the rails'. In social conversation we never stick to one topic consistently. Observe next time you find yourself around the bar or the dinner table how each contribution, be it opinion or anecdote, is answered by another which will refer to one idea in that contribution – usually the last. This new contribution will actually be about a slightly different subject, as will the next and the next. After 10 minutes the conversation will have 'drifted' far away from the original theme. The same can happen with meetings.

Questions directed at enlarging group knowledge of the primary subject will always tend to re-focus the attention of participants. They also serve to make contributions relevant and often shorter. If they are accompanied by summaries – see below –

they make contributors clarify and develop their ideas. Above all, questions are unthreatening and flattering and will encourage people to develop ideas rather than defend and argue for their initial contribution. In short, questioning is creative: argument is destructive.

Summarising is a skill not widely practised but it is most useful both in formal groups and in everyday social intercourse. At first, when we are introduced to summarising, it all seems forced and we feel embarrassed, but by repeating back to others what they have said, they get the chance to re-emphasise or correct it, or if agreed the discussion can be moved ahead. It is remarkable how summaries remove tension and defuse arguments because they always speed understanding. It is virtually impossible to argue with someone who responds with a summary followed by a question.

The most important aspect of summarising is its power to reinforce learning. As children we are encouraged to repeat our lessons so that they are committed to memory. If we repeat what we have heard in our own words we already begin to gain ownership and we will remember it.

In a group, summarising is far more than just a recapitulation of decisions taken or a rehearsal of other people's views. It is the process by which all members of the team can regularly review their progress in identifying the real issues under discussion. Good summaries 'package' the discussion so far and almost inevitably end with a question. This is because the summary is like constructing a jig-saw from the pieces of the discussion. If a piece is missing from the picture this will occur to the summariser – hence the question. Summaries, like questions, also help to keep the discussion 'to the point'. They remind the participants about the topic and encourage them to direct their next contribution to it.

Summaries can be encouraged and enhanced in a number of ways. It can be a regular routine of the chairman to make or call for a summary. Flipcharts and white-boards can be used to make notes and lists which will help to organise summaries. Note-takers can call for summaries in order to keep the record. They are also important for the chairman himself because they enable him to agree decisions, ensure that there is a consensus and identify any key differences of view which must be resolved. They invariably form the basis of any report or set of minutes.

145

Effective listening is much more than just hearing what another person has to say. There are occasions where larger chunks of knowledge or information have to be transmitted. Often we find ourselves in conversations where one side has the knowledge and the other wants to learn. In such cases the learning happens when there is active listening.

Think about what you do when someone else is talking. Probably you first pay full attention to their opening sentences. You decide whether you have heard it all before, or if new material is being presented you rapidly decide what points the speaker is making or is likely to make. Because your brain can process information very quickly you have some spare time. You use this either to think about something quite different, or more likely, to work out what you are going to say next when you get the opportunity.

Effective listening is more demanding. It requires considering why the speaker is saying what he does, particularly if you do not agree with him. Because he is unlikely to be giving sufficient information to determine fully the reason for his views, you will need to ask questions before putting forward your own viewpoint. Thus effective listening and questioning are closely linked and, used well, can progress a discussion quickly and without unnecessary acrimony or confrontation.

These skills are also an important part of the group process itself. It is very difficult to argue with someone who asks questions. Everyone feels included and encouraged when singled out in a discussion and asked their opinion. If conflicts do arise then a judicious summary can be very useful in isolating the cause. If someone has just made an extreme and unsupported statement, and they then hear its contents reflected back as a summary, it is often hard for them to sustain their position and the conflict evaporates.

Working in a group

Successful group behaviour does not depend on continuous conformity. In fact the group will benefit from diversity as long as it can make use of it. As we have seen, working in a group means performing a wide variety of roles. However, the basic skills described above lie at the heart of the process.

Let us now distinguish between roles and the essential tasks which must be undertaken in group activity. During its work the group has to process a wide variety of information and reach conclusions efficiently and effectively. To do this a number of tasks must be undertaken by the members. It is part of group behaviour to ensure that such tasks are assigned and undertaken.

- *Organising.* This is done by someone called a 'chairman' who is there to enable the group to programme its work and assign tasks within the group's limited resources, the scarcest of which is often time. However, there will be occasions when others perform this task more appropriately. For example, when the group's task involves a specialist technique such as accounting, it may be more efficient to let the group member with this skill take the lead.
- *Enquiring.* Somebody has to ask the questions which enable the group to start its work. In fact, each stage will probably be initiated by a question. Enquiry is the key way in which data and information are extracted and organised. Groups work well when someone sets out to be the enquirer rather than when individuals spend time telling everybody else what they know regardless of its relevance. The giving of information, which includes the telling of anecdotes, can often be a way of trying to establish status – thus it becomes a competitive rather than collaborative activity.
- *Information-giving.* On the other hand, questions do have to be answered and usually every member of the group finds he is an 'expert' on something or other and will be able to help with answers to the questions as they are posed. Nobody should be afraid of being an expert but knowledge must be put at the disposal of the group in an orderly way.
- *Ideas-generating.* Once the group begins to understand its task and information is being traded, it will need to generate ideas. There are many techniques for implanting ideas. Simply dropping them into the discussion is seldom effective. All too often people shy away from good ideas because of the way they are expressed. So experience teaches that groups who explore ideas systematically usually do well. Techniques such as 'brainstorming' are relevant here.

147

- *Clarifying*. The group has to subject all the ideas generated to critical review. As we shall see, there has to be order and criteria for this to work. All the time someone has to be reminding the group why it is there.
- *Synthesising*. The work of the group has to be put into shape so that objectives can be properly achieved. Often there will be one group member who shapes the ideas and pulls everything together and begins to make sense of it all. (This is often done by the Belbin 'shaper' described in Appendix V.)
- *Detailing*. Management groups who deal only in broad information and ideas tend not to be particularly successful. Someone in the group must undertake the detail and help it to examine the minutiae.
- *Completing*. Every group task must be finished and it needs a particular skill to bring the various contributions to a successful conclusion. (This is the Belbin 'completer/finisher'.)
- *Presenting*. The work of a group always has to be communicated to someone. Whether this is a written report or a live presentation, it takes skill to put it together and good communications are seldom achieved by a committee. Someone has to take the lead.
- *Recording*. But without the essential note-taker nothing can be achieved. Management is nothing if it is not a written activity. The work of every group must be recorded in a well-ordered fashion. This too requires particular skills.

However, as well as these tasks directed towards successful outcomes the group itself has to be maintained. If the group is to take full advantage of its own dynamics, the members have to feel good about what they are doing. There are a number of behavioural tasks to be performed. These are:

- *Harmonising*. This tends to be done by the chairman, who will seek to ensure that the work of individuals is incorporated with the group activity in ways which avoid clashes, give due reward and further the overall task. In short the group should avoid unnecessary friction.
- *Encouraging*. Every group needs its 'teamworker' (See Appendix V) who tends to be as much concerned with the health of the group as with the achievement of its main objectives.

He knows that by maintaining a high level of motivation, good outcomes are more likely.

- *Resolving.* This is the key activity for the group. It was Mary Parker Follett, an American social scientist, who pointed out at the beginning of the century that 'compromise' usually results in the worst of all worlds.[1] She suggested that 'resolving differences was the key to success'. By this she meant that through discussion a new view of a problem and a course of action would emerge which would be, at least, acceptable to the various parties. A group which has the ability to resolve differences is likely to be very powerful.
- *Processing.* This is the behaviour which gets the job done in the end. It is important that the group works on problems and progresses the work without allowing debate and argument to become personal. This is always possible because groups are social. Someone has to remind them about the purposes of the group.
- *Gate-keeping.* This means keeping the 'gates' open and ensuring that every member gets to participate or maybe rejoin the debate after they have been silent. The channels of communication have to be kept open and this is only possible if someone is actively remembering the various contributors, bringing everyone into the discussion and keeping the discussion open.

All these tasks are not only a necessary part of the work of a group tackling one issue at one time, they are also the essential stuff of the continuing relationship between managers and their staff. Every day managers meet together and as they learn to practise these skills, both individually and collectively, so their meetings become more successful – and shorter. No matter what the agenda – briefing groups, working parties, business meetings – group skills enhance performance. But it is our observation that the single most frequent activity undertaken by management groups is the solving of problems and that this is generally not done well. As well as the usual skills it requires a set of quite specific techniques.

Meetings are usually to solve problems

Do you take part in weekly meetings with your colleagues and your manager? Are they effective, or do you regard them mainly as a means of keeping each other informed? This constant quest for information, almost for its own sake, seems to us to lie at the heart of much managerial frustration. 'I wasn't told . . .' leads to meetings and endless copies of memoranda to anyone who might be interested. This in turn leads to 'We spend too much time at meetings' or 'I'm deluged with paperwork'. It is a vicious circle.

To break the circle managers need to recognise that information is only useful when it leads to action, or confirms successful actions. Excess information either leads to 'overload' (i.e. one cannot do anything with it) or is a manifestation of inquisitiveness. Managerial meetings should focus on problems and always lead to action, but so many degenerate into one-to-one conversations between the chairman and one other member, while the rest of the meeting looks on. One reason for this is that at most management meetings the chairman is the most senior manager present, in fact he may be the boss of most present. This makes it very difficult for him to be other than a tribal leader – even if he wants it otherwise – and very difficult for the others to contribute as much as they could.

Let us remind ourselves of the two key roles of every manager:

- To deliver the output for which he is primarily responsible;
- To contribute to the attainment of the goals and outputs of the management groups of which he is a part.

In the first case he will probably create a group or team to enable him to achieve the necessary outcomes. In the second he will be part of a management team, often led by his boss. We all have to be able to perform both roles – frequently in quick succession. Each requires a keen knowledge of how groups work and how to tackle problems. Meetings are so much a part of the life of every manager we tend to take them for granted. If, in our experience, meetings are ineffective, we seldom analyse why. Rather, we tend just to complain.

The situation becomes one in which time is wasted in meetings while the company staggers from one crisis to another, mostly caused by a lack of clear policy and poor communications. In short, the very problems the meetings are called for seem to increase with the time spent in meetings. What are needed are useful meetings which will enable managers and supervisors to do a better job and reduce the number of unplanned disadvantageous events, i.e. crises.

Participants also often feel unable to contribute through the form and procedure of the meeting. Out of frustration these meetings become either monologues by the chairman or post mortems on the problems of yesterday. Clearly such a gap cannot be closed by a simple edict to 'get it right'. If meetings are to be useful, the participants have to be prepared to 'buy in' to the process. They all have to be aware of the advantages of co-operating. And the key to that is an agreement about the content of the meeting. This is the agenda.

It is just as frequent to hear of agendas set entirely by the chairman as it is to hear of no agenda at all. Agendas are not merely ritual. A good agenda provides the framework for successful teamwork. In short there has to be a clear understanding of the purpose and expected outcome of every meeting and this is the agenda. *The agenda of a good meeting is one where everyone at the meeting feels involved all the time.*

How should we deal with problems?

We all think we are good at solving problems. We do it constantly, every day, all the time. Whenever you say 'They should do this . . .' or 'If only they realised . . .' you are proposing a solution to some problem. Our whole national debate is conducted in terms of solutions. In most cases the problems are assumed, often in the face of what little evidence is available. In fact the power of a 'solution society' is now so evident that adherence to particular problem definitions has become an article of political faith.

How often do we hear a problem stated in what we would call a straight binary form? For example:

– There are a great many homeless because the government no longer builds subsidised housing.

therefore

– The government should house the homeless.

Here is another:

– There are extensive waiting lists for hospital treatment and the National Health Service is under-funded.

therefore

– More tax revenue should be diverted to the NHS.

Or:

– Hooliganism by young men happens at football matches.

therefore

– Rebuild football grounds to make such behaviour difficult during matches.

When stated like this we can easily see that the way in which the problem is stated predetermines the available set of solutions. Furthermore, a moment's thought would reveal that each problem could have been stated to produce a different set of solutions. In fact we would argue in all these cases the problems as seen by those involved have never been properly analysed. For example:

– There are a great many homeless made so by the repossession of houses by building societies.

therefore

– The government should subsidise a scheme for renting by the building societies and cut interest rates.

Perhaps the most telling evidence for our preoccupation with solutions in the United Kingdom today is the almost complete passing of Royal Commissions. For a century and a half governments had such Commissions appointed to enquire into any great public issue. They spent a great deal of time investigating the problems set and frequently produced reports of historical significance. They tended, if anything, to be weak on solutions but after such recent reports as Fulton or Donovan we could have been in no doubt about the problems of the Civil Service or industrial relations respectively.

Governments prefer solutions to ill-defined problems and act accordingly. Policies are no longer about how the government will behave on such and such a matter or towards a particular section of the population, they are merely lists of solutions. It is therefore no wonder that we all tend to join in the endless discussion of solutions most of which cannot solve the problems which have never been properly specified. Thus we are locked into the theory of reverse consequences which states that every political action tends to have the opposite consequence to the one desired.

Perhaps, fortunately, no-one takes much notice of our individual views. But we do tend to take this behaviour into our managerial lives. If you don't believe this, count up the number of proposals for action suggested at any meeting. Most proposals are met with a response 'It won't work because . . .' or 'We've tried that before . . .' The trouble lies in the fact that we have not considered fully and exhaustively the real nature of the problem we are trying to solve. Kepner and Taylor explore this facet of management.[2] Their ideas may be represented by this little diagram:

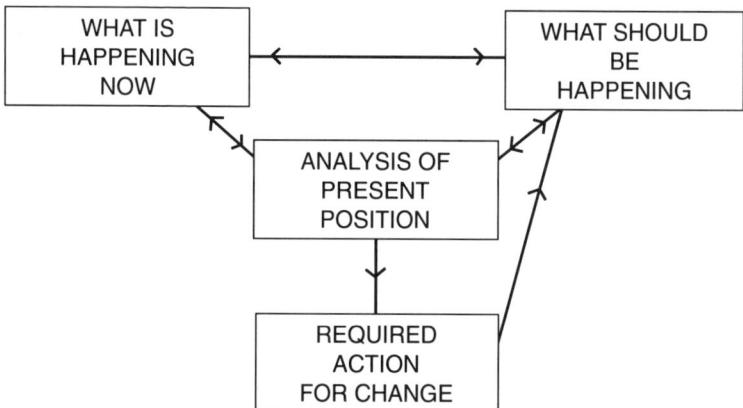

The arrows linking the boxes are two-way, because clarification of one box leads to the need for further consideration of another. The important thing to remember is that most problems are more complex than appears at first sight. The real danger is that we call 'the reciprocal solution'. Here is an example:

Present position – Sales are falling.
What should be happening? – We must increase sales.

The discussion then proceeds rapidly to solutions – ideas on how to increase sales.

This is not good enough. We need to spend considerable time on determining 'what should be happening'. The first step in this process is to define the criteria for what will be happening when the desired result is achieved. This can be matched against 'what is happening now' and an analysis of why what is happening is taking place. Inevitably this discussion leads to a modification of the criteria for 'what should be happening'. Only when the group is really clear about this should solutions be discussed – and then most of them are self-evident.

A real-life example will help to clarify what we mean:

In 1974 the British motor industry was in serious decline. Its home market share was being steadily eroded by car imports. The Government commissioned a study by the Central Policy Review Staff in which one of the authors became involved.

Before beginning an extensive series of visits to car plants in Britain and Europe, a number of senior executives in the industry were interviewed. Almost without exception they saw the problem in technical terms. The foreign imports were, they said, technically inferior but cheaper. They were worried lest they caught up technically with no increase in price. They blamed their workers for many of their ills. There had been very poor industrial relations for years and, they said, the general standard of performance was poor – the workers were simply not skilled and not motivated. Their solution was more investment in car design, to create better cars, and in car production, to produce cars using fewer workers.

It was widely believed that the market required a great diversity of types, models and options and that cars were bought primarily on their technical specification. At that time in the British inventory were some of the most advanced passenger vehicles in the world. There was also a large model range. All that was needed was

Government help with the investment and the industry would 'kick start' into success.

The team then started to collect data to support this thesis. Not only were factories visited, a great deal of data was made available. Detailed production schedules and costs were analysed, work practices investigated and sales and marketing data scrutinised. While there was no doubt that many customers saw the imported cars as better value for money, they were not markedly cheaper. They were also, in many respects, not technically inferior. There was little evidence to support the industry's own thesis other than the demonstrably better industrial relations in Europe. This was 'explained' as resulting from higher pay levels which, too, turned out not to be entirely true.

The team were not problem-solving in the structured way described here, but there were similarities of approach. Let us, however, apply our schema to it:

The current position:
The British car industry was losing market share to imports because of perceived inferior value for money.

The desired position:
British cars should become competitive with foreign cars to the point where they were able to regain market share.

Analysis of the present position:
Poor labour relations, poor quality of workmanship, outdated production techniques and machinery. In addition, it was argued that the terms of trade were against the industry and that overseas manufacturers were subsidised.

Action needed:
Subsidies for investment because the industry could not raise the money.

The team remained unconvinced by the evidence. There were, however, a few clues as to what the real problem might be. A Consumer Association Report in early 1975 revealed that British cars occupied almost all the top twenty positions in a poll of unreliable cars. It also revealed that the cost of after-sales service was high for the British cars, the guarantee periods short and the service slow. The industry itself had information which reinforced this. Their own market research showed that reliability was an important market requirement and was not thought to be good among British cars. Their response had been to spend more on the distributor network and the parts organisations.

155

The real problem appeared almost by accident. If reliability was the symptom, what was the disease? The industry said that it was constantly improving its products with reliability as well as performance in mind. The design engineers were encouraged to 'develop' every car in production in the pursuit of 'high technical standards'. This meant an almost continuous process of modification to the design. As part of the routine data collected from the British factories, the team received the schedules of product change orders. These are the detailed and itemised changes to the specification of a car which is in production as a result of design changes, which are sent to the assembly shops. The lists were very long indeed.

Every model was being modified every week. In one assembly shop there had been over 800 change orders in a year. One model had three different light fittings and dozens of detailed changes to its engines. The workers were perpetually having to learn new routines; they could never settle down and learn to build a standard car – there was no such thing – and so they were always low down on the learning curve. There was always difficulty with parts since the new ones were invariably delayed. This often meant cars clearing the lines incomplete and having to be fitted with parts later. Good workmanship was being sacrificed to design at every stage. As a result there was little satisfaction and no motivation.

The situation in the parts inventory was worse. Because of changes, there were always holdings of obsolete parts. Every model had so many versions requiring different parts that whole new information systems had to be created and storage requirements were huge. No dealer could possibly stock a representative selection, so customers would always have to wait. This led to low motivation here too.

It was now possible to define a new problem:

> The dominance of the design offices meant that technical advances always tended to be made at the expense of production and reliability. As a result customers, while recognising the excellence of British design, had no confidence in the cars produced.

Once stated like this, solutions presented themselves. The problem would be solved only when there was a measurable improvement in customer confidence. However, old habits die hard and it was another decade and more lost markets before reliability and consistency in production, not to mention customer care, began to be valued more highly than technical performance.

Incidentally and by contrast, the team found that in a well-known German car factory, in one assembly shop there were just seven change orders that year between the annual model change.

The lesson is clear: *it is more important to define the problem correctly and to set criteria, than it is to develop elegant solutions to the wrong problem.*

We have found in practice that one extra stage is often helpful in developing solutions. The clarification of 'what is happening now' and the examination of the criteria developed for 'what should be happening' leads to a *gap* where actions are required. Being formally aware of this gap often highlights the fact that it is unlikely to be closed by taking one solution in isolation. What is required is a series of sequential actions which, over a period, will close the gap.

There is nothing which concentrates the business mind like a shortage of cash. A small company with three directors, all with the right to sign cheques, and with an enthusiastic buying department suddenly realised that cash flow was below expectations. The business was inherently healthy and sales were up to expectations. Stock levels were on target and the sales ledger staff were busily collecting money. So what had gone wrong?

A simple statement of the problem, namely 'insufficient cash', might lead to either a simple solution – 'get debts in faster' – or no solution at all, merely resignation. However, the directors had used problem-solving techniques before so they asked themselves 'Where do we want to be?' and gave themselves the answer 'About a quarter of a million better off'.

This dramatically demonstrated a 'gap'. As yet the problem remained unclear. So they began to analyse the nature of the shortfall. In fact the ratio of invoices to debtors, and debtors to cashflow looked about right. So they looked at payments and the creditors list. To their surprise they found outstanding creditors far lower than expected. Many suppliers had been paid almost on delivery; days of grace had been ignored and the company was not taking the credit due to it.

It transpired that, in their enthusiasm, the members of the purchasing department had all been 'looking after' their suppliers; and though each director had been very careful to sign only those cheques which he or she deemed essential, they each had different criteria for what was essential. So they had been manipulated by the staff – always with the best of intentions.

The problem was now revealed to be the lack of a policy and procedure for making payments. No short-term action was actually possible, only the creation of a system which would control payments and a policy for deciding priorities.

Even though this gap was closed by the action planned, it is clear that new problems would occur. Purchase staff might resent the restrictions, suppliers might become less friendly. This illustrates a great truth about problem-solving: *every solution is itself the basis and cause of the next problem.*

We suggest that problem-solving is always helped by using flipcharts or white-boards to write up the stages as they evolve. Frequently, there will be a number of specifications of where we are now and often more than one of where we want to be. The analysis of the path between may cover many sheets. Eventually, however, solutions must be listed. If these are all framed as strategies and tactics for crossing the gap, they will invariably lead directly to a specification of the conditions for success: *that which must have happened for the desired state to have been arrived at.* These are the criteria for testing solutions.

Teamworking

Since working in a group is so central to management, we have concluded that the training of managers must be largely done in groups. It is an essential part of the design of all our courses that people should work in groups. *Not only does this make for more effective learning but the participants learn some of the techniques of working in a group.*

Typically, on the Monday morning of the British Rail Midland Region Course, as soon as the groups had settled down we would visit them. It was essential that they begin to organise and plan their work. To a certain extent we had done a good deal of this in the course design. It can be seen from the course documents in Appendix I that the work had been divided into manageable chunks. Each stage contained very specific instructions which formed the basis of the agenda for each stage.

For a group to work effectively it needs time. So meetings which are to lead to action should have limited agendas. Often the implications and ramifications of a task appear daunting. That is why many people tend to concentrate on quick solutions to apparent problems rather than analysis. We encouraged our groups to spend a high proportion of

---

their time at the beginning analysing and pooling knowledge.

One of the key skills of a Chairman is to help the group to 'get its arms round a problem' – to reduce it to manageable size. The most effective way of doing this is to ensure that the group concentrates first on criteria. What is it that they want to have happened by the time the task is complete? It is amazing how often setting criteria concentrates the work into a manageable size. Side issues are seen for what they are – distractions from the key essentials.

On one occasion, in the early days of the courses, we created a group in which the youngest member was the chairman. We had used the Belbin test to locate our chairmen and this young trainee manager, by expressing the necessary preferences, was chosen. At the end of the week we were, of course, curious to know how this had worked out. During the course review sessions on the Friday it came out. At first the older men had been affronted because they had an essentially 'tribal' view of chairmanship, assuming that it bestowed on the holder the right to be right. It should therefore have gone to the most 'experienced'.

The young trainee, on the other hand, knew he did not know that much. Nobody had told him about the traditional chairman's role. He was used to working in groups of his peers and getting the job done. It transpired that that was exactly what he did. He encouraged the others to share their skills and experience, he set agendas and organised the work with flair and enthusiasm. It hardly needs adding that they produced a star presentation and performed very well in the later exercises.

Effective groups work as a team. We set out to show that every team member would have something to contribute. This placed a heavy responsibility on the chairman to ensure that 'silent' members were encouraged to talk and that the discussion was not monopolised by a few dominant people. From the outset we encouraged chairmen to look for signs that a person had something to say. Some people who could make significant contributions were either too shy, or felt too junior, to speak out. We reminded them that people learn by voicing their thoughts.

During the early stages of the week we also took every opportunity to develop the individual skills required for successful working as a team which we have discussed in this chapter. These are not, in themselves, difficult to acquire, but they need self-discipline. The structure of our courses gave ample opportunity for coaching and feedback.

By using group working as the main medium of training we

came to understand how four or five individuals, starting out the week as a group, gradually become a team. We believe that the process we set in train, which placed the responsibility for the course firmly in the hands of the course members, had a dramatic effect on the performance of all the groups.

The process of invention itself draws the members together. If ownership enhances the efforts of the individual, it positively illuminates the group. For a group to be effective it needs to focus on the problem it has come together to solve. If you think that this is a self-evident truth, ask yourself why it is that so many meetings appear to be used to further the ideas or views of individuals. Our groups had clear task goals to achieve and definite time limits. This forced them to keep focusing and avoiding side tracks.

As the week developed most groups began to coalesce. One very important turning point was when the invented business was given a name. Very quickly corporate identities would be created and logos invented. From then on the business and often the group would be referred to by name. We even had cases where printing work was commissioned and a group appeared with headed notepaper.

Wednesday was invariably the presentation by the group of its 'company' and the business plan. This illustrated another aspect of identity. By owning the invented company in public the group at once gave itself an identity. We even noticed that by that stage groups had begun to eat together and even express friendly rivalry with others.

Immediately after the presentation, the groups would be asked to review what they had done and, in the light of the other group presentations and our feedback, tell us what they would have done differently – not in respect of their plan but in the way it had been presented. We showed them that in such cases a management must always review its performance and modify future conduct.

This was followed by exercises on three important management skills, namely communication, interviewing and negotiation. It is worth remarking at this point that once a course has reached this stage it can be set any appropriate task designed to develop whatever skills are thought to be appropriate by the client or even the course members themselves. Having created a 'living' company and an environment, the possibilities for management exercises based on it are almost limitless.

For the communication exercise we asked the groups to compose a succinct and attractive announcement about their plans which could be used either to inform staff or as a press release. This gave them the opportunity to review techniques of communication and understanding something of the different needs of various audiences. Once again we used the resources of the whole course by posting each communique and asking the other groups to read and comment. One very common feature was the way a group would veer away from their plan as presented and return to the conventional style of the railway organisation. This was usually spotted by the course members, who often saw in other communiques the very faults they were committing themselves. The groups were learning from each other.

We believe that one-to-one interviewing skills are so fundamental for all managers that some practice in these should always be included in training. Our approach was pretty conventional using the invented companies. We asked the interviewee to take a role within the company. The interviewer then had to find out the details of the management problems which that manager would experience in undertaking the modernisation plan. We always ran these exercises in groups of 10 and used closed circuit television to film the interviews. Once again we used the course members to help with the feedback (the interview observation guide is Document 26 in Appendix I).

[We have included the briefing material on Communication, Interviewing, Negotiations and Problem-solving in Appendix I (Documents 25, 28, 31 and 32.)]

For our negotiating exercise we invited the participants to become advocates for their own railway and its modernisation plan, and judges of the others. Once again we used the roles which the group members had assigned to each other – operations manager, finance, engineering and so on. Working now in five groups of four, one from each railway, each with the same responsibility, they had to decide which modernisation plan was the best. They were not allowed to compromise or reconstruct a plan out of the four, they had to decide *unanimously* which was best.

The point here was that they had to make objective judgements, decide on a strategy and then win. Success was not ensuring that their own railway won, but that the one they judged best did. What the participants found was that it was very difficult to come up with a 'winner'. More often, in spite of the instruction to the contrary, they built a proposal with the best elements from the four – a solution they could all live with. Thus an important lesson about negotiation was learned.

The process was recorded on CCTV and when everyone had finished it was reviewed by the whole course. It was remarkable how quickly defence and hostility switched to conciliation and resolution as soon as it was realised that success was 'getting an agreement' not winning. Many participants discovered hidden strengths because this exercise required negotiating on their own and reacting instantly to the situation as it developed. Those with experience of negotiating were used to operating as part of a team and this exercise threw them back on their own resources.

On all our courses the problem-solving session became the high point of the week. It always took place on the Thursday afternoon by which time the groups had been together for four days. By then they were familiar with their company and its plans and had become used to working together. Now they were put in front of the video cameras and asked to tackle some catastrophe, minor or major, which had befallen their railway. Each group would tackle a different problem, handpicked to highlight the strengths and weaknesses of the group and its fictional railway. (In some cases the problems were written that very day.) After each 20-minute session there would be a period of feedback using the recording. The whole exercise was observed by the other groups in another room and they were always involved in observing and feedback.

We found that by focusing on the positive aspects of what we observed but never avoiding the mistakes, there was a wide acceptance of this learning process. We always had a member of another group counting solutions. No matter how often we emphasised that the art of problem-solving is to analyse the problem, every time without fail the first group to do the exercise would dive for solutions. The worst case was 32 solutions counted in 20 minutes. Once the lesson began to penetrate, solutions gave way to problems. The best was a group that did not talk about solutions until the last two minutes because they became so absorbed with the problem and its ramifications.

The most fascinating thing about these sessions was the opportunity to eavesdrop on the groups. They soon forgot the cameras and went to work unselfconsciously. We were able to see chairmen at work, to observe 'plants' and admire 'completers'. The material gained went far beyond developing problem-solving skills and enabled us to give positive and detailed feedback to the groups about their performance. It also demonstrated to the whole course the undoubted power of the group at work. Here were teams, only created four days before, going to work on management problems in a way they had probably never seen and demonstrating many of the lessons which had been introduced that week.

We were always surprised. In 27 such courses and with 108 groups no two ever behaved the same. We remember one group who were so taken with SWOT that they adapted it for problem-solving; we watched another group timetable the whole thing; and another group use brainstorming. We saw many groups perform below what they would have liked but almost no total disasters. Every occasion was a valuable learning experience.

Summary

Managements tend to make too little use of active groups to manage their businesses while allowing business meetings to eat up valuable hours. Everyone recognises that most work is performed in a group; in a learning organisation the tremendous potential of management groups will be tapped. Conventional management meetings tend not to release all the creative energy and drive available within a typical management team. A group does best when it makes the maximum use of each individual's contribution. To do this requires the performance of specific roles by group members and the understanding of a set of tasks by the group. Its work has to be purposeful and organised. The group itself has to be harmonised and cared for by its members. In all this the group shares an equal responsibility no matter who takes the role of chairman. There are three key skills required of all members of a group: questioning, summarising and effective listening.

Problem-solving is the paramount activity for management groups. Management consists of a stream of problems and groups are far better at solving them than individuals. The exercise of simple techniques which focus on identifying problems rather than trading solutions has been found to work successfully. The group must identify where it is now, where it wants to be, what the steps are to move from the first to the second and how they will judge that the move has been successful. Group work is an essential part of management training for thus it becomes group learning. Such activities have to balance the need for structure with the need for individuals to create their own learning situations.

Groups need chairmen but not to dominate and decide, rather to enable the group to achieve its end while making the maximum use of its collective resources. This quality is leadership and is the subject of our next chapter.

References

1 FOLLETT, M. P. *The New State*. New York, Longmans Green, 1918.
2 KEPNER, C. and TAYLOR, B. *The Rational Manager*. Provincetown N.J., Kepner-Tregoe Inc. 1965.

Leadership is not Optional

A manager is also a boss

Think about the bosses you have had in your career. Which ones earned your respect and which ones made you want to scream with frustration? One thing is probably certain – there is unlikely to be an exact correlation between your view of your boss as a good or bad boss, and your view of him or her as a fellow human being. You may, or may not, like a boss as a person – but that does not necessarily match your opinion of his or her behaviour as your boss.

What are some of the things which you liked when working for a 'good boss'? They are likely to include at least some of the following:

- He or she developed clear objectives with you, and then allowed you to get on with the job with a minimum of interference.
- When you went for help or advice you got it.
- You were made to think about solutions to your problems, and you knew that he or she would back you up if you had discussed them with them first.
- He or she shared decisions where it was possible and, when it was not possible, he or she told you why they had made a particular decision.
- He or she gave you good information about the results of your actions.
- You knew that you were accountable for your actions.

And what of the other kind of boss? Do any of the following ring a bell?

- He or she gave you orders and instructions rather than objectives.
- You could never get an answer to a question.
- He or she always seemed to change their mind.

- He or she would take work away from you in the middle of a job, and then blame you for the mess.
- He or she told you they were giving you responsibility, and then kept 'nit-picking' about the way you did it.
- You hardly ever saw them, and if you did he or she was not very interested in you.
- He or she never 'listened' to your point of view.
- You never knew how you had done – good work was greeted with the same silence as bad.

Sometimes these are individual instances of good or bad behaviour by bosses; more often they are simply reflecting the 'culture' of the business. We have frequently found that when a manager had complained about his boss, his own subordinates have made similar complaints about him. But it is also the case that managers who have a poor view of their own bosses' behaviour normally think that they treat their subordinates much better.

Thus being a 'good' or 'bad' manager has as much to do with the way a business behaves corporately as it does with individual behaviour within the organisation. This corporate behaviour tends inevitably to be set from the top. The way leaders behave not only provides the model for all those lower down, it sets an example to be followed by those seeking promotion and career advancement. This is not to say that everything is 'the bosses' fault', but rather that leaders set the standards by which the whole business judges itself.

Some years ago a major British publicly owned corporation was being prepared for its return to the private sector. A new Chairman was appointed and he in turn appointed a Chief Executive. Both were noted for their 'tough' approach to management.

That particular business had a well-recognised culture based firmly on the considerable expertise of those that worked for it. Not the most efficient, it nevertheless had a world-wide reputation for reliability and integrity and its managers were individually highly respected. Almost all saw themselves as lifetime employees, and their security was an essential feature of the culture. The business is one where security is very important and this was well understood. Its customers felt comfortable about using its services even when it let them down.

The new leaders decided to use these feelings about the company as a major promotion feature and have ever since described the business to its customers in terms designed to underline the familiarity, reliability and sense of dependability which had existed up till then.

They also decided, on some flimsy evidence, that the management, having grown up in the public sector, would not be appropriate for a private sector corporation. So in great secrecy they planned a major reorganisation and one summer's day they fired one-quarter of the senior management. Most hardly had time to clear their desks; many have not got over that experience to this day.

Subsequently, other managers have been sacked for a wide range of transgressions of which poor performance has been only one. In many cases, not having been given criteria for success, the management axe has fallen as a complete surprise. There have been many more reorganisations and re-shuffles. The secrecy surrounding all such activity has increased.

The change from a highly secure and task motivated management to one motivated by fear was immediate. Within a few years the younger managers had learned to behave in a similar fashion and industrial relations began to be conducted in the same way – secrecy, insecurity and sudden unilateral action replaced consultation and openness. This approach had a superficial and short-term success. It always does. In the short term everyone is fearful of losing their job. But gradually the customers have come to realise that the company they knew has changed. It is no longer one that can be trusted. It is secretive and capricious. It says one thing and does something different. Above all a mere customer can no longer rely on a business that treats its own employees badly.

There is a most important lesson here. *A business has a single culture, it cannot behave one way to its managers or staff and another to its customers; and, bad behaviour always overshadows good – eventually the customers find out.*

Business culture

Just as it is individual behaviour which enables managers to get from where they are to where they want to be, so it is the sum of these behaviours, the culture, which enables a business to move from where it is to where it wants to be. Once a management has analysed a problem and decided upon the appropriate course of action for itself to move to the desired situation, it must also enable all the staff involved to make the same move. The approach adopted defines the culture.

Broadly speaking two contrasting styles of management can be identified in businesses.[1] These are distinguished by the assumptions made by managers about people. Theory X assumes that work is inherently distasteful; most people have little ambition, no desire for responsibility, do not exercise creativity in problem-solving, and are entirely motivated by earning rewards and avoiding punishment. As a result most people have to be controlled and coerced to achieve business goals.

On the other hand, Theory Y assumes that work is a natural pursuit of man; people like to achieve group goals through self-discipline; creativity in problem-solving is widely distributed and motivation is a complex reaction to many personal needs, including esteem and self-actualisation. So people can be self-directed and creative at work if properly motivated. The reader will be in no doubt where we stand in this debate. However, the continuing widespread practice of Theory X management, not to mention widespread political and public espousal of its alleged virtues, compels us to examine it in more detail.

The first and most obvious defect in the Theory X approach is that it flies in the face of the overwhelming social philosophy of the majority of societies on earth today. No leader who applies it to his workforce would wish it applied to him. It simply cannot coexist with such ideas as, for example, freedom of opportunity, workers' rights and democracy. It implies that there are two kinds of people and the leaders are always of one kind.

But still we hear about 'the smack of firm management', or that management 'must be allowed to manage'. Such phrases are usually used by those who have themselves never managed anybody. They have some primaeval memories of school or the scout troop where they enjoyed the benefits of imposed discipline. This reveals a major confusion between the exercise of authority and the art of management.

In spite of all their sophistication, the British are a peculiarly tribal nation. They give enormous emphasis to leadership – even professing to want strong leaders. While claiming to be democratic, success is nearly always attributed to individual leaders who graciously acknowledge the contribution of subordinates, or not. Leaders' utterances are carefully reported, they are allowed to decide, often as a majority of one. In modern politics one might even be forgiven for assuming that party leaders had made up the whole of their party's policies themselves, so strong is the attribution. It is axiomatic in British life that to be made chairman of a public committee is to be given the right to determine the outcome of its deliberations.

> A recent British Prime Minister once remarked, in reference to a Royal Commission, that all you had to do to ensure a satisfactory outcome was to choose the right Chairman.

This confusion about the exercise of authority by leaders arises mainly because when it comes to immediate crisis management, or the real-time operation of a 'fail dangerous' process, or, above all, when fighting a battle, nobody has much difficulty in accepting the leadership of the best qualified.

> Many years ago one of the authors was caught in the Lewisham train disaster. He woke to find himself at the bottom of a pile of wreckage pinned to the railway track. Over the next five hours railway workers painstakingly delved down through the wreckage extracting the dead and injured. At last a hole was opened above him and he could see the stars and there on a high point of the wreckage stood a railwayman with a lantern directing operations. His voice had been a constant background to other and more gruesome noises for many hours. He was directing the location of survivors and organising medical help and stretchers with a loud-hailer.
>
> Many days later and after a number of enquiries it emerged that the individual concerned was a modest shunter who had run from the Hither Green marshalling yards with a sodium lantern when the crash occurred. Apparently he stood on the top of that wreckage for over 10 hours with hardly a break. It was clear that somehow everyone trusted him and accepted his authority and that night he gave leadership to a whole section of the rescuers, many of whom were senior to him.

This is the kind of authority exercised by the captain of an aircraft or the shift leader in a nuclear power station. It was the norm throughout the armed services, for in wartime such authority is essential. However, such autocratic behaviour does not necessarily lead to disharmony and disaffection. Aircrew may enjoy extremely egalitarian and harmonious relationships, recognising nonetheless the distinctive roles to be performed according to a laid down schedule. The important point is that in all these cases the arrangement is entered into voluntarily. The railwayman on the wreckage was simply recognised as the best person for the job; aircrew accept that only one person can be captain. Even the army has had to modify its approach so that authority is only exercised autocratically in defined situations.

Procedures and standards of behaviour will have probably been the subject of detailed discussions and agreement by the participants. Such situations always lead to the development of a distinctive hierarchy of competence. Often this is signified by ranks and regalia. The rank is accepted as an indication of authority since there is no time or opportunity to test for competence and agree procedures anew each time. Such exercise of authority is self-evidently right and useful. The trouble is that too many people then extrapolate back to management in general. Theory X argues for the exercise of autocratic power in the absence of consent; in fact it argues that such consent will not be forthcoming and so coercion is necessary. We see no evidence for this whatsoever.

Theory X makes assumptions about people which are simply not true. There are lazy people, but threats and bribes do not stop them. In almost all cases it is simply that the right motivation has never occurred. There is a young man known to us who at 32 years old has never had a job. However, he works tirelessly for his community, his family and his hobby. Somehow he has never been able to link his own satisfactions to the earning of money.

There are a great many people who apparently shun responsibility and simply want to go to work, be told what to do, get paid and go home. Nevertheless, it is the experience of countless managers that once given the opportunity and the skills to take some responsibility, virtually everyone will. It was certainly our experience when running the British Rail courses on which there were many men who had taken orders all their lives. It can be argued that the whole of life is one huge problem-solving exercise. Certainly, in the hundreds of problem-solving sessions we have run together and separately, we have never found anyone who was unable to make a creative contribution once they knew how.

At the level of practical management nobody now believes that money is the only motivation. Feelings of insecurity and insufficient money can undermine motivation, but pride in work and satisfaction from those that benefit from it provide a far more powerful motivation than financial reward.

Theory X is a thoroughly bankrupt approach of which the

most damning indictment is that it simply does not work. In time the level of demotivation and lack of ideas leads to a spiral of inefficiency. In British Rail, where a certain amount of autocratic and authoritarian management is absolutely necessary to get the trains to run on time, we found that the style persisted at all levels of management. Deference replaced discussion and staff tended to be more concerned with obeying the rules of the organisation than with achieving its objectives. In commissioning the programme described here, British Rail management had clearly recognised the need for behavioural change.

The Human organisation

A model of organisational culture developed by Renis Likert[2] is based on the view that different systems of management behaviour have developed in response to the need to manage people effectively to achieve business goals. He differentiates four systems based on the investigation of more than 200 firms:

System 1   Exploitative; Authoritative

System 2   Benevolent; Authoritative

System 3   Consultative

System 4   Participative; Group

Each of these has a different structure and behavioural characteristics implying a different leadership process. The way in which decisions are made, and goals set, distinguishes the different systems, as well as communications, interaction and influence. Above all each implies a quite different pattern of motivation.

Likert established not only that a particular culture can be identified for each business but that System 4, resting on the principles of supportive relationships, group methods of supervision, involvement in decision-making and delegation of responsibility, is the most effective system of management judged against the firm's financial, operational and market performance. The leadership style which characterises System 4 has precisely those attributes which we suggested at the top of this chapter the good boss would display. It really contains three key tasks – selection, delegation, and motivation – and has as its prime group role that of Chairman.

Selection

Nowadays management is usually given a great deal of help and support in recruitment. The actual process of describing the job and its role, converting this to a person description, developing selection criteria and interviewing or assessing candidates is well covered in management literature. Like so many management activities, it is the domain of specialists, but every manager must retain control of the process.

A manager who simply fills 'slots' on the basis of straightforward skill criteria may end up with an unmanageable team. One of the key attributes of a good leader is the ability to select a team. This means understanding how members of the group interact and what group skills are necessary. (This was covered in Chapter 10.) The extent to which this can and should influence selection is a matter of judgement. However, it is possible to specify such skills and add them to those required by the post. Perhaps even more important is the placing or promotion of existing staff, a situation in which leadership skills can be sorely tested.

> There was once a brilliant Production Controller in a large manufacturing plant. He could be relied on to ensure that everything possible was done for the factory, to make targets and to keep within budget. If he had a fault it was that he preferred to deal with one problem at a time. The only trouble, however, was that his manner was so abrasive that he became more and more isolated. His loyalty and commitment to the company was without question, but he seemed to have no future.
>
> His Managing Director decided, after the most searching review – which at one time nearly led to the Production Controller being asked to go – decided to make use of the undoubted energy and commitment and so made him Head of Materials Management *and* put him on the executive board.
>
> The result was a stunning success. Removed from the need to undertake endless personal negotiations to keep the production process going, his reforms of purchasing and supply produced large savings.

This was the exercise of leadership skills in selection. In fact the Managing Director in question is described as one who can 'get those who are cleverer than he to work for him'.

Frequently, to get the best out of an individual, a manager will change the job to fit the man or woman. Once again it is a leadership attribute never to waste potential resources. Recognising real skill is important, and creating and re-creating the team is a prime managerial function. This is understood in sport but often overlooked in business. Nevertheless, every leader needs to bring into his team playmakers, defenders, ball carriers, and of course, goal scorers. It is recognising all these different skills and combining them to creative effect that marks out the leader.

Delegation

Both the hallmark of good leadership and its most difficult feature, delegation is fundamental. But how few managers, judged by their performance, really practise skilful delegation.

Here is a box:

```
+-------------------------+
|                         |
|                         |
|     Y   O   U   R       |
|                         |
|                         |
|     R   O   L   E       |
|                         |
|                         |
+-------------------------+
```

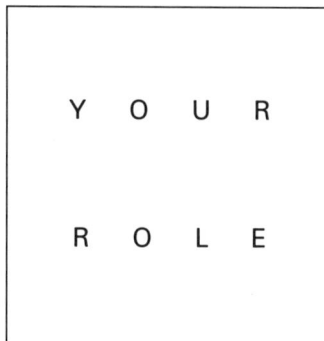

It encloses all your responsibilities as a manager. It encompasses all the things you are paid for; in other words your role (remember Chapter 4). But, you will not be expected to get results by yourself – there are not sufficient hours in the day – so you will have to share some of the work.

Let us divide up the box:

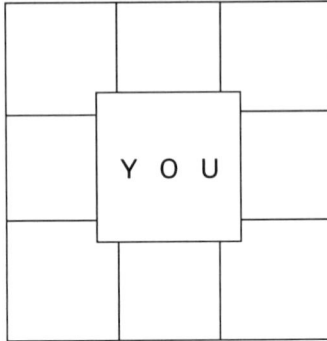

Now you are the centre of a set of boxes and these are the responsibilities of your immediate subordinates. Each box belongs to one of them and is created by you. The boundaries would need to be agreed and described as part of a role description, as we described in Chapter 4. As soon as you have done this you have delegated some of your responsibility.

A great deal of rubbish is talked about delegation. When people find themselves overloaded, they often say 'I must delegate more', when what they really mean is that they want people to do their bidding. They want someone to do the work without taking responsibility for it – they want the right to grab it back. The problem is not one of delegating more – it is one of delegating well. The mere fact of paying a subordinate implies that you want to share your work. But we have argued that people only work well when they want to and they only want to when they feel that the job *belongs* to them. Managerial leadership consists in creating the conditions whereby work for which the manager is ultimately responsible becomes work for which others also feel responsibility.

In Chapter 1 we used the analogy of the orchestral conductor and it is true that a manager exists to 'conduct the working of a business'. However, all managers do more than conduct. They actually do some work, and by work we do not mean sweat. Work in a business is anything which adds value to the product or service destined for the customer. In a large part of the business this means producing something, selling, buying materials and so on. People in these occupations spend most of their time *working.*

Managers, on the other hand, spend most of their time 'conducting' – but they all do some work as well. Every manager has an 'in-tray'; they all do calculations; interviews and negotiations are work too. The Managing Director who sees an important customer is working; so is the Finance Director who negotiates a bank loan. Nowadays at trade fairs you are as likely as not to be served by the proprietor of a small or medium company.

So we need to amend the box:

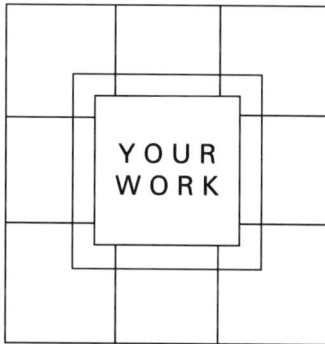

```
 _____
|      |        |       |
|    __|_____|__     |
|   |   |     |   |     |
|___|___|_____|___|_____|
|   |   |     |   |     |
|   | Y O U R |   |     |
|   | W O R K |   |     |
|___|___|_____|___|_____|
|   |   |     |   |     |
|   |___|_____|___|     |
|      |        |       |
|_____|_____|_____|
```

The shaded bit in the middle represents the *work* you decide not to delegate, but to undertake yourself. Determining what this shaded area will comprise is essential if your subordinates are to be clear about the limits of *their* work and responsibility. The size and shape of your retained responsibilities will depend on the degree to which you can trust your subordinates. But the paradox here is that until you really trust them you will probably never know whether you can.

It has been argued that trust and control are managerial opposites. The less you trust the more you are likely to exercise continuous control and the less your subordinates will feel trusted. The less you control and the more you trust the more the subordinates will grow into their jobs and reward your trust – if you get it right.

The act of delegation implies:

- The transfer of initiatives, responsibility and authority to another for the performance of an agreed role;
- The retention by the delegator of the means of exercising overall control and for checking the performance of the subordinates;
- The willingness of the delegator to delegate and the willingness of the subordinate to accept the responsibility for the tasks so assigned.

We see no reason to amend this definition, penned by one of the authors in 1974, save to add that delegation can never be temporary. It always carries the implication of a long-term transfer of responsibility.

Motivation

In Chapter 3 we argued that motivation comes from the knowledge that the business is a worthwhile activity which satisfies customers. But it takes a leader to make this manifest for everyone who works for the business. We can describe what should happen but each leader has his own way. There are no rules – just what works for an individual manager. The 'new' management we have described puts a high premium on group and interpersonal skills. It is more time consuming and probably more stressful, but research shows[3] that the consultative style of management and leadership is not only more successful, it correlates with higher job satisfaction. In short managers are more highly motivated.

Leadership is not really a trainable skill – it is hard enough to describe – but it can be enhanced. A manager is a bit like an actor. He must have some talent for it, he can be told the basics, coached through the rehearsals, but once on stage he is on his own and only the applause at the end tells him how successful he has been.

Leadership is itself behaviour, and behaviour is a function of the personality and the situation. We have not attempted to suggest changes in personality – if such changes are possible only the individual can effect them. We would not attempt to specify the skills of leadership – they are specific to each manager. But we would suggest ways of approaching their development and here are some pointers:

- Be practical: get to know what you did when it worked for you.
- Be reflective: listen to those who can give feedback on your own performance.
- Be confident: it's expected of the boss even when he is not so sure.
- Be selective: ask always whether what you intend is going to further your department's objectives.
- Be disciplined: if you are not then neither is anyone else.

Creating the situations which allow for the development of such skills was always one of the objectives of our courses.

Leadership development on the courses

We have tackled the issue of leadership at this stage in the book because it really impinges on every aspect of what happened during our short five-day courses. *In a very real sense the whole course was a demonstration of how to exercise leadership in management.*

From the Monday morning each group had a leader, but it was made clear both through the selection and in our briefings that this did not bestow particular rights on the particular individual. Rather, he had an obligation to the group to perform a particular role. Of all the roles described in the Belbin schema, that of the chairmen is most crucial. It was obvious how far the performance of a group could be affected both positively and negatively by this individual. In Chapter 10, we briefly described the role, now we must look more closely at the behaviour required to perform that role and how we encouraged its emergence.

Our first visits to the groups would take place within the first 30 minutes of the exercise. In most cases the chairmen – remember they were self-selected – would already have begun to impose some order on the proceedings. They would have sought to create a framework. Sometimes the group would be sitting quietly reading the copious briefing notes; on other occasions the reading of the notes would have been delegated and preliminary discussions begun. Others would be deep in discussion about how they were to tackle the task.

As the week progressed and we observed the groups, we were always conscious of how far they were being managed by their chairmen. Sometimes we would have to encourage or steer the chairman, at others we might have to speak informally to the group members. The aim was always to encourage the chairman in his task of enabling the group to perform at the top of its ability.

At the end of the course there was always discussion of the chairman and his style and effectiveness. This was deliberately engineered during the feedback session. Often the comments on how they had performed and what had worked were among the most valuable made. It was clear that both the first-hand experience of those that had been chairmen and the experience of their colleagues, as well as the reports from the other groups, all combined to widen the experience and the practice of the entire group.

It is our view that any course of this nature should have a consistent group chairman throughout for only thus is the situational experience large enough have a material impact on performance. We believe that while leaderless group and syndicate work is valuable, groups specifically structured around a particular selected leader provide the basis for real practice. It enabled us not only to specify leadership skills but also to indicate where they had been demonstrated. Frequently we could show how the exercise of such skills had benefited the group, even though it simply thought itself lucky.

But all successful leaders are lucky. They have developed the untrainable knack of being in the right place or taking the right decision at the right time. But as Gary Player said when told he was lucky: 'It's real funny how the more I practise, the luckier I get.'

Summary

Leadership is an essential quality in a manager. The way this is exercised depends on the culture of the business. Those that believe in Theory X tend to encourage autocratic and coercive behaviour. That style of leadership, which has superficial attractions, is, in our view, not only inappropriate today but largely ineffective. Theory Y requires the exercise of the more subtle arts of management which we have described in this book. Although the exercise of unquestioned authority may be relevant in situations which are 'fail dangerous', when such a style permeates all management it tends to demotivate and encourage obedience and conformity rather than energy and creativity.

Leadership is a key characteristic and skill in the successful functioning of groups. In particular, selection, delegation and motivation are important areas where the exercise of leadership improves business performance. Thus, selection can never be just an objective process, it must always allow for the intervention of a leader who must create a balanced team. Delegation requires the leader to divide his work – to give responsibility but retain ultimate authority. The key to motivation is to create a situation where every individual experiences in some way the market feedback from satisfied customers and this is most likely to occur in a 'learning' organisation.

Now we turn to consider how learning becomes fixed as a practical change in behaviour and an enhancement of skills.

References

1 MacGregor, D. *The Human Side of Enterprise.* New York, McGraw-Hill, 1960.
2 Likert, R. *The Human Organisation: Its Management and Values.* New York, McGraw-Hill, 1967.
3 Owens, J. 'The Uses of Leadership Theory'. *Michigan Business Review.* University of Michigan, January 1973.

12

Behaving Differently and Liking It

Turning lessons into action

You are nearing the end of this book. We wonder if you think that you have learned anything – picked up even one idea which is worth considering. If you have, what are you going to do about it? Unfortunately, you will have learned nothing unless you now translate what you perceive to be useful into action. *Learning only takes place when behaviour changes.*

In Chapter 1, we stated four propositions about learning. First, people must want to; second, they must see the point; third, they must try it out for themselves; and finally, they must have knowledge of results. We have discussed the first three in depth and we have described how numerical data describing the business should be assembled and distributed. But that data has to be used actively by the business to improve management performance. We have all had the experience of returning from a conference or training course full of enthusiasm only to find that life and work are exactly the same and, what is worse, the things we would like to do differently simply do not seem to fit. But unless you do something differently when you return to work you will have wasted your time and learned nothing other than the fact that you heard about a 'good idea' or two.

It is the word 'differently' which is important. Even though we seem to live in an age of perpetual organisational change, much of that is imposed from above with a wide range of often contradictory motivations. Local change is often discouraged and many excuses are made for keeping things the way they are. So we hear about good ideas which cannot be put into practice because of time constraints. But any worthwhile idea should not mean additional work for an already busy manager, rather it should result in some other work becoming redundant. Or, alternatively, the new idea may displace some well-liked but less productive activity which colleagues nevertheless prefer and so the expected benefits are simply not accepted. Some good ideas are stopped before they can even be tried because they do not suit the boss or do not fit the culture or policy of the business. In any event some persuading is necessary.

And even if we do persuade our boss, or our colleagues, to try something different, the battle is only half won. The usefulness of any change must be demonstrated. We have argued that management is an integrated activity with a clear objective – the production of goods and services which meet customer needs. The way in which a business judges new ways of managing, or how we know that our brilliant new idea will result in better performance, is by the response of customers to our product in the market place. All our actions, whether routine or innovative, must be judged by those responses. Thus any changes in behaviour must be measured through integrated responses which are driven by the customers.

It is now increasingly recognised that companies should create well-founded channels of feedback to staff at all levels. At first such communications – through notice boards, house newspapers, and other media – were seen as little more than ways of reinforcing feelings of loyalty and identity as well as putting across the organisation's policy. Then it was recognised that formal communications structures enabled staff to know essential information which would improve understanding and performance.

Since the prime motivator for all good performance is the approbation of customers in the market, information about that market must become an essential part of feedback at every level in the business. Every member of staff must be aware of such responses and be able to contribute. In that eventuality every new idea will be subject to the same criteria. It will be declared to work if it makes a positive contribution to market performance. In such an organisation each managerial development can be tested against the company's criteria of success and change within a learning culture can happen.

Feedback in a company is like competitive sailing. When a boat is under full sail there are a large number of adjustments which can be made. While the helmsman knows what he wants to achieve he never knows exactly which combination of course, sail setting, rig tension and tactics will actually make the boat go faster or reach its destination more quickly. What he does is to make small adjustments to everything under his control and then to measure the result. In the old days, judgements were a matter of feel and experience and frequently the results of a particular tactic or adjustment would not be known until much later or even when the race was over.

Now all that has changed. The development of integrated on-board electronic instruments means that every change and every adjustment will show on instruments which give instant read-outs of speed, location, heading and even progress towards the objective. There is continuous feedback and every new idea is tested against immediate knowledge of results.

In Chapter 9 we described how an integrated feedback mechanism was developed for the management of the British Airways cabin crew. With such a system in place it was possible for the first time to test out ideas for improving staff and management performance. There was little risk because within a month the effects could be measured. While such general feedback mechanisms can be dramatic and important, the feedback with which we are all more familiar is that provided by our immediate superior.

Knowledge of results

A common form of feedback in business is performance appraisal. In most cases this is a one-to-one interview in which a manager or other worker is informed about his performance by his superior. All too often these interviews are embarrassing exchanges of half-formulated opinions. Even though much has been written about them, many managers have received training and even John Cleese has made training videos, they still tend to be unstructured discussions based on generalisations. They are frequently viewed as irritating diversions from important work done to humour the personnel department.

Another kind of feedback is given to those who participate in formal training. Most courses include a review in which the individuals are encouraged to look at their own performance. This rarely provides solid feedback and hard evidence about the participants' performance because such reviews frequently lack focus and the process is often reversed with the participants giving feedback to the tutors.

The review part of a performance appraisal or the review at the end of a training course are not optional extras or a sort of relaxation after the more stressful parts. They are essential. In fact, we would say they are the most important part of both processes. *A review must point the way to changed behaviour.*

There are three guiding principles in all management reviews:

(1) *A review must be based on facts.* Nobody is really going to take seriously comments about their performance or experience which are based on hearsay or opinion. Whether it is an individual, group or course review it must start from a set of agreed data. 'This is what happened while you were doing your job, let us discuss it'; or, 'The group response to this question was . . . what do we think that means?'

(2) *A review must be by the subject himself or herself.* Nobody responds well to being told what to do. A review does not consist of the boss or group leader expatiating on shortcomings and misdemeanours and then informing how things should be done. Instead, it should be a series of questions which enable the subject to discover what has happened and why. In most cases they will know what went well and what went badly, and they will usually know why.

(3) *A review must look forward to action.* The one thing a review must never be is a catalogue of recriminations. A colleague of ours, Bob Thomas of Ashridge, has Ten Management Commandments, one of which is: 'Never punish mistakes, but you may have to punish fools.' Everyone makes mistakes and these can always be put to good use in modifying future behaviour. It is only repeated errors and deliberate misdemeanours which need to be dealt with.

We cannot reiterate too often that the purpose of a review is to change future behaviour beneficially and not to make the reviewer feel better. Thus the method of review is important. It must not be threatening. Those being reviewed must be comfortable and in a position of equality with the reviewer. Thus bosses should come out from behind their desk and tutors should go and sit or stand with the course. Everything possible should be done to gain the co-operation of those involved, even to the point of encouraging them to set their own agenda. In the end they have got to *want* to change.

There are a number of important points to make about a person's willingness to change his or her behaviour. The first is that people will only do something differently if they find that their present behaviour is not achieving the results they want (Point 2 about learning – 'What's in it for me?'). This means that good ideas are often seen as 'all right in theory'. The practicality has to be demonstrated to and accepted by those who are to change.

The second point is that people do not change their behaviour over a whole range of issues all at once. Not only is behaviour change gradual, but it is also selective. This means that in any group each individual is likely to pick out different things which they view as important and which they wish to try out. A review session where nearly everyone says that they have learned the same thing is unlikely to lead to mass changed behaviour. Learning is a very personal process.

The third point is that changes in behaviour result from trying something out and discovering whether it works. This means that we try something out consciously and then 'review' the result. If it works, or nearly works, we try again. Gradually, if the results are satisfactory, the new behaviour becomes second nature, or part of the system, and takes place automatically. This is the stage when learning is complete.

In practice, managers achieve improved results more from constant small changes in behaviour than from a cataclysmic change in a system. Personal self-appraisal is an important key to learning. Consider what you do before a meeting. No doubt you plan what you want to get out of the meeting and how you will achieve it. Now ask yourself whether you review what happened after the meeting. Do you ask yourself whether you achieved your objectives and if not, what you might have done differently which could have been more successful? Equally importantly, do you ever ask yourself what you did which led to success?

Progress comes through change. But people will only alter their behaviour when they recognise that the results they seek cannot be achieved without a change in behaviour. It is of no value to say to someone 'You ought to do this . . .' That person must be helped to understand the existing situation and have the potential for change demonstrated to them. Advice to effect a change will only be accepted and acted upon if the individual is convinced that a change is necessary. If this acceptance is not present, all that will happen is a cosmetic alteration which reverts to previous behaviour once the pressure is off.

We use the word 'ownership' a great deal nowadays when talking about management changes. This idea encapsulates the real key to success, for people only behave differently when they want to. Therefore the success of any review process, whether it be appraisal in a company, or discussion at the end of a course, depends on creating situations where people themselves offer suggestions about what they might do differently. But this is not enough – it is also necessary to find a way of helping the individual to assess whether the change in behaviour will lead to the results desired.

Reviewing also serves quite another purpose. It is part of the process by which people 'belong' to their work group. We all do it for our children. We not only seek to improve their performance, we do it to encourage them and reinforce good outcomes. People who work together are always watching each other's work and giving and receiving comments about it. Much of this contributes to a mutual learning process, but positive approbation by one's peers is a crucial part of the motivational process which we described in Chapter 2. Managers have a very particular role in this because their seniority and authority gives added importance to what they say, and their praises will affect how the group sees and values its members.

A young graduate in her first year as a Research Officer in the Civil Service had become increasingly unhappy. She felt that her work had no meaning and she was becoming very demotivated. She explained to her boss that throughout school and university each piece of work had been 'handed in' and a few days later returned with comments and often a mark. Even examinations provided feedback through the grades awarded. Suddenly she found that she was asked to undertake quite specific research tasks on which she lavished care and energy only for them to disappear without trace.

She was quite right. The British Civil Service has very poor feedback mechanisms because a great deal of the research and administration in Whitehall has no obvious output. Even the decisions based upon it are taken through an arcane process involving Government Ministers and senior Civil Servants, much of which is even secret from those that have contributed to it. This makes it essential that a specific feedback routine should be put in place to encourage those who do the work.

Helping your subordinates to learn

No manager can succeed unless he has good subordinates. Helping one's subordinates to learn is, therefore, a prime activity for any manager. Reviewing achievement and fostering behaviour change is an essential continuing process. Formal, overall appraisal, conducted annually, can be useful in helping to see the wood for the trees, but day-to-day coaching to improve performance is of equal value.

Thus every manager has an important role in developing a 'learning organisation' – one where there is constant questioning and a continuous drive for improvement. The key to success lies in having a clear perception of the outputs desired and this was discussed in Chapter 4. Equally essential is knowing whether the outputs have been achieved. This is much more than simply providing control information, which often arrives in the form of computer print-outs presenting facts that the manager ought to know already.

> A Production Superintendent in an engineering factory was supplied regularly with sheets of computer information which he never read. Instead, his office walls were covered with charts, updated daily or weekly, showing the essential features which he wished to control, such as levels of rejects, absenteeism, late orders and so on. He remarked that these charts enabled him to take action – the computer print-outs he regarded as history.

Any manager who wishes his subordinates to learn needs to encourage them to review their results on a continuing basis. It is not enough to say 'You did not achieve this . . .' because the subordinate manager ought to be aware of the fact already. Nor does it really help to say 'You must do better'.

What is required is an environment where subordinates are encouraged to review constantly their own achievements against the outputs planned. This means encouraging them to develop their own control information mechanisms, which will be personal to them and may not form part of the company's formal reporting system. Ideally no subordinate should be surprised to learn that something for which he is responsible has, or has not, happened. In fact, he can often take corrective action in time to ensure that the boss never knew that something was going wrong. Better still, in a real learning environment, a subordinate will go to his boss when something is amiss, which he is unsure how to rectify, in order to discuss the problem before it gets out of hand. The superior manager's objective in review is, therefore, primarily to help a subordinate solve his current problems, not to make judgements about success or failure.

It would be idealistic to suggest that continuous feedback by managers about their subordinates' performance was easy or convenient. However, it can be built into everyday activity more easily than may be imagined. If delegated responsibilities have been set up in terms of measured outcomes and there is regular formal and informal contact, it is quite possible to discuss progress and give information about an individual's performance. In fact every meeting and interview can be adapted to contain some performance feedback.

Since reviewing is so central to the development of good management skills, the way it is done on training courses must stand as an example for those who attend. This is another case of the training process teaching as much as the content. In this case the participants are all going to experience the process themselves. They will judge first and only learn afterwards for such personal experiences always trigger the question: 'What's in it for me?'

Training course reviews – continuous feedback

On our courses we do not limit ourselves merely to running a course review on the last afternoon. In fact, our experience is that the conventional approach to course reviews leaves a great deal to be desired. On the one hand, it is a kind of informal popularity contest to make the tutors feel better, or worse, as the case may be; on the other, it is used by the organisers to provide them with feedback so that they may develop better courses. There is nothing intrinsically wrong with either of these approaches. The problem is that they do not usually add to the learning process and they may even negate some of the beneficial parts of the about-to-be completed course by irritating the participants.

If a group of managers is asked to comment on and rank the performance of their tutors and then go on to discuss the course in general, it is human nature for them to concentrate on those aspects about which they feel strongly but which give them no discomfort. Our experience is that this invariably triggers a wave of congratulation if the course has been enjoyed, or a session of 'ain't it awful' if the course has not been popular. Neither of these addresses the question of whether it has been effective.

The other approach, which asks what the participants thought of the course and invites suggestions about its future, may be of great benefit to the organisers and usually prevents the traditional complaints session, but it too does little for the participants. As we have stressed throughout, training must mimic life and to hold back all feedback to the end is not like life. We all need knowledge of results as we go along.

The first rule is to give both qualitative and quantitative feedback at every stage. This must be positive in tone even if it has to be negative in content. We have seen some trainers involved with behavioural exercises only able to criticise. They find it impossible even to remember the good points and only say what was wrong. This is not to imply that we should only look on the bright side. It does mean that for feedback to work it has to be accepted by the recipient. Our tenets of learning apply here too. The individual has to *want* to hear the message and has to *see the point*.

The second rule is that feedback has to be in context and that context has to be set by the participants. Thus, it is always better to visit a group while it is at work, ask one of its members to summarise what has happened, then ask questions and then comment positively on what has actually happened. While every tutor has his favourite prepared material and 'hands-outs' which contain his 'pearls of wisdom', course participants are, in our experience, particularly open to learning when they want to know something and when they ask the questions. That is the moment for the tutor to become, briefly, the teacher even if the subject is not one of his favourites.

The purpose of all feedback is to reinforce learning which in turn leads to behaviour changes at work. Such changes require that the individual make a commitment and thus our third rule is that course members need to make their intended changes public. The very fact that you have told someone you are going to change makes that change more likely.

This is where training in groups has an added advantage. It makes it much easier for people to give and take feedback and for them to declare what they intend to do differently when they return to their jobs. We have also found that groups of those with similar jobs provide a good forum within which the specifics of returning to work with new skills can be discussed. But the most important is the public declaration to a whole training course or one's colleagues at large, that a new skill is being acquired and will be used.

On the British Rail Midland Region Courses we developed a number of ways of providing feedback which all came together in the final review. And that itself took up the whole of the last day. In fact we would argue that if learning is to take place, review and feedback should occupy at least 25 per cent of all training time; it should be built into the structure of the course.

Continuous feedback had taken place all week. From the very first stage we visited the groups frequently, not only to encourage and explain anything they did not understand, but also to watch and listen and let them know how they were doing. During these visits a great deal of coaching took place – there is a fine line between reviewing and coaching. On such occasions it is often the unspoken agenda which is important and only by sympathetic listening will this become apparent.

After every formal presentation or exercise there was a period of feedback and discussion. Here we always included the other participants in the process. In fact it was usual for them to be asked to comment first on what they saw. It was remarkable how such discussions by the participants about their fellows in front of the rest became a very important learning experience. Naturally it was carefully controlled and structured.

At intervals during a course we gave out little questionnaires which made the participants think about their performance and what they had learned. A typical one given on the third morning is reproduced below.

PROGRESS QUESTIONNAIRE

We want you to comment on your response to the course so far – please answer the following:

1. Name one new skill which you have used this week.
2. Give one new and significant fact which you have heard this week.
3. State one misconception which you have identified this week.
4. Specify one thing you have learnt about working in a group.
5. State one new action you will apply in your own job.
6. What particularly would you still like to get from the course?

From time to time other questionnaires about group working, management style and specific topics were given. All of these were retained by the participants at the end of the course. This enabled them to keep a record of their progress after the results had been used in both group and individual feedback during the course.

The formal review process at the end of the courses started with a couple of questionnaires. The first was to test how each individual had reacted to the process of learning in a group. The second was to test how the groups had actually performed together. (Both are reproduced in Appendix II.) They were first completed individually and then the groups were sent away to discuss not only what had happened but what they intended to do about it. The questionnaires were then filled out by the groups working together. All this took place on the last evening (usually a Thursday). Overnight the results had to be processed and the individual scores compared with the group ones. However, it was our experience that the discussion of these questionnaires often went on into the small hours and a great deal of further learning took place about the working of groups.

The last morning started with an open feedback session which concentrated on how the groups had functioned and which role each individual had performed. At last the results of the Belbin test were revealed and could be compared with what had actually happened. It was remarkable how often there were quite frank admissions of difficulties overcome or personality differences solved. Few were in any doubt that they had experienced management work at a higher intensity than they did normally or that it was a valuable learning experience. They would tell us of their insistence that everyone contribute, that no idea, however slight, got overlooked. In short, they appreciated each other's contribution.

Frequently, it would be revealed that personal goals had begun to overshadow those of the group. It was recognised that this might lead individuals to try to dominate the group or, alternatively, to withdraw. Sometimes there were even sub-groups and rivalries. However, there were opportunities to see this happening and to deal with it in completely safe circumstances. The teams made their imaginary world so real that they could see and understand problems and deal with them, so learning valuable lessons for their own management life.

These discussions, together with the previous evening's questionnaires, sometimes revealed inconsistencies between what the group said had happened and what its members *thought* had happened. It was often instructive to see how individual views had to give way to group ones in describing what had happened. This was a valuable demonstration of a common phenomenon in management and demonstrated why groups should not only agree, but should also agree the record of what happened.

But while such reminiscences were often entertaining, the importance of the experience and its effect on future performance was always emphasised. The aim was to concentrate on the process they had all gone through in order to extract all the relevant issues. Remember, on this course how things happened was just as important as what. The session ended with each participant deciding which specific lesson or lessons he or she would go on to apply.

After a short break, the course members were asked to complete one more questionnaire. This was the Knowledge Inventory taken on the first evening which was repeated as a comparison. The original had been analysed and used as guidance for the tutors through the week in both group and individual coaching. It would be copied and handed back, with this second sitting at the end of the course as an indication of changes in knowledge and outlook.

The next session started with group discussions in newly created groups of those with similar jobs. Now they had to consider the managerial and commercial lessons they would apply when they returned to their own jobs. This again was followed by an open session to underline the commitments.

Finally, the general applicability of the course was discussed so that each participant was reminded of the overall objectives (Chapter 1) and could assess how far these had been met.

In the event, we usually found these review sessions to be the most intense of the week and to require the most concentrated input from the tutors. We know that this is in contrast to the usual management training course review, but we do have plenty of evidence that only thus was a permanent learning process initiated.

Action planning and post-training audits

We believe that all management training should be post-audited. In the live management context there are regular reviews when intentions can be checked and performance assessed. After a training course the participants disperse and may never see each other or the course tutors again. It can take only a few days for the commitments to wear off and the lessons to be forgotten. We, like many others in the field, have tried to involve company managements in the process. Ideally every boss should be so involved in his subordinates' development that he knows in advance what to expect from the course. He should receive a verbal debriefing after the course which then becomes incorporated in the regular reviews. Sadly this is not generally the case.

Some training establishments have tried individual action planning, which involves written commitments to undertake certain action as a result of the course. They then arrange for the course members to keep in touch by correspondence and report their progress. Time and distance, not to mention the tenuous connections established in a week, usually defeat this. Furthermore, this depends on promises and objectives set in the heat of the moment at the end of the course.

We believe that the best way of providing long-term support for managers who have started the process of change on our courses is to bring them together again afterwards. Regrettably we have only been able to do this once. It was a tremendous success. We found that of the 30 or so who attended all had carried something from the original course into their managerial performance. But through the process of sharing over a short weekend, they were reminded of so much more and determined to develop further.

In our other work with senior management groups this problem has, we believe, been more successfully tackled. Since the whole point of our seminars is for the group to learn through working on their own current problems, they have every incentive to see their hard-won solutions come to pass. In these cases action planning is an essential part of the exercise. Planning action is more than just distributing work to individuals. The person responsible for ensuring that action takes place need not necessarily be the individual responsible for the management line activity. Nor, indeed, need the volunteer actually perform most of the tasks involved in the action. His job is to ensure that they are performed and by a target date. The key point is to ensure that the person who accepts responsibility for seeing action takes place is committed to that action.

We have found it helpful to ask 'Who would like to be responsible for this action?' We have never failed to find a volunteer. The main problem has been setting target dates for completion. People normally under-estimate their work loads and suggest dates which are unrealistic, apparently ignoring that they have a normal job to do as well. Some actions cannot realistically be completed in under six months or a year. In these cases it is important to set staging posts. It is also important to persuade those responsible for actions to set criteria, *at the beginning*, for what will have happened, or be happening when the action has been completed.

The remarkable effect of planning future work like this is that, because it springs from the committed work of a viable and energetic group, the members feel a great sense of obligation to fulfil their undertakings.

In Chapter 5 we described how the management group from the rubber products company had worked with one of the authors to develop a strategy and that this involved the members in making specific commitments to undertake particular work by certain dates. In this case, as with many similar, the matter did not stop there. The seminar was one of a series and so review could become built in to the process. We left the group, who had enjoyed their first experience of open-ended group activity to create a strategy, committed to return in six months. This too could be just more enjoyment. The acid test would be – *did anything happen during that time which might not if the workshop had not happened?*

Before the second workshop each participant was asked to fill in another questionnaire. Once again this provided the basis for the opening session. Here is a sample of the points which emerged:

- *What is the biggest step the business has taken to achieve its mission?* The creation of management working parties which were successful in problem solving and team building.
- *What has given most personal satisfaction?* A real sense of achievement in completing a task allocated by peers and publicly committed to; and also being able to work together in new ways.
- *What should have happened which did not?* Insufficient effort to open new accounts with the multiple store chains, even though that would be outside the quality market.
- *What barriers to progress still exist?* Credit control.

This session gave rise to the sort of opportunity which frequently happens at such workshops. Because a particular inhibitor had been specified – credit control – it was used as the basis for an exercise in problem-solving – such occasions can give rise to real training 'on the hoof'. It is our experience that when management skills are sought by a group of managers as the result of a directly perceived need, the lesson sticks.

But what had actually happened between the two workshops? The chairmen of the working parties were all anxious to report. They were proud of what they had done and wanted the rest of the group to know about it. The remarkable feature of these was that they did not read like management reports but described in narrative form how ideas had been arrived at. One was written by the Marketing Manager, a young woman in her twenties; it showed already a broadening of approach away from the merely managerial towards the thinking required of directors.

The workshop then discussed the following questions in groups:

- How can we defend our gains in the UK market?
- What do we need to do to enter selected European markets?
- How can we stimulate the industrial contract market?

Once again action plans were drawn up, agreed and tasks allocated – all to be reviewed at the next meeting.

Since these first seminars these workshops have become a regular feature of the way that business is run. Not only has the group become a 'learning team', other groups in the business asked for similar treatment. This is how an organisation begins to develop a learning culture.

Summary

We have argued throughout that learning can only be said to have taken place when behaviour has manifestly changed. Management is itself a process of continual change and the ability to learn new skills as one goes along is, perhaps, the most important attribute of a manager. Because this process of learning is so central to good management, the most beneficial change is the establishment of the learning process itself. Those businesses that manage change best are those that have developed such a learning culture. It is an essential attribute of such a culture that everyone has good knowledge of results on which to base their assessment of past performance and their expectations of future developments. There has to be constant and structured feedback which must inform and modify the process of change.

Reviews must be based on facts, be made by the subject and look forward to action. Reviews can help managers to recognise areas where new behaviour can be developed; where such change will do most good; and how to try out the new-found skills. The whole process must be one of co-operative progress where every step is 'owned' by the subject. Reviewing performance, therefore, is a basic part of our training process. It has to be continuous, but at the end it has to be formal and structured. It has to embrace both the understanding and acknowledgement of the lessons learned and also a commitment to put them to use.

Finally, we turn to how the whole process of learning to manage better may be created and fixed within a business.

13

Towards Being a Better Manager

Making management better

There is a new expression widely used by those who buy and sell companies. They speak of 'turning a company round'. What they mean is that a company judged by them to be underperforming, that is making insufficient profits based on their valuation of its assets, is to be made more profitable. The phrase has now been taken up by the management consultancy fraternity and expanded to imply any action designed to enhance company performance quickly. There is now a whole battery of measures which are employed, ranging from simple staff and wage cuts right through to the latest management panacea. There are armies of consultants willing to offer the 'quick fix' provided by the current fashion in management techniques; there is a whole library of books with advice and suggestions.

When management was first declared to be a 'science' we had the Hawthorn Experiment which focused on *how* people work. More recently there was the Tavistock Institute with its emphasis on organisational theories. After that we had Profit Centres, Management by Objectives, Job Evaluation, Quality Circles and, right up to date, Total Quality Management. And this list is by no means exhaustive. They were all based on valid and sensible observations and they have all contributed to our better understanding of how people should behave at work. But none of them could provide that quick fix, an instant turn-round in performance. What they all have in common is that they require managers to implement some newly acquired behaviour, and that means someone has to learn to do things differently. No matter what solution may be offered by outside consultants – what old truths newly packaged – in the end a management must never forget that *if a business is to succeed it must learn.*

It is all very well to change and develop individual managers, but we work in organisations. It does not help very much if one

196

manager sees the light on the road to Damascus while the management of which he is a part is still in Jerusalem. So now we have to examine how business organisations both nurture the learning process and enable useful changes in behaviour to come about. A successful business is not created simply by finding the best way to manage; it happens when the organisation has acquired the *ability to find and implement the best way for it to be managed.* There are no quick fixes. Good management is only achieved by the careful and painstaking application of the principles we have discussed in this book. They are not themselves original. Our claim is that they can only be applied in an organisation that takes learning seriously.

> One of the wonders of the twentieth century has been the emergence of Japanese business, which seems to be able to produce outstanding products at competitive prices manufactured by a willing and satisfied workforce. At one time it was believed that there was some kind of secret. There is. One of the authors saw it on a visit. They simply do it right, day after day after day – and this is possible because their whole culture emphasises learning.
>
> Thus they tend to innovate gradually, learning from experience and making only those changes to both their products and their production processes which can be shown to yield benefit. They introduce new products with caution and great thoroughness. They seldom make any large changes thereafter and they never undertake major reorganisations all at once. Everything is a learning experience and so change must be within the capacity of those involved to absorb it.
>
> There is a well-known Japanese saying that: 'The thrifty farmer winnows his crops down to the last grain of rice.' They have even called their style of management 'the grain of rice', which means the painstaking attention to detail. Excellence is rewarded not by quick promotion or by being lured away to other companies, but by the satisfaction of pre-eminence in the marketplace. The pursuit of excellence is seen as a lifetime of learning to improve performance, and everyone is involved.

Developing good management takes time. Businesses cannot be 'turned round' with a few quick fixes. It has been estimated by the McKinseys[1] in 1993 that 75 per cent of Total Quality Management schemes in the United States have failed after only a year or two. It is not the first panacea to be found wanting.

Management by Objectives, introduced unwisely, did so much harm to some businesses that no management development was attempted for many years after. All these techniques have something positive to offer. They are *an* answer not *the* answer. When they fail it is because the context is wrong and the commitment is missing.

To succeed they need two things:

- The business must introduce the particular scheme as a learning process and evaluate it as it proceeds.
- Behaviour from the top must be in line with the new scheme which is to be introduced.

Such changes cannot be introduced by edict, no matter how slick the presentation or glossy the brochures. It is no use, for example, introducing TQM to improve communication between internal 'suppliers' and internal 'customers' while the top management responsible continues to pass down decisions ignoring the very behaviour it seeks to introduce. We cannot repeat too often that managements are groups of people who seek to affect the lives of others positively, and that the process of change is a learning process in which every member of the management is involved. A business has to be committed to the continuous and purposeful training of its managers throughout their careers.

Why train managers?

There is nothing more frustrating in management than knowing exactly what has to be done and simply having nobody to do it. Most managers at some time find the job too much and simply have insufficient time to do all the things which are needed to reach the chosen goals. They become tired, their private life suffers and, in the end, their work deteriorates. They are told to delegate but they laugh and cry out that they are 'surrounded by idiots' and if 'they don't do it' there will be a disaster.

But many of us have had that blissful experience of going home on a Friday knowing the week has gone well. We have completed our own work and successfully delegated the rest of our responsibilities to colleagues who were competent and confident. Problems have been faced and difficulties overcome but we are not exhausted and can enjoy our weekend.

The difference between these two scenarios is one word – training. The second manager had a staff trained to do the job, one on whom he could rely. But a manager, or a director, can only have confidence in subordinates who are skilled in the work which they are called upon to do. In other words *the ability of a business to function successfully is dependent on the skills exercised by the staff appropriate to the jobs they actually do.*

Management education is now a mature academic and educational discipline. Business schools on both sides of the Atlantic are busy turning out over 8,000 MBA graduates each year and beyond this are thousands of more junior management and commerce degrees and diplomas. Almost every business of any size at all is sending managers on courses to management schools and colleges. Nevertheless, there is still a strongly held view that the standards of management, certainly in Britain, are not adequate. And for all their qualifications and knowledge of 'how the numbers work out', our young managers still do not perform well when faced with day-by-day real life management. The Director of the Chicago Business School said recently that management is a practical skill which can only be perfected by doing it and the business schools have no 'workshops' in which to practise.

While a business can itself be a 'workshop' it may sometimes be necessary to create such a learning environment while training and that is what we set out to do by creating the courses and seminars which we have described here. The problem with so much management training is that it seeks to fit the candidates to the training rather than the other way around. Most training courses are general and are concerned with generalised concepts and skills. Even, so-called, bespoke or tailor-made courses are often simply a selection of existing lectures, exercises or 'modules' which are thought to be appropriate for that client.

The whole thing is a compromise, justified on the grounds that 'management' is a general skill which can be applied to any business. This is indeed true up to a point – there are general skills but when it comes to managing real businesses these have to be modified to fit actual situations. If we return to our orchestral analogy, there are general skills in music like reading it, or keeping time, and then there are specialised skills like playing the oboe. But no conductor would attempt to play a symphony in public with 60 musicians just sent to him by an agency. First the concert master has to train them to play as an orchestra and only then can the conductor rehearse them in a particular symphony.

A young General Manager in a recently reorganised large public corporation was faced with a management team with very varied backgrounds and skills. Some knew the work well for they had been there a long time. Others had come in from another, taken over, company and did things differently. Still others were new recruits to the department. All of these managers and supervisors were good at the job and the General Manager was satisfied that he had the right mix of experience and skill. However, the performance of the team was very patchy and he had difficulty getting his policies adhered to and his objectives met.

There were internal consultants available for advice and they diagnosed a training need. They also noted that almost every manager and supervisor had an apparently different need – a different deficiency. What was needed was more assessments and a careful selection of 'training opportunities' for the identified deficiencies.

However, what the General Manager saw was that *as a group* they were only semi-numerate, they had difficulty running efficient meetings, they could not communicate with each other, and their staff counselling was terrible. In other words the *group* had a set of serious skill deficiencies. In fact some of the managers and supervisors were individually good at some of the necessary skills, such as communicating and counselling. The problem was that to carry out the General Manager's objectives they all had to exercise their skills as a *team*. They had to sing the same tune from the same song sheet and do it in harmony, even if the voices had different pitch and range.

So the General Manager told the training experts that he himself would design the training and he would be the trainer. A series of practical exercises was developed based on the actual experiences of the department. These were incorporated into a series of training days and some longer residential blocks. At all of these the General Manager was the main trainer. He led the sessions and ensured that the skills developed and the lessons learned were appropriate to the departmental strategy he intended to follow. Naturally, there had to be specialist input from professional trainers. But this was all incorporated in the framework after being tested for relevance.

The training itself was a success. Not because the courses were enjoyed, or they 'thought the sessions useful', but because the performance of the department showed measurable advance from the very first. But there was a second, and, at that time, unexpected benefit. The whole team got to know its leader and each other. They began to behave consistently because they wanted to support each other; they began to work as a team.

It is not only the form of traditional training or its relevance which is at fault, the method too is frequently ineffective. We have shown throughout this book that we believe that the traditional lecture is entertaining but ineffective as a learning method, and in Chapter 2 we explained why traditional case studies teach little. But there is a bigger problem. It is widely believed by those who teach knowledge that if you tell people good things about management then they will go away and apply them at once to become good managers. If this were true there would be no need for any adult training because the libraries of the world are full of good advice.

In fact, society works by giving instructions. The enormous complexity of our whole technology demands instructions about everything. The computer on which this is being written requires a whole library of instructions. A great deal of the output of the food processing industry requires that we follow the instructions printed on the packet. Even our clothes will be damaged in the wash if we ignore the instructions sewn into them. Because of our dependence on instructions, those that will not or cannot read them are at a severe disadvantage. This fundamental reliance on instructions has, therefore, had the effect of considerably widening the gap between the literate instruction-reading minority and the rest. Our amazing modern technology is in practice only understood by a small minority. The rest either pretend or give up.

A characteristic of instructions is that they only fit the particular case for which they have been written. It is not really possible to give approximate instructions. Only by knowing how it works and how to use it can we modify and adapt – and that implies real learning. But a great deal of training takes the form of instruction. We even refer to the trainers as 'instructors'. They say 'do this or that' to get a result and then assume that the instruction will be followed. One even hears in management courses: 'Never mind if you don't understand why, just do this to get results.'

The trouble is that all too often training is *either* about theory applied to circumstances *or* about 'skill' to do a particular job. In practice, management is about both. *The skill of a manager consists in turning the theories of management into practical action to achieve particular ends.* Thus training starts with the creation or acceptance of ends by the subject who then is enabled to develop the skill to achieve them.

We place the whole emphasis on outcomes. For us the only judgement of the efficacy of a particular management initiative is 'will it work?' Theory and skill are about means but it is the outcome which makes a particular action 'work' even when it violates the expected norms. But this is not to say we take an entirely instrumental view of management. In the determination of ends managers must reflect the ethical norms of their society. Business is not just business – it is a part of society and businessmen must behave accordingly.

Our approach to training therefore starts by making managers state and face their objectives. Training starts with the decision about ends. Of course managers need knowledge; they also need some pretty complicated skills. But all this is only useful if it is encapsulated in a framework where actual learning takes place, and we have specified that that can only be said to have taken place if there is *a clear and measurable change of behaviour and performance afterwards.*

The making of better managers

We now bring together the whole message of this book. While we have not intended it as a primer or a do-it-yourself training manual, we do intend that those of our readers who are responsible for designing management training courses will take note of this material and use it to their own advantage. For this reason we have printed in full the material for the British Rail courses in Appendices I and II and the Senior Management seminars in Appendix III together with a summary of the framework which underlay all our work in Appendix IV. We have argued that everything we describe here is inherent in good management itself *because a manager is principally an enabler and a coach who provides the means, the opportunity and the skills for others to do the job. Management and training require parallel skills and the process of training is itself as important as the lessons of the particular course or session.*

While ours is a demonstrably practical approach, it is based on a clear set of principles, the crux of which is our belief that the process of learning has to be understood and embedded in the structure of a management. We do not favour organisational solutions to business problems nor do we believe that questions of legal ownership or regulation have much part in determining whether a business is well managed. The goal of good management will be attained by those who seek to fulfil the simple objective of satisfying their customers in the best way for each particular business. And that can only be done by discovery and learning.

Let us remember the question we posed in Chapter 1. How do managers do the job of making business work and how can they learn the skills they need? In many ways this book has been a bit like trying to explain how to ride a bicycle. Maybe you have tried yourself. How far did you get? Did you explain the theory; or maybe the physical process; or maybe you relied on poetry and described how it feels?

In the end the only way to learn to ride a bicycle is to get on it and try . . . and try . . . until, after a few falls, you succeed. You cannot actually explain about balance – you just have to do it. Only after you 'know how' can all the necessary associated skills, such as roadcraft and safety be added. So it is with many other acquired skills, such as walking, swimming and skating, and, we would argue, so it is with management. However, we go a step further.

When someone can ride a bicycle we know he can because we see him do it and after a bit he does it in order to go somewhere. Then he uses the bicycle to go to places chosen for a reason other than a pleasant cycle ride. Again, so it is with management. When someone can do it we can see it because their business or department is going somewhere, namely towards its chosen objective, purposefully and successfully. Furthermore, as with a good cyclist, the good manager is effortless.

It is this combination of a personally acquired knack joined to a set of skills and knowledge which makes management special. To make a manager we have to create the circumstances where both kinds of learning can take place. We have to describe, show and demonstrate – and then give him or her the bicycle. But this is not all. We believe that the knack which the manager must learn is very close to that required of the good teacher. Remember our principles of learning in Chapter 1! People learn when they want to – the same goes for people at work, they do it well when they want to. People learn when they see the point – and at work we all do better and work longer when we understand. They learn by doing – and that is the heart of management, giving people the chance to take on their own tasks and to 'own' them. And finally they need to know how they did – and without that there can be no continuing commitment to high-quality work.

So the process of acquiring this amazing skill is itself an analogue of the skill itself and that process must itself serve as part of the learning process. This is why we let the participants invent their own cases and eventually believe they are running their own courses, for that is what we believe good managers should do. In a successful business the staff may come to believe that they do not need the managers at all; while all the time it is the managers who are enabling it all to happen that way. That is how a good manager does his job well.

Summary and final words

There are no easy options for improving the management performance of a business. There are many useful techniques and organisational theories but a business must first find the best techniques for itself. The process of changing and developing in business is a gradual one with learning at its heart. There are a large number of particular and general disciplines and skills which must be present in a competent management. However, the key to successful management is to enable those who must do the work to learn those skills in ways which make them relevant and memorable. While a great deal of training must happen at work there will always remain the need for managers to draw back and learn away from the business. Such courses and seminars must themselves provide for the appropriate and intelligible practice of the skill of management.

We have argued that development must be self-directed and manifestly useful and that training courses based on cases invented by the participants, or seminars which use real issues from the members' own company, will always be seen to be useful and relevant. Furthermore, because they adhere to our basic principles that people learn when they want, when they see the point, when they can practise and when they get good knowledge of results, they are a demonstration of all the essential ingredients of a learning company which will develop good management and is likely to have good results. In other words, it will be successful both for the individual and for the business.

The management of change and the management of learning are two sides of the same coin. In a well-directed business this truth will be well understood at all levels. Staff will feel supported and nurtured, their capabilities respected, good performance supported and their inherent talents released. Such a business will tend to have satisfied customers and a well-motivated workforce – the only real criteria of success.

References

1 Quoted in 'TQM Revisited'. *Business Week*. Number 3297-628, 22 March 1993. Page 51.

British Rail – Midland Region Management Development Programme

COURSE INSTRUCTIONS AND BRIEFING NOTES

This appendix contains all the principal documentation for the second and most successful version of our course. These documents were handed to the participants in the sequence printed here throughout the week starting on the Sunday evening and following through to the Friday morning.

Sunday 20.00

DOCUMENT 1

INTRODUCTION

Objectives

This course is designed to provide you with the following outcomes:

1. A demonstrated ability to work better in multi-disciplinary groups – taking decisions and making choices on the basis of wider considerations than those within your own departments.
2. A more disciplined approach to problem-solving – being more likely to define and to analyse the causes of problems before considering solutions.
3. When considering solutions to problems, a willingness to think in terms of the effect of the solution on business results and customer service, as well as on the purely operational aspects of running a railway.
4. The capability to answer the questions:
   (a) What are the purposes of my work?
   (b) How can I judge my performance?

Content

The five-day course will cover the following areas of managerial activity in sequence.

1. The understanding of most important financial and operational variables and parameters.
2. The setting up and interpretation of market surveys.
3. The specification of railway services and standards.
4. The setting of targets and measurements of performance.
5. The creation of operating plans.
6. The development of marketing plans and sales programmes.
7. The making of business reports and presentations.
8. The techniques of good staff relations.
9. The nature and content of good communication.
10. How to tackle problems.

Finally you will be asked to look at your own performance and given guidance in self assessment. This will enable you to continue the development processes initiated on this course.

General Guidance for Course Members

This week you will be engaged as part of a group on a continuous series of exercises concerned with a single case study. Most of what you will work with you will invent yourselves. A basic set of data and information will be provided but from then on you will accumulate your own information. You will work together to make up a railway operation.

We do not expect you to have knowledge beyond what would be consistent with the positions you have occupied. However, we know that railway managers have a great interest in what they do and within each group there is bound to be more than enough expertise to create credible railways. However, beware of overloading yourselves with too much detail.

Neither do we expect you to exercise management decisions outside your experience. You may need to project yourself into the position of your immediate boss, or even beyond, but we are sure that in your minds many of you have already done so. Indeed the capacity to visualise an issue from your boss's viewpoint is an important personal skill.

There are two basic rules of this week's activities:

1. Once your group has invented something and the stage has closed you may not go back and disinvent it later. The same applies to the decisions you take and the negotiations you conclude. Your group must live with its own history.
2. You are to be the management of a real part of British Rail – this is not a role-play exercise – nor are you to indulge in idealisation or fantasy. As far as possible you act yourself. Your group must believe in what it is doing.

The exercises are divided into 14 stages. For each one you will receive quite specific instructions. On only three occasions will you be required to make formal presentations as a group. Otherwise, your work will be monitored and observed by the tutors and you may be asked to make short informal presentations.

It is essential that you document what you do as you go along. Make use of all the facilities available to you. Your group will occupy one syndicate room for the whole week. You may, therefore, put material on the walls as well as accumulating written records.

How your group is organised and how the work is tackled is up to you. A Chairman will be appointed but all other activities are up to the group. Remember you will be under time constraints all week and organising your work will be a most important activity. Your time must not only be planned but all your activity must be monitored otherwise you will fall behind.

You will be given a briefing on group working at the beginning of the exercises. Since learning more about group activity is part of the course objective you will find it useful to keep notes on your own performance, reactions and feelings. Finally, although the week is structured, it is a learning experience and the timetable can be changed if necessary. Your group should review progress each day and if problems arise there should be immediate discussion with the tutors.

DOCUMENT 2

STAGE 1 – INVENTING A RAILWAY

The attached briefing (B1) gives details of two urban railway lines linking suburbs to a large city. It is currently a conventional operation using diesel multiple unit trains on lines which have changed little since before nationalisation. The decision has been taken to modernise the lines; details will be given to you later.

You are asked to invent the railway before modernisation. In particular you must answer these questions:

1. What are the names of the city and the towns it serves?
2. What is the current level of service and how is it provided? (Specify: frequency, punctuality, reliability, number of trains, etc.)
3. How are the lines organised? (Provide an organised chart: give names, ages and pen portraits of principal managers; give numbers of staff at all levels directly employed on these lines).
4. In general are your industrial relations good, average or bad? (You may enlarge on this as you choose.)
5. What are the current levels of absenteeism?
6. What is the current level of business (e.g. daily traffic levels, growth or decline)?
7. What competition exists? (Describe competing roads and associated bus services.)
8. Make a SWOT summary (strengths, weaknesses, opportunities and threats to your railway).

You will be asked to tell us about your railway. This is to take no more than five minutes. (In that time you will only be able to introduce your railway and outline the SWOT summary.)

Monday 09.45

DOCUMENT 3

BRIEFING NOTE 1 – TWO URBAN RAILWAYS

A large conurbation (M) has a number of surburban rail ser-vices. Some have reasonable patronage while others are in the latter stages of decay. This study is concerned with two – one to the north and one to the south. The geographical de-tails are shown on the map and the dimensions and popula-tion are given on Information Note 1.

The main station at M was substantially rebuilt when the main east–west line was electrified. It has nine platforms and also supports three other local services and a number of cross-country stopping services.

The northern line is served by such a service. It is a non-electrified main line with considerable goods traffic as well as frequent fast passenger services. It has four tracks as far as the Comet Aviation Plant. This complex of factories employs 10,000 people and is the hub of the economy of that part of the city. Nearby the County Authority has set up the Galaxy Industrial Park. This has attracted a large number of high technology industries. While both attract workers from areas to the north, a great deal of commuting takes place *through* M.

The northern line passes through the suburb of B. This is a sprawling commuter area with no real town centre. It has a large park and there is a project to build a new stadium at C. The three stations here have been served only morning and evening by stopping trains coming in from a neighbouring city.

The inner part of this line used to pass through a heavy in-dustrial area now mostly derelict or vanished. In its place the new university at X accommodates 15,000 students and staff, while at Y there is a large office development. The line here passes through a maze of old sidings and cross-overs and a viaduct.

The service on the northern line has been provided by trains operating from a city to the north. It has been barely re-liable and ridership has steadily dwindled. There are no car park facilities at A, B or C. Parallel to the line is the main road from the north. The whole area is now well served by trunk bus services as well as local routes. There is a lot of car com-muting.

The southern line is a complete contrast. Because it serves S it has always maintained ridership. This thriving town has a wide variety of engineering and manufacturing industry and generates traffic at all times of the day. Both the satellite stations at J and H serve mixed residential-industrial areas.

The line then passes through a tunnel, crosses the motorway and enters a densely populated inner suburb. Just south of the motorway is a large newly built shopping centre. The stations at G, F and E though a bit battered, are well used since car ownership is relatively low. However, unemployment has hit the area and economic activity is low.

Just before joining the main line, the line passes across a viaduct with a seriously vandalised and hardly used station on it at D. It then uses the slow tracks on the south side of the main line and regularly terminates at platform 9. In spite of good use by commuters this line has less than 100 car park spaces and the road access to the stations is generally not good for car drops.

The service on this line has been by three-car diesel multiple units (DMU) built in the late 1960s. They are serviced and stabled in the depot at T. While they are mostly depreciated, there is a good deal of remedial work to be carried out on them and, therefore, engineering costs are expected to rise. The present operation provides for a six-day regular operation with extra capacity in the peaks.

The map shows that there is a network of roads to the south of the city and these support a wide range of bus services. However, the wooded hill to the south means that the bus services have a circuitous route while the railway is more direct.

Apart from a summit at the north end of the tunnel and a slight rise between A and P, the lines are virtually level. The track is not modern nor is the signalling. The main line has four-aspect signalling controlled from the power box on the main line west of M. However, the southern line has a few tight curves with consequent poor clearance for long vehicles.

Rail servicing around M now falls within the responsibility of the Metropolitan Authority. They have been reluctant to sanction fare increases and have, therefore, provided annual revenue grants for the operation of the southern line. Two years ago a travelcard was introduced for the whole conurbation. BR is remunerated at the rate of 30 pence per passenger journey calculated on the basis of monthly surveys of numbers of passengers and average journey length.

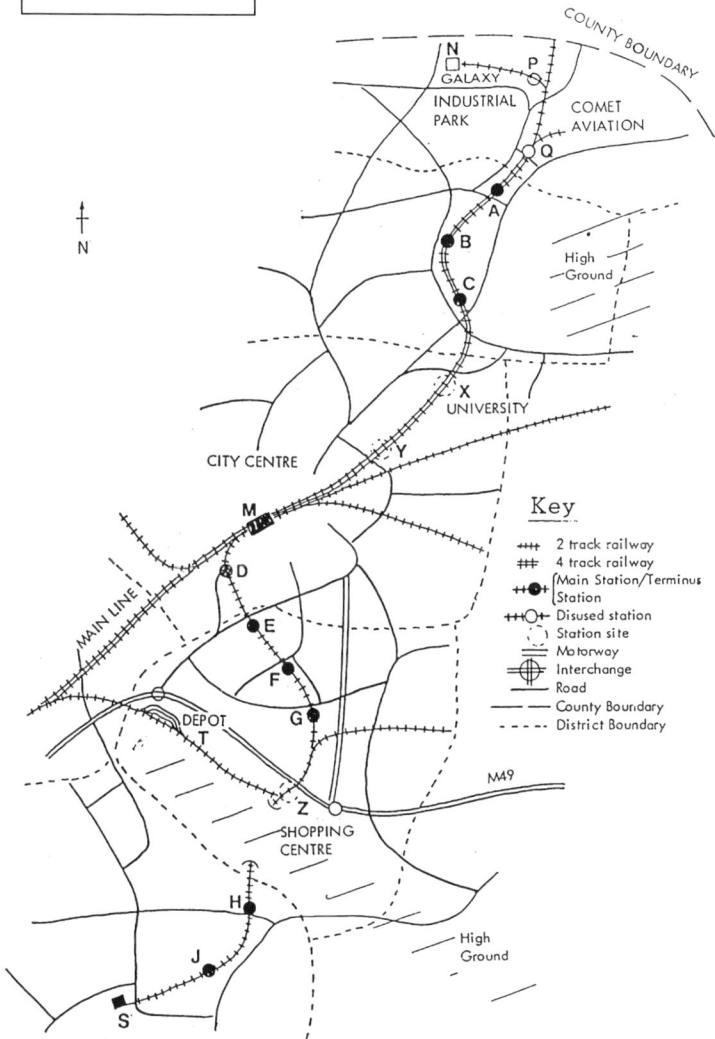

SKETCH MAP
OF TWO URBAN
RAILWAY LINES

COUNTY BOUNDARY

N
GALAXY
INDUSTRIAL
PARK

P
COMET
AVIATION

Q

A

B

C

High
Ground

X
UNIVERSITY

Y

CITY CENTRE

M

Key

D

+++	2 track railway
++	4 track railway
+●+	Main Station/Terminus / Station
+++O+	Disused station
	Station site
	Motorway
⊕	Interchange
	Road
— —	County Boundary
- - -	District Boundary

E

F

MAIN LINE

G

DEPOT
T

Z

M49

SHOPPING
CENTRE

High
Ground

H

J

S

Monday 09.45

DOCUMENT 4

INFORMATION NOTE 1 – THE URBAN RAILWAY LINES
SPECIFICATION

Station	Status	Facilities	Miles to M	Time to M (minutes)
N	Disused	3 platforms – ground-level access	9.50	26
P	Disused	2 platforms – ground-level access, level crossing	8.50	24
Q	Disused	2 platforms – road bridge access, disused sidings	7.25	21
A	Optional	2 platforms on outer lines, road bridge access, dilapidated buildings	6.25	19
B	Optional	4 platforms on 2 islands rebuilt 1966 but heavily vandalised	5.50	16
C	Optional	2 platforms on outer lines – footbridge access, unmodernised buildings	4.75	13
X	Site only	Space available for station in cutting	3.25	9
Y	Site only	Space available using disused lines on viaduct	1.75	6
M	Optional	9-platform central station, built in 1969 beneath office development	0	0
D	Optional	2 platforms on viaduct buildings almost derelict	0.75	3
E	Optional	2 platforms – ground-level access, large disused marshalling yard adjacent	1.75	5

Station	Status	Facilities	Miles to M	Time to M (minutes)
F	Optional	2 platforms – footbridge access	3.00	8
G	Optional	2 platforms – road bridge access, old derelict coalyard	4.25	11
Z	Site only	Ground-level site available	5.75	15
H	Optional	2 platforms on an island from a road bridge	8.00	21
J	Optional	2 platforms outside of tracks with ground-level access	9.00	24
S	Optional	4 platforms – centrally located town station. Formerly a junction with a large amount of BR land	10.00	28

THE URBAN RAILWAY LINES' CATCHMENT AREA POPULATION

The resident population of the territory directly served by the commuter railway is currently 600,000. This comprises:

Area served by	Stations Included	Total Population	Economically Active
N District	N,P,Q	65,000	35,000
B District	A,B,C	80,000	45,000
Central District	X,Y,M,D	90,000	40,000
G District	E,F,G,Z	145,000	70,000
Borough of S	S,J,H	220,000	130,000
		600,000	320,000

Economically Active: This is defined as all able-bodied males and females between 16 and 60, *less* students and those in full-time education, *plus* males between 60 and 64 who are still at work.

Monday 11.00

DOCUMENT 5

STAGE 2 – BASIC DATA

You should now complete the Operating and Financial Data Worksheet. This is to provide the basic data against which your plans will be made and judged.

The worksheet is to provide a minimum and you are certainly welcome to add any other data or numerate descriptions to the picture you have built up of the urban railway lines.

There should be a systematic relationship between revenue, passengers, traffic and costs. Ensure that there are sufficient, but not excessive, trains to handle the business. The lines are making losses but these are not unreasonable.

Monday 11.00

DOCUMENT 6

BRIEFING NOTE 2– COST AND REVENUE BRIEF

The problem with developing good financial data in the railway business is allocation. So many costs are incurred jointly and so much revenue is for more than one journey. This has developed the concepts of escapable costs and attributable revenue. Put simply these mean that we attempt to isolate those costs and revenues which would not occur if the operation ceased.

Where an operation uses a specific set of vehicles, operates alone on one line and has passengers who rarely transfer, the whole problem is much easier. In this exercise we have not used the usual BR conventions but all the figures are *based* on current BR costs and revenues and the answers will be realistic.

Staff costs

It is possible to calculate quite precisely the numbers of train crew required to man a discrete fleet. The terminal staff are only working for the one service and they too can be costed. The problem arises when services are performed by other departments such as signals or permanent way. In this case the staff costs will be lost in the allocation process.

Operating costs

It is very easy to calculate the running costs of a trainset. The engineering costs are much more difficult. In this case we must simply accept an allocation based on train miles since we do know that costs increase with mileage.

Track and signalling

The provision and maintenance of track and signalling tends always to cross operating boundaries. These are allocated again by train miles. However, this would penalise more intensive operations which often use the facilities more efficiently without substantially increasing the costs. Thus a fairer system is for a specific operation to be charged at an annual rate.

Terminal costs

The cost of maintaining buildings and estates is at present allocated within BR. However, these are services which could well be brought in from outside. It is very likely that managers will increasingly be given a budget and be able to spend this where they can get the most advantageous prices.

Administration and overheads

The generality of all BR administration costs has to be spread over the whole operation and this usually entails some very crude allocation. Some activities can be more accurately costed such as printing, issuing and accounting for tickets, which is directly related to traffic.

Capital charges (Depreciation and the cost of capital)

In BR accounting capital costs tend to be lumped together because the usual problem of joint use is aggravated by the varying age of the many assets. Nevertheless, in the case of a specific service, some attempt must be made. Railway investments have a very long life and nobody expects them to yield a high rate of return in cash. (In general they are undertaken for notional social benefits). Thus a charge of 4 per cent of accumulated fixed capital less depreciation is a reasonable approximation.

Revenue

The critical issues when estimating revenue are price, capacity and frequency. Rail travel is not very price-sensitive. This means that it takes quite large increases in price to discourage people from using the trains. But it is probably the most important variable and used creatively can be used to stimulate the market. On the other hand, rail services are very expensive to provide. A view has to be taken about capacity and frequency in order to get the largest loadings per train.

Price

The average fare or yield (found by dividing revenue by passengers) is only a very simple measure of price. The composition of that yield will be crucial, especially where cheap fares become available to those who would be prepared to pay more. Yield can, therefore, be increased by altering the balance of fares favourably. Yield is also a function of the average length of passenger journey and an increase will automatically increase the yield.

Conclusion

Developing a budget of costs and revenues is a balancing act between many variables, the most important feature of which is to try to understand and use those over which you may have control.

Monday 11.00

DOCUMENT 7

WORKSHEET 1 –
OPERATING AND FINANCIAL DATA – CURRENT OPS
(All prices are 1988 and constant)

Traffic Data

Weekday passenger one-way journeys	:	
Saturday passenger one-way journeys	:	
Average passenger journey	:	4.9 miles
Weekday one-way trainset journeys	:	
Saturday one-way trainset journeys	:	
Annual Revenue train miles	:	
Trainset availability	:	70%

(Remember when calculating annual
figures to allow for public holidays)

Current Revenue

	Annual Passenger Journeys	Average Fare per Journey	Annual Revenue £000
Travelcard		0.30	
Season Ticket		0.25	
Ordinary Single/Return		0.50	
Day Returns		0.28	
Concession Fares*		0.20	
Others (children, etc.)		0.12	
Contribution from through tickets and the network		0.09	
TOTALS		0.29 – 0.35	

(* These are OAP and scholars' passes paid for by the Local
Authority)

Capital

Notional Fixed Capital	£2,000,000

Current Cost Data

Average cost of staff per annum (including employment costs and overheads)

Terminal staff	£9,000
Train Crew – drivers	£12,000
– guards	£10,000
Supervisory staff	£14,000

Operating costs £ per train mile (3-car DMU)

Fuel	0.32
Maintenance	1.05
Overhaul	0.25

Track costs £ per year

Northern Line	nil
Southern Line	62,000

Signalling costs £ per year

Northern Line	nil
Southern Line	42,000

Terminal running costs £ per year

Northern Line	24,000	
Southern Line	65,000	
Central Station	25,000	(notional contribution)

(N.B. Track, signalling and terminal running costs include their staff content)

Ticketing costs £ per passenger (Accounting, printing, machines, etc.)	.0075

Capital charges at 4 per cent of Fixed Capital (BR overhead contribution £ per train mile)	0.45

Current Costs

£000

Staff

Operating and Maintenance

Track and Signalling

Terminal

Ticketing

Capital Charges

BR Overhead

Current Revenue

Annual Profit/Loss

Monday 14.00

DOCUMENT 8

STAGE 3 – MODERNISING THE RAILWAY

It has been decided to modernise the two lines. They are to be operated as a single through service with new rolling stock and many new and refurbished stations. Both the Metropolitan Authority and British Rail will be investing in this programme. You are not invited to examine this decision itself since it has been taken at the highest level against national criteria. You are concerned with implementation.

The plans for modernisation, as set out in Briefing Note 2, concern the major strategic decisions. You should examine these for any inconsistency with your own railway. You may recommend modifications but these will only be allowed subject to consultation (with the tutors).

The Capital Programme, Information Note 2, gives the current estimate of the costs of all the investments now under consideration. You will see that there are many options and many choices. Do not attempt to make them yet, this information is to enable you to understand the overall plan. There will be plenty of time to develop your plans in detail later.

You are asked to consider the implications of the proposal, its timing and any special circumstances. Then express in one sentence what you believe this investment will achieve.

Monday 14.00

DOCUMENT 9

BRIEFING NOTE 3 – THE MODERNISATION PLAN

The Metropolitan Authority has decided to finance the modernisation of these two lines in conjunction with British Rail. This has been accepted by the BR Board who will invest £12.5m while the Authority will invest £7.5m.

The proposal is to operate the two lines as a single high-frequency seven-days-a-week service connecting N and S to M. The project will take two years and will include the following:

1. The provision of new 'Sprinter' diesel multiple units which will all be either two-car or three-car.
2. The improvement of the slow track north from M and the renovation of the branch to N.
3. Resignalling of the line south of G and north of A and full integration into the power box at M.
4. The building of up to three new stations, the complete rebuilding of three disused stations and the renovation of the remaining stations on the line to enable it to have a single unified product image.
5. The building of bus stations, car parks and access roads.
6. A major advertising and promotion activity.

The Authority has decided to integrate the new line with the bus service which it operates. Trunk routes from N, A, C, G and S will be cut back and new routes will centre on the stations. There will also be a substantial traffic management scheme on the roads.

The scheme shows a good return on the basis of social accounting. However, it is also expected to be a modest comercial success. While the line will be supported by a revenue grant from the Metropolitan Authority for up to five years, the target is to break even on current cost before then.

Monday 14.00
DOCUMENT 10

INFORMATION NOTE 2 –
NEW RAILWAY CAPITAL PROGRAMME
(The following cost data includes the available options for
allocating the £17m available for modernising the railway).

Stations

Renovate: Repair and decorate existing buildings and
fixtures to BR standard

Utility: Renovate platforms, demolish buildings and
replace with utility structures/build new
utility station

New Build: Rebuild or build to high standard using common
design theme

Capital Cost in £000

	Renovate	Utility	New Build
N	–	220	850
P	–	110	440
Q	–	125	470
A	180	95	280
B	·130	110	245
C	145	155	260
X	–	150	425
Y	–	210	490
D	150	180	540
E	40	75	275
F	25	125	240
G	30	110	380
Z	–	155	360
H	60	150	290
S	75	200	360

Depot

Essential renewal and re-equipment   £1,100,000

Track and Signalling

Resignalling one half of Southern Line
Essential work at M power box
Track and signalling work both at A,
including new crossover   £1,800,000

Additional work for 23-metre coaches   £320,000

Trains

New class 15X stock available in two configurations:

15x2:   Two-car, high-density unit, each car
        23 metres, seating capacity 160
        Prime cost with spares, each unit   £520,000

15x3:   Three-car, high-density unit, each car
        20 metres, seating capacity 214
        Prime cost with spares, each unit   £720,000

Car Parks

Construction of car park on railway property £80 per space

Construction of car park on newly purchased land £2,250 per
space

(There is space available on BR land at N, P, Q, A, B, C, E, G, J
and S)

Ticket Equipment

Automatic ticket equipment may be purchased. It will cost
£280,000 to equip the whole line.

Further Capital Expenditure

Any capital investment beyond the £17m now budgeted must
be remunerated through additional traffic. The rate is £1 of investment to £0.15 of additional annual revenue or, put another way, each £1,000 of investment must produce 8 extra
passenger journeys per week.

Examples of Capital Cost Items

(These are approximate and depend on spec.)

Special waiting room on Platform 9 at M	£22,000
Heating in station waiting rooms – per room (Do not forget running costs)	£1,500
Design of special logo and full set of station signs	£75,000
New 'high-tech' signs at M	£2,500
Electronic train indicators on all stations	£110,000

In addition, the launching publicity programme will be treated as a capital expenditure. Thereafter, the line must cover its own publicity within the budget.

The construction of bus stations and access roads will be undertaken by the Metropolitan Authority as required and will not be subject to this capital programme.

Monday 16.00
DOCUMENT 11

STAGE 4 – REPORT ON THE MARKET

You are asked to specify the following about the market *you now serve:* (Use Worksheet 2)

(1) Give the size of the total passenger market in this corridor, decide how much of it is along the corridor and, therefore, available to tail and estimate how much is *now* travelling by car, public bus, bicycle and rail.
(2) Divide your markets by journey purpose, for example work, shopping, school, social and leisure.
(3) Give the levels of competing services and fares; describe the services provided.
(4) Write a brief for a market survey paying particular attention to point 1 on the market survey brief (B4) which you must decide. The rest would normally be advised by your contractor. You will want to know about such things as: journey times, comfort, frequency, off-peak services, early and later journeys, car parking, interchange facilities.
(5) Now invent a report on the market survey findings covering those issues covered in your brief. You may add any other information you might reasonably expect to obtain through such a survey.
(6) Make a SWOT summary of the market survey from your railway's viewpoint.

Monday 16.00

DOCUMENT 12

BRIEFING NOTE 4 – MARKET SURVEY BRIEF

A market survey is a way of testing customer reaction to what we do or plan to do. The simplest market survey is to add up what is actually sold on the assumption that the purchasers are satisfied. More complex surveys involve asking some or all customers what they like. The construction and enumeration of surveys is a complex business, however the kind of surveys which can be attempted and the form of the answers is easy to reproduce.

In drawing up a market survey you should pay attention to these questions:

(1) What exactly do we want to discover?
(2) Do we observe current behaviour or ask questions?
(3) What sort of a survey shall we mount, e.g. postal questionnaire, open interview or discussion?
(4) Do we interview existing or potential rail travellers or everyone who might travel?
(5) Do we ask opinions, offer multiple choices or seek a rank order of product features?
(6) Do we ask concrete questions or offer hypothetical possibilities?
(7) How do we tackle the price of travel?

In interpreting the results you will need to consider these points:

(a) The results can only reflect the questions asked.
(b) Conclusions only apply to those surveyed.
(c) There should be some form of cross-check with existing information.

All surveys are only as good as the questions asked. They should therefore avoid these:

(i) 'Motherhoods' – i.e. those which express the obvious.
(ii) Leading questions – i.e. those containing the answer in a way which encourages it to be given.
(iii) Aggressive questions – i.e. those which assume a poor response by the subject or which are accusatory.
(iv) Ambiguous questions – i.e. those whose object is unclear and whose answers are open to many interpretations.

Finally, in all surveys a healthy scepticism is a good thing, however, even the poorest survey is preferable to unrestrained managerial prejudice or 'decision by anecdote'.

Monday 16.00

DOCUMENT 13

WORKSHEET 2 – THE MARKET

Total population: 1,050,000

Population Profile

	Male %	Female %
Pensioners	7	10
Adults	30	30
Children	9	8
Infants	3	3

Employment Profile

% of adult population	*N & B*	*G & S*
Managers	3	3
Professionals	4	3
Non-manual	17	15
Skilled manual	11	11
Unskilled manual	6	11
Housewives	44	34
Others	1	3
Unemployed	10	12

Modal Split (before new service)

Journeys to work and school

	North Section %	South Section %
Bus	–	17
Train	1	4
Car Drive	26	–
Car Passenger	–	–
Walk	23	–
Cycle/Motorcycle	–	4

Journey Purpose on Public Transport (before new service)

	North Section %	South Section %
Travel to work	48	–
Shopping	–	16
Visiting friends and relatives	–	–
School children and students	–	10
Leisure	–	–
Feeder to Inter-City	2	–

Present Line-users' Profile

	Annual Passenger Journeys	Average Journeys per Customer	Number of Customers
Travelcard			
Season Tickets			
Ordinary single/return			
Day Returns			
Concession Fares			
Others			

These figures should match those which you put into Worksheet 1.

Monday 20.00

DOCUMENT 14

STAGE 5 – PRODUCT SPECIFICATION (Part 1)

Brainstorming

The railway product has often been defined as simply transporting people and goods from A to B. We know that it is much more complex than that. It actually covers every part of a passenger's experience from the moment he decides to travel; it covers for a freight shipper the total involvement of the railway in logistics and distribution.

You are asked to use the full resources of your group to create lists which cover every aspect of the *passenger* rail product as you see it (e.g. frequency, comfort, passenger service, etc.). Include not only what is, but also what might be. Include as many ideas and inventions as you can.

The purpose of the exercise is to produce a product specification for your new railway.

Tuesday 09.00

DOCUMENT 15

STAGE 6 – PRODUCT SPECIFICATION (Part 2)

Now you are asked to define the new service in clear numerate and qualitative terms. Draw on the lists of product features which you have generated to put together a composite description of the rail product which you feel is appropriate to the market you have defined.

The specification must be consistent with the resources which are available but need not be constrained. Superior service levels may be proposed but bear in mind that additional costs will be incurred and, therefore, revenue justification will be necessary. The product need not be kept within either current British Rail practice or technology. But innovations will require both financial and specific implementation.

Tuesday 09.00
DOCUMENT 16

WORKSHEET 3 – THE NEW OPERATION
(All prices are current and constant: 1988)

Traffic Data

Weekday passenger one-way journeys :
Weekend passenger one-way journeys :
Average passenger journey   :
Weekday one-way trainset journeys   :
Weekend one-way trainset journeys   :

Annual revenue train miles :
Trainset availability   :

Current Revenue

	Annual Passenger Journey	Average Fare per Journey	Annual Revenue
Travelcard			
Season Ticket			
Ordinary Single/Return			
Day Returns			
Concession Fares			
Others (children, families, etc.)			
Contribution from through tickets and network			
TOTALS			

Capital

(Add the Capital Programme to the £2,000,000 Notional Fixed Capital.)

Current Cost Data

Average cost of staff per annum (including employment costs and overheads)

Terminal staff	£9,000
Train crew – drivers	£12,000
– guards	£10,000
Supervisory staff	£14,000

Operating costs £ per train mile

	15x2	*15x3*
Fuel	0.40	0.60
Maintenance	0.64	0.81
Overhead	0.14	0.21

| Track costs £ per year: | 110,000 | |
| Signalling costs £ per year:* | 35,000 | (contribution) |

(* This figure will depend on the programme but will be about £100,000.)

Ticketing costs £ per passenger –
Accounting, printing, machines, etc.

| Traditional method: | 0.0075 |
| Automated technology: | 0.0100 |

Capital charges 4% of Fixed Capital

BR overhead contribution, £ per train mile 0.45

Current Costs

	£000
Staff	
Operating and maintenance	
Track and signalling	
Terminals	
Ticketing	
Standing charges	
BR overhead	_____
	_____

Current Revenue

Annual profit/loss

(Year due to open)
Estimates for further years may be added)

Tuesday 10.30

DOCUMENT 17

STAGE 7 – OPERATING PLAN

Develop an Operating Plan to deliver the product you have specified. This will describe in detail how the proposed service will operate.

You may include whatever investment you choose up to the limit provided by the Metropolitan Authority and British Rail. Any investment beyond that must produce more traffic and be remunerated through additional traffic at the rate specified. You will also be required to justify your figures to the Authority and the Board.

Clearly your Operating Plan will reflect your Marketing Strategy. You will need to decide your overall philosophy before deciding how to spend money on the station modernisation programme. The depot expenditure is mandatory as is the main part of the track and signalling. The extra track work to accommodate 23-metre coaches depends on your trainset decision. You may only purchase *either* 2-car *or* 3-car sets, *you may not have a mixed fleet*. The remaining capital expenditures are all options.

While you are expected to plan a cost effective and efficient operation, it has been established that the agreed level of investment is necessary to attract passengers and provide the expected benefits for the Metropolitan community. In other words, you are not expected to reject investment or cut down to a utility service.

You may take full advantage of the cost savings which the new facilities produce. Total operating costs of the line may be expected to be between £4m and £5m. The plan must look forward to a situation of profit within five years.

(1) Give details of the full investment package.
(2) Describe the train service (full details not necessary).
(3) Specify all resource requirements.
(4) Detail infrastructure and terminal implications.
(5) Give details of staffing.
(6) SWOT summary.

Tuesday 14.00

DOCUMENT 18

STAGE 8 – COST ANALYSIS AND PERFORMANCE STANDARDS

You now have an operating plan and a marketing plan, which are both feasible in terms of the constraints given to you. The next task is to produce a cost/revenue summary using the data given to you in Worksheet 3. You will then need to set a number of key performance targets which will enable you to monitor your progress from the situation which exists to the situation you wish to achieve. These targets must be realistic, i.e. the current situation is the one you described yesterday, including the current key operating data. This is your starting point. Now ask yourselves what are the key targets along the road to the situation you wish to achieve in your operating plan? Define these in both quantitative and time terms. You may wish to consider how the information to monitor progress will be obtained.

The worksheet provided is a guide. There are other possibilities and you may wish to add both comprehensive and particular targets relating to your operating and marketing plans.

Tuesday 16.00

DOCUMENT 19

WORKSHEET 4 – PERFORMANCE STANDARDS WORKSHEET

Line-user Profile

	Current Number	Target Number
Travelcard		
Season Ticket		
Full Fare		
Day Return		
Concession Fare		
Other		

Proportion of market using train for journeys in corridor

	Current %	Target %
To and from work	2	
Shopping	3	
Visiting friends and relatives	1	
Schoolchildren and students	1	
Leisure	2	
Feeder to Inter-City	26	

Opening Standards

	Current	Target
Availability of rolling stock	70%	%
Arrival within 5 minutes of published time	%	%
Proportion of services cancelled	2%	%

Tuesday 16.00

DOCUMENT 20

STAGE 9 – MARKETING AND SELLING PLAN

The Metropolitan Authority's target is to break even on direct costs within five years. This can only be achieved if all the potential of the new investment is explained. It is now your task to work out how this is to be done.

Marketing is about the whole process of designing the product to meet customer demands at a price which can be afforded. It embraces all activities from market survey to actual daily operations. (To help you, information about the costs of the new line are given in Worksheet 3 – this should *not* be filled in until later.)

A marketing plan is to be developed which starts from the specification of the product and then considers how sales are to be maximised.

(1) Specify the market segments to be exploited.
(2) Detail methods by which the core market will be expanded.
(3) Describe the methods for expanding other existing markets.
(4) Examine potential for exploiting new markets.
(5) Decide what you will call your new line and how you will promote it.
(6) SWOT summary.

Tuesday 16.00

DOCUMENT 21

STAGE 9 – BOARD PRESENTATION (Preparation)

You are asked to give a presentation of your plans and targets to a joint meeting of the Metropolitan Authority and British Rail top management tomorrow morning. You will have *twenty minutes only* followed by a period of questions. You may assume that your audience has a basic understanding of your railway, so there is no need to give background information unless it is needed to justify a particular plan or target.

Note the following points:

(1) Choose your best presenter and build around him. It is not necessary for everyone to take part.
(2) Decide precisely the points you want to make and stick to them. (Generally it takes 3–4 minutes to make a point. Your SWOT summaries will help you to choose the relevant points).
(3) Make maximum use of charts and other aids.
(4) Do not pad.

[The presentations took place on the Wednesday morning followed by feedback from the whole course.]

Wednesday 14.00

DOCUMENT 22

STAGE 10 – HANDLING PEOPLE AT WORK

You will now be asked either to conduct an interview or to be interviewed. This will last for 12 minutes followed by a review. The rest of the participants will observe (see Worksheet 5). You have 15 minutes to prepare yourself.

Wednesday 14.00

DOCUMENT 23

STAGE 10A – INTERVIEWEE BRIEF

You will be interviewed by a newly appointed senior manager about your job in the new railway. You must be prepared to talk about the plans for renewal and your role in them *as if he knew almost nothing of the detail*. However, since you only have 12 minutes, you must be clear beforehand about the specific points which you wish to make. Be prepared to be asked about your personal targets.

For the sake of this interview you are to be yourself and you may, therefore, use all your past history and experience. Imagine only that you have been appointed to the position on the new railway.

Wednesday 14.00

DOCUMENT 24

STAGE 10B – INTERVIEWER BRIEF

You are to adopt the role of a newly appointed senior manager in British Rail who has to assume responsibility for the newly refurbished urban railway. The man before you is one of the five-man management team. In the next 12 minutes you are to discover:

(a) Who he is and what he is responsible for;
(b) How he views the development of the refurbished railway;
(c) What he considers his role will be in that;
(d) What key tasks he expects to tackle.

At the conclusion you may wish to agree some targets to be attained in the short and long term.

Wednesday 14.00

DOCUMENT 25

BRIEFING NOTE 5 – INTERVIEWING

A great deal of management activity is concentrated in one-to-one interviews. The main problem is that the strain is focused upon one individual. To be successful, an interview must enable both parties to practise appropriate behaviour. The interviewer is in control and, therefore, it is he who must create the correct circumstances. It is only when both parties are comfortable, with stress minimised, that a good outcome is likely.

Here are some brief guidelines for successful interviews:

- *An agreed content.* The two parties must both be clear from the beginning about the purpose and content of the interview. Therefore, the interviewer must introduce the issue and explain exactly how the interview will proceed.
- *A sense of mutuality.* Having agreed the content and form of the interview, each must respect the contribution of the other. The stronger our feelings the *less* likely there will be a mutual element.
- *An understanding of the other.* We must avoid self-protection. If we anticipate what is said, seek only to make our next contribution and do not listen, then interaction is unlikely. Self-revelation to a modest degree is a sensible way of countering this.
- *Raised motivation.* The interviewer has to get the interviewee to *want* to participate and this is done by *questioning* and *listening.* In addition, the interviewer must be neutral rather than registering astonishment, disapproval, boredom or impatience.
- *Frame of reference.* No two people will view things in the same way. Furthermore, on average we only really understand 10 per cent of the words we hear. The only way we can be sure that some understanding, involving language and point of view, exists is by frequent *summaries.*
- *Creative silence.* In flowing conversation we never say all that is on our minds. The interviewer must give his subject the chance to say and *think.*
- *A clear conclusion.* Every interview should finish with an agreed summary, an understanding of the consequences and specified future action.

Wednesday 14.00

DOCUMENT 26

WORKSHEET 5 – INTERVIEW OBSERVATION GUIDE

This guide is to help observers to focus their attention on different aspects of the interviews. Please record your observations on a separate piece of paper.

1. *Objectives*
   Were the objectives of the interview clearly stated? In what way was it clear that the interviewer had prepared properly?

2. *Factual Information*
   Did the interviewee offer sufficient factual information? How did he react to information supplied by the interviewer?

3. *Questioning*
   What comments have you on the way the interviewer framed his questions? Please give factual examples.

4. *Listening*
   In what ways did both parties try to understand the other's point of view?

5. *Summarising*
   What summaries were made during the interview and by whom?

   (a) to check understanding?
   (b) to regulate the progress of the interview?

6. *Silence*
   Were there any points in the interview when either party used silence effectively?

7. *Results*
   Were the objectives of the interview achieved? Please give examples.

8. *Overall assessment*
   Please state *one* important lesson you learned from observing this discussion.

Wednesday 20.00

DOCUMENT 27

STAGE 11 – TAKING RESPONSIBILITY

In order to be accountable for an activity in management we must first be given authority to act by our superiors. They do this by delegating power to us and making us responsible for a specific area of activity.

1. You are asked to assign by agreement one of the following roles, which are listed together with a prime objective, to each member of your group.

   (a) *Marketing Manager.* To maximise revenue by continuously assessing all categories of demand, advising on the product specification and pricing and monitoring performance.

   (b) *Operations Manager.* To ensure operational targets are fulfilled by planning the operation and utlilising resources so that the traffic is carried at minimum cost.

   (c) *Staff Manager.* To allocate the manpower resources to the operation in such a way that manpower efficiency is maximised while ensuring the best possible working conditions and industrial peace.

   (d) *Rolling Stock Manager.* To allocate trains to the timetable in the most efficient way, ensuring the highest levels of reliability and the lowest maintenance costs.

   (e) *Track and Property Manager.* To ensure that all track and signalling meets the required product and that all stations and other property required for the operation are provided within the specification and properly maintained.

If possible do not assign a task to a group member whose current job is similar. However, experience is no bar and some knowledge of an area is both sensible and useful.

2. As a group you now have the rest of this period to help each individual prepare himself for the role he will play in the next exercises. We suggest the following steps:

   (a) Review all the work done by the group in your area.
   (b) Identify all the work done by the group in your area.
   (c) Seek agreement on any additional information or other details which you wish to add.
   (d) Assemble the material into a logical framework.
   (e) Prepare a *short* brief with the three most important features of your role in the management of this railway.

Wednesday 21.00

DOCUMENT 28

BRIEFING NOTE 6 – CONFLICT AT WORK

In business activities 'conflict' is defined as that situation which arises when the specific or general goals of individuals or groups at work are apparently incompatible.

Resolving conflicts is one of the most important tasks which face a manager. He has to achieve a unity of purpose between staff and managers. He must ensure that individual goals match those of the business. He must bring his own objectives into line with those of his colleagues. Finally, he must adjust the firm's internal goals to those of the outside world.

All these activities involve negotiation. We are familiar with trade union negotiation. Many of us participate in commercial negotiation about prices and product definition. However, the skills which we deploy there are just as valid as when we find ourselves arguing with colleagues about objectives and targets.

Negotiation is about gaining agreement, it is not about compromise. In order to arrive at a solution with which everyone can live the criteria for deciding the issues *must* be agreed. This is the first priority.

Negotiation is a special type of group activity. Most of the points made in 'Working in Groups' are relevant here too. Even the most disparate group when given a specific goal will act together to achieve it.

Negotiation is a social skill and not an end in itself. We need to become skilled practitioners of the process.

Thursday 09.00

DOCUMENT 29

STAGE 12 – GROUP NEGOTIATION

[For this exercise five new groups were formed, each containing one representative from each of the task groups who had been given the same role.]

Each of you works for a newly refurbished railway and you have all been assigned the same role. Arguing only from the standpoint of your own jobs, your task is to agree to support one of the railways as being the best.

You will each have 2 minutes to describe the key points of your railway *from your particular point of view*. You will then have 16 minutes to discuss together and decide which is the best. You may use any criteria but you must stay within the area for which you are responsible. *You may not vote*; the group recommendation must be unanimous.

The buzzer will sound to start each mini-presentation (2 minutes each). It will sound at the end of the last one. It will sound again when you have one minute left to make your decision. No matter how far you have got in your discussion we ask you to come to a conclusion.

Thursday 12.00

DOCUMENT 30

STAGE 13 – STAFF COMMUNICATION

The plans for the new railway have been agreed. You must now make the announcement to the staff in order to both inform them and win their support.

You are asked to compose a 150-word statement to every member of British Rail staff affected by the new operation. As long as you stick to the plans and programme put forward by your group, you may include anything that you judge will benefit the development of good staff relations.

The group should work together to produce this statement, but it may be that you prefer to leave the final writing to one member. Please write up a fair copy which can be posted on the wall at the end of the exercise.

Thursday 12.00

DOCUMENT 31

BRIEFING NOTE 7 – STAFF COMMUNICATION

Good communications between management and staff are an important factor in modern management, in the management of transport they are essential. We have to communicate with every individual exactly what the job is. We have to communicate information about the system every moment we operate. We have to know about the views and performance of every member of staff. But most of all, we must tell our staff about the business so that they understand what is going on and can identify with it. That is the basis of a motivated workforce.

Management has great difficulty with communication. Here are a few reasons why:

- *The sheer size of the business we manage:* the number of people involved is so large and the distances so great that the effort overwhelms us.
- *Communication takes time:* the daily responsibilities of managers and staff take so much time and effort there is not any left over for communication.
- *People tend not to like to communicate:* especially when they think it will provoke difficult responses or make more work.
- *Management and staff talk a different language, literally:* since they tend to read different newspapers and move in different circles they actually use words differently.
- *Communications are often garbled:* one man's jargon is another man's gobbledegook.
- *People have different points of view:* since we see things differently we talk about them differently and we assume everyone else sees things our way.
- *Managers love to hoard information:* knowledge can be power and far too many managers believe that information is like the family jewels – to be locked away and hidden from sight.
- *Information makes conflicts obvious:* if people know things they will know things with which they disagree – tell them and you have to cope with the situation instead of ignoring it.

Why is good communication so important?

- *It actually reduces misunderstanding:* at work, ignorance is not bliss; misunderstandings take time, cause delays and are inefficient.
- *It involves the participants:* the very act of knowing means we are included.
- *We discover information and views:* as soon as the debate is started by the management they soon discover that others have knowledge and ideas which are relevant.
- *The debate becomes knowledgeable:* the processes of management are bound to be improved the more information and data becomes available.
- *It improves decision-making:* more knowledge and more participation means a better decision is likely.
- *We can control 'the grapevine':* it can never be eliminated but spurious inferences and outright lies can be minimised.
- *It reinforces management:* as the source of most information it makes our staff more, not less, dependent on us.
- *It helps us manage change:* which can only happen with support and co-operation born of the confidence of being part of the decision.
- *It improves commitment:* because we share ownership of information, we also share consequences – decisions and actions.

So how do we set about good communications? They have to be *systematic, relevant* and *intelligible.* The rest of this note is about the third criterion and that starts with what we say and write.

- *Tell the truth:* credibility is very hard to achieve and very easy to lose. We do not have to tell the *whole* truth at once – there may be good reasons not to, but only sometimes – but we must always tell the truth if for no other reason than that our information is so easily checked.
- *Be authoritative:* we not only have to be believed, but also believed in. It is no use delegating communication, especially when the message is unpleasant, we have to be acknowledged as the source.
- *Be clear:* short simple sentences are always better than long and involved ones – one message on one topic is far better than a whole series of different points in one communication.

- *Use the appropriate language*: know your audience and use their idiom, do not use words and phrases which they are unlikely to understand.
- *Only give the main reasons*: do not give lots of reasons for doing something – it confuses people and invites them to challenge your weakest point.
- *Do not flood with data*: pick out a few telling numbers to make your points, supporting tables and figures are ignored or misunderstood.
- *Be brief*: by all means tell it all but do so in the shortest possible communication.

Finally, remember feedback. Communication is a two-way process and so every initiative from management must include an invitation to respond.

Thursday 14.00

DOCUMENT 32

STAGE 14 – PROBLEMS AND ISSUES

Each group will be faced with a problem which has occurred during the introduction of the new service.

You will have 20 minutes to work on your problem as a group. There will then be an open coaching session.

Your aim in each case is to create a workable contingency plan.

[For this exercise the groups were observed on closed circuit television by the rest of the course who then participated in immediate feedback sessions. Once in front of the cameras each group was handed a problem tailored to the railway it had invented. Four examples follow.)

14A Problem 1

The Inter-City Management have decided, as part of their 'product development', to operate all their trains on an 'open station' basis. All tickets will henceforth be collected and inspected on the trains. Your new line has proved a considerable success and is now carrying a large number of transfer passengers (about 500 per day) who interchange at the Main Station. You have opted for closed stations and automated tickets. Not only will this development cause problems with passengers changing trains but there will also be substantial accounting difficulties.

You are asked to suggest a way of ensuring easy connections and sensible cross-accounting between your own system and Inter-City.

14B Problem 2

After many months of negotiations, the Board have failed to reach agreement with the trade union about the operation of your new service and its inauguration is postponed once more. However, the local staff are committed and enthusiastic about the new services. They have become increasingly impatient about the delay and are threatening to work to rule unless an agreement is concluded and the service started.

You are asked to review the situation and make proposals for coping with it.

14C Problem 3

It is some months since the new service opened. The response has been good and traffic is building up. However, this success has stimulated two competitive thrusts from the bus and coach industry fearful of losing business. To the north a regional coach company has announced a new luxury service of limited stop coaches serving the whole surburban area and using the dual carriageway main road; and to the south a rival bus company plans to 'cover' all the trunk routes which were vacated as a result of the feeder services agreement which you concluded with the main local carrier. There is also the threat of more mini-bus operations aimed at shoppers. Your whole market is threatened.

You are asked to reconsider your marketing plans and make contingency recommendations.

14D Problem 4

Your new service has been in operation for three months and has had considerable success in attracting commuters to the northern section. Just north of the new University Station the railway lines run through a cutting. During construction it was necessary to carry out substantial earth moving in that area. There has been heavy rainfall all week and last night there was a serious landslip which has blocked both up tracks. All trains must now use the down fast and slow tracks. As they pass the slip, all trains must operate at very reduced speed. Remedial works will take at least a month. You are asked to develop a contingency plan to minimise the damage to your new service.

Thursday 14.00

DOCUMENT 33

BRIEFING NOTE 8 – THE ANALYSIS OF PROBLEMS

1. *What is a Problem?*

A problem arises when there is a difference between a state of affairs which exists and the state which we think ought to exist. In every case there are a set of factors which cause this difference. In most problems the difference is the result of some change which has taken place. If there had been no change then there would be no problem.

In analysing problems we need to identify as well as we can the nature of the changes which have taken place and which result in our having a problem. When the problem relates to 'improving' a situation we need to identify what changes are needed to move from what is happening now to the new situation we wish to achieve.

Thus we remove the differences between what is happening and what we want to happen by removing the things or circumstances which cause the differences.

2. *Steps in Analysing Problems*

There are a number of logical steps which will help us in analysing problems. These are:

(i)   Identifying the difference between what exists and what is required;

(ii) Specifying this difference in precise terms:

    (a) WHAT is the object or unit involved? is wrong with the object or unit?

    (b) WHERE is the object or unit located? is the trouble located on the object or unit?

    (c) WHEN did the trouble begin? is there any pattern about when the trouble occurs?

    (d) SIZE How important is the problem?

(iii) Identify any patterns which can be observed. This means identifying what can be observed and what cannot be observed. For example:

WHO   is concerned and not concerned?

WHAT   is the object involved and the surrounding objects not involved?

WHERE is the object located and not located?

WHEN   does the problem occur and not occur?

(iv) Consider the answers to these questions which will help to specify the exact changes which have been occurring.

(v) Suggest what the causes of the problems are and check these against Step (iii). If there is a match you have probably identified the causes of the problem.

3. Doing Something about the Problem

There is usually more than one possible solution to a problem. We need to choose the solution which will remedy the situation in the easiest way. However, it is unlikely that any solution will give us all we want so we need to be clear about what MUST be happening in the new situation, and those things we would like to be happening in addition to the MUSTS.

The steps in formulating what action we need to take are:

(i) Identify those things which MUST happen in the new situation. These things may include things which must not happen.

(ii) Check these against possible solutions and discard any solutions which do not match completely.

(iii) Draw up a list of desirable things we would like to be happening which are in addition to the MUSTS.

(iv) Choose a solution which gives us all the MUSTS and as many as possible of other desirable things.

Course Review Questionnaires

DOCUMENT 1

MANAGEMENT GROUP CHECKLIST

To assess how the individual members of the group functioned.

Under each of the six headings below are listed five statements – a to e. According to how you assess the performance of the group allocate 100 points to the statements under each heading, distributed as you think best. There is no need to allocate points to every statement, unless you so wish, provided the aggregate score is 100.

Here is an example: *Control and Direction*
a   20
b   30
c   0
d   5
e   45

Please complete this working entirely on your own while reviewing your group's activities over the whole week.

Control and Direction

(a) Discussion went round in circles with little evidence of commitment.
(b) People were agreeable and the discussion was pleasant and harmonious.
(c) One or two individuals took over and controlled the meeting and the topics raised.
(d) The Chairman stepped in to try to keep discussions organised and on time.
(e) A lively exchange of ideas took place with each person regulating their own contribution.

Deciding

(a) Contributions were not picked up; they were lost in haphazard discussion.
(b) After support of an idea by one or two, a course of action developed; individuals were concerned to agree and maintain good relationships.
(c) One or two individuals 'steam-rollered' their views.
(d) Decisions were a compromise.
(e) Decisions were based on understanding and agreement with everyone convinced.

Discussion

(a) Ideas and opinions were expressed with little conviction or enthusiasm.
(b) Polite give and take resulted in a friendly meeting.
(c) Discussions were on a 'win or lose' basis; personal victory mattered more than getting the best solution.
(d) Although different opinions and ideas were expressed, reasonably acceptable positions were reached; people changed their stance to make progress.
(e) Points of disagreement were identified and thrashed out logically; members were honest and open.

Atmosphere

(a) Going through the motions; flat and lifeless.
(b) Easy-going and pleasant.
(c) Competitive, critical and tense.
(d) Interesting and satisfying.
(e) Penetrating, rewarding, challenging and committed.

Objectives

(a) There was quibbling over unimportant detail; objectives were never clear.
(b) Keeping the peace was more important than getting the best result.
(c) People were vying for power.
(d) Objectives were modified in line with what could be most easily accomplished.

(e) Objectives were clearly understood, accepted and the group worked constructively to those ends.

Review

(a) Little or no attention was given to discussing group effectiveness throughout the exercise.
(b) People were supported and complimented but faults and weaknesses were ignored.
(c) There was unconstructive and negative criticism.
(d) Some suggestions were made about improvement and doing things differently.
(e) There was an on-going review of the work of the group seeking to improve and learn from experience.

DOCUMENT 2

EVALUATION TEAM ANALYSIS

To assess how the group worked as a whole.

Which of the following statements best describes the way in which the group functioned. You are asked to complete the first column *without consulting the other members of the group* and then you will meet together to complete the second column *as a group.*

Please circle one letter for each question

	Individual Assessment	Group Assessment
Objectives		

The objectives of the group were:

completely clear	a	A
very clear	b	B
clear	c	C
fairly clear	d	D
not clear at all	e	E

Relevance

The relevance of discussion has been:

complete	a	A
high	b	B
fairly high	c	C
moderate	d	D
low	e	E

Utilisation of time

Utilisation of time was:

efficient	a	A
reasonably good	b	B
fair	c	C
involved 50% wastage	d	D
very poor	e	E

Participation	Individual Assessment	Group Assessment

The level of participation meant that:

	Individual Assessment	Group Assessment
everyone listened	a	A
there was some 'steam-rollering'	b	B
there was frequent 'talking-down'	c	C
potential contributions were suppressed	d	D
a few members completely dominated	e	E

Tolerance

Examples of individual views being disregarded were:

	Individual Assessment	Group Assessment
non-existent	a	A
rare	b	B
few	c	C
frequent	d	D
a permanent feature	e	E

Frankness

Group members were being:

	Individual Assessment	Group Assessment
completely honest with each other	a	A
moderately frank	b	B
tactful	c	C
guarded	d	D
highly inhibited	e	E

Commitment

The group's commitment was:

	Individual Assessment	Group Assessment
complete	a	A
very high	b	B
high	c	C
moderate	d	D
low	e	E

Performance	Individual Assessment	Group Assessment
The performance of individuals has in general been:		
open, helpful and enthusiastic	a	A
reasonably objective and useful	b	B
cautious, but sometimes valuable	c	C
negative and critical	d	D
obstructive and unhelpful	e	E

Top Managers' Development Workshops

These documents were used for the management workshops run for the rubber products company referred to in Chapter 3.

FIRST WEEKEND

DOCUMENT 1

VIEWS AND OPINIONS

This questionnaire is to provide material for the forthcoming workshop. It is based on the recent series of interviews with each of the participants individually. Please answer the questions as frankly as you can and complete and return it before the workshop.

Please tick the *one* statement that you believe to be most 'correct' about your company:

A The business is in a static market and the best we can do is to maintain our market share.

B The market opportunities in the UK and Europe are so great that in order to survive, we need to become a dominant force.

C The over-riding need in the business is to develop improved ways of meeting the needs of our traditional customers.

Here are some other statements, please indicate whether you think that they are *predominantly* true or *predominantly* false.

| T | F | 1. Our market share in the UK can only be expanded by introducing new product lines. |

| T | F | 2. Whatever developments take place in selling to large retail groups, our dependence on wholesalers will remain paramount. |

| T | F | 3. The immediate key issue is to increase sales in traditional lines. |

| T | F | 4. There are no major problems between the Sales and Operations Departments. |

| T | F | 5. We have a good understanding of all our present and potential competitors. |

| T | F | 6. We have little understanding of our potential markets. |

| T | F | 7. It is more important to ensure the success of our branded line than to develop new 'unbranded' lines. |

| T | F | 8. If we are to expand in Europe it will be necessary to 'change' customer buying patterns. |

| T | F | 9. In general our customers are well satisfied with our administrative systems. |

| T | F | 10. Our warehouse and distribution system is inadequate and needs a fundamental re-appraisal. |

| T | F | 11. The market for most of our products is fixed, the only debate is the share gained by the various suppliers. |

| T | F | 12. We would gain better control of the market by dealing directly with retailers. |

| T | F | 13. There is a sense of purpose and direction about the business and morale is high. |

| T | F | 14. Bearing in mind the locations where people work, the company's remuneration system is fair. |

Now complete the following sentence:

'My dream for the future of the company's business is ....

....

FIRST WEEKEND

DOCUMENT 2

COMPANY CULTURE

The following characteristics of the company will affect the way in which our business plan will be implemented. We need to judge how effective the company will be in coping with the demands of the next three to four years. Please consider the following carefully and rank each one on a scale of 1 (relatively ineffective) to 10 (highly effective):

1. Encouraging new ideas
2. Evaluating and implementing ideas
3. Containing expenditure
4. Introducing new systems
5. Gaining the commitment of staff
6. Rewarding employees for above-average performance.
7. Achieving upward communication
8. Achieving downward communication
9. Providing management control information in a usable form
10. Giving staff a challenge
11. Achieving a well-respected performance appraisal system
12. Technical training
13. Management training
14. Setting clear objectives
15. Producing a first-class product
16. Focusing on the needs of its customers
17. Producing a consistently first-class product
18. Setting a clear pricing policy
19. Controlling cash flow
20. Offering the right incentives to employees

Appendix IV
The Framework of Management Training

All our courses have been built up using a framework which embodies all the essential elements of active learning.

A. *Self assessment by the participants*

It is essential to know where you are before you start. In the case of general courses this should take the form of some sort of self-administered test of management style or performance. It should also face the participant with what he already knows and what he does not know.

More specific company-based courses, especially those involving directors, must make the participants explore their feelings and perceptions about the business they run together. This enables them to attempt to eliminate misconceptions and to try to create a level field.

B. *Agreed objectives*

Even on a course which has been developed by a firm in order to achieve a particular policy development, as ours was for British Rail, the participants must know and accept those objectives. In more general courses, polling the individual course members for their objectives is more likely to lead to an acceptance of the process and may modify the course to everyone's benefit.

At more senior levels it is not just the objective of the particular course or seminar which must be explored, those of the firm itself must be examined and, if necessary, reappraised. We often ask participants to 'describe their dream' in order to draw out the live objectives from the conventional dross. Not surprisingly, once it is seen that it is the future of the business they run together which is under consideration, there is usually a vigorous discussion leading towards convergence of views.

C. *Carefully constructed groups*

While we favour a self-administered test, such as Belbin or Kurtin, any systematic way of constructing groups with a range of knowledge, experience and group skills will provide solid learning opportunities within groups. And groups are essential because much more learning takes place than ever could in a large class. At the very least there is nowhere to hide.

When dealing with senior managers, the group is usually predetermined, because the whole course consists of one management board. But even here it may be necessary to break down into groups of two or three. Some form of behavioural polling is necessary so that viable groups can be created which may even give new slants on the behaviour of the parent group.

D. *Relevant content*

While invented companies are not essential, we believe they are the best way to make a course relevant. In practice, they are not invented at all but simply the course members' own company the way they would like it to be – and that is often a useful experience in itself.

For directors it is often necessary to build the seminar around their latest crisis. In this case, relevance is not a problem; information overload may be. They may simply know so much that they have no room for learning. In such cases the tutors have to help them to simplify.

E. *A set of structured tasks*

There must always be an agenda. In management this is set by the events of the business. An important management skill is determining how to cope with these demands, many of which will be unexpected either in circumstances or outcome. A course has to start out with a structure and in many cases the structure has to be maintained. In our experience there should never be quite enough time – there never is in real life – and participants should be made to make choices.

With directors and senior managers, an internal agenda is more likely. One must still start with a complete programme and all the relevant material. In fact, the seminars never turn out like that and new agendas have to be created as the event progresses.

F. *Knowledge and information inputs in response to requests*

Almost every task set on such a course will require some input. We believe very strongly that there can never be tricks or exercises which result in deliberate failure. There is, we know, a school of training which believes that 'throwing people in at the deep end' produces learning situations. After the group has failed, because it did not know what it was doing, the clever tutor will 'give creative feedback' so that they will learn what to do.

This does not work. Such events demoralise the participants and switch off learning. In short the group drowns. Success is the real

267

spur to learning and that depends on knowing at least the theory of how to do it. People have to feel good about the process, not disappointed.

Always explain first how to do it. Then answer any request for knowledge or information as soon as it arises, for the act of questioning is the first stage in learning and one has to 'strike while the mind is hot'. During both courses and seminars, it is necesary to give mini-lectures frequently and often, through questioning participants, thereby releasing knowledge that the group or individual already has.

G. *Constant feedback on progress*

Feedback should be live and immediate. Such information becomes stale if stored too long. Detailed notes of every stage have to be maintained by course tutors so that feedback becomes concrete and not just opinion. With more senior groups it is, in our experience, better to have two enablers present so that one can observe and take notes while the other is working with the group. Then later the observer can feed back to the group his view of what took place. Sometimes this can be so startling that the whole seminar changes direction, or, as in one case we had, the board concerned was subsequently reorganised.

H. *Exercises designed to practise acquired skills*

There are now a large number of exercises available in all fields of management, many utilising CCTV. These can be adapted to the needs of a particular group, provided they can be made relevant to the company concerned, either real or imaginary. The important thing is that they have intelligible instructions and plausible outcomes. In other words, the participants must believe in what they are doing. Such exercises may be for groups or individuals, they will seldom be for a whole course. Most important of all they must be relevant to the learning experience and seen to be so.

I. *Structured review of the whole course*

We have described in Chapter 12 how this may be done for a management course. For management and directors' seminars, while a final review is essential, because such seminars invariably include action planning, there also has to be a written record in the form of a detailed report and a timetable for specific action. It is our experience that unless directors are committed to specific new action in front of their peers, and such action is recorded, then it does not happen, changes do not occur and learning will not have taken place.

J. *Post audit of performance*

This is perhaps the single most important element both in training and management itself. The regular monitoring of performance and change not only reinforces good behaviour, it continually stimulates the learning process so that often only part remembered lessons from a course or seminar appear years later.

Boards of directors who decide to work together to improve their performance will usually come together for a whole series of seminars, in which case the review of one often provides the basis for the next.

Appendix V

Group Behaviour Models

The process of management is essentially a communal or group activity. It is therefore essential for individuals to understand how they perform in a group. We have found a number of models of group behaviour useful both in explaining how groups function and in creating good working groups. Although we have the hard evidence of practice that groups created to have a balance of participating types are very successful, such a circumstance is an ideal which may be far from attainable in a real work situation.

Of all the models of group behaviour available, we have found that of Belbin[1] to be the most useful. It satisfies our basic approach of being self-defined, but provides some useful and recognisable stereotypes. Belbin defined eight group roles or personalities. He argued that while every role might not be present as a primary attribute – if for no other reason than that not all groups have eight members – each role was bound to be performed by someone if the group was to be successful.

His eight group roles are:

- *Company Worker* – The one who takes ideas and initiatives and organises them into practical applications; displays common-sense and self-discipline; is likely to identify with group goals and to expect loyalty from the others.
- *Chairman* – The one who concerts the activities of the group; the organiser and co-ordinator; the setter of agendas and timetables; will seek to include every group member and draw out their contributions; the main summariser and definer of conclusions while not imposing own view.
- *Shaper* – The most active player, the one who develops every contribution and moulds the work of the group; a high contributor who will demand from all of the others and will 'keep the show on the road' but will probably develop the workable strategies which achieve the group goals.
- *Plant* – The one who has the ideas, always adding a new slant, never completely baffled; unlikely to be a 'good' group player and may remain a marginal contributor for long periods. However, once attention is engaged will probably make the one contribution which makes the group's goal attainable.
- *Resource Investigator* – The one who explores and develops ideas and strategies, responding to challenges and often 'providing' for the group. Is gregarious, makes easy contacts and carries forward the process activities.

- *Monitor/Evaluator* – The one who subjects all the group's activities and ideas to sober evaluation; recognises that resources are finite; exercises judgement and keeps a level head; usually neat and orderly and often the group's 'keeper of records'.
- *Teamworker* – The essential extrovert whose highest priority is the welfare of the group rather than its activities or achievements. The one who ensures that all the members of the group integrate and likely to be the 'housekeeper'.
- *Completer/Finisher* – The essential one who is determined to complete the job; no matter how much fun or how difficult the task, this is the member who keeps it going to the very end and makes sure that even 'little things' are not forgotten.

In order to identify which role we each perform, Belbin developed a 'self-perception inventory' which indicated which roles (or types of job) an individual *preferred* to undertake. On our various programmes, the 'teams' comprised between four and six individuals and we found that the inventory indicated that an individual rarely preferred only one role. Normally, people indicated a preference for two, or sometimes three, group roles. Thus we realised that people are quite adaptable in a group situation and this made the formation of teams based on the Belbin hypothesis a practical proposition.

The questionnaire itself simply offers a choice of behavioural responses to eight different circumstances. These are ranked by the respondent and the consequent scores are matched with the expected behaviour of the eight role models. From this it is possible to predict which roles would be most likely to be taken by each individual. We then went one step further and used the results to construct groups which placed everyone in a position where they were likely to play the part they most preferred.

As far as we are aware, this was the first time that this model had been used in this way. Generally it had been given as a diagnostic exercise to help individuals to understand their behaviour within an existing group. We took the results and constructed balanced groups to which we gave projects and exercises.

There were two consequences. The groups were very successful at learning to work together quickly. In general, members performed the 'Belbin roles' we had expected them to. Most importantly we were able to select as chairmen those who were not only generally good but actually wanted to be a chairman.

The balance of group behaviours also produced some outstanding performances from individuals who were wholly surprised by what had happened. Because most groups included a highly articulate contributor working alongside an organised achiever, clashes were minimised and output maximised.

The second consequence was that on the rare occasions when we were unable to include someone who had expressed a willingness to perform an essential group role, this would emerge through an individual changing his normal behaviour. This demonstrated an extremely important and dynamic feature of managers at work. Once the needs and goals of the business are understood, individual managers can often show remarkable adaptability. It is surprising how often this is denied in large organisations, to their detriment.

One important aspect of this approach was that the results of the Belbin test were only revealed after the groups had worked together for some days. This did not really violate our principle of openness, because the test itself consists of preferences expressed by the subjects, and it was essential that behaviour in the groups be spontaneous otherwise the exercise would have simply been a self-fulfilling prophecy.

In the event we have found that over 80 per cent of participants performed the role predicted by the Belbin test and the others, almost without exception, performed that role in part. In all the courses we have run using this method of group construction we have only once had a failed chairman who had to be replaced. After this experience many participants were not only convinced of the need for a variety of roles within a group, they accepted that well-balanced groups work well. In management, the importance of a team cannot be understated.

From over 200 groups constructed using Belbin, one particularly worrying piece of feedback emerged. Many young managers reported that in their own companies they were often placed in jobs requiring behaviour and aptitudes directly contradictory to what they preferred. Whereas in our groups they had been able to shine by exercising their talents comfortably and creatively, back in their jobs they felt stressed and uncomfortable. This illustrates the perverse tendency of management to hammer square pegs into round holes.

This is not the only way in which the behavioural aspects of management can be tested and used in a learning context. We have also used the Kurtin Adaptor-Innovator Test[2] to create groups. Again this is a self-assessment. It aims to get the individual to describe *how* problems are tackled or creativity exercised. It does not purport to measure creativity itself. The test consists of over a hundred binary options which the respondent can use to describe himself.

Kurtin argues that we are all creative in one way or another; the real interest lies in *how* we exercise that creativity. He postulates a scale reaching from 'adaptors' to 'innovators'. Adaptors are those who accept the world as it is and seek to solve problems by using the skills, methods and materials that they can see and identify. Innovators are those who do not accept anything as it is but seek to solve problems by changing the very basis, even the nature, of the world as they see it.

There are very few pure adaptors or innovators. Most people approach problems using both approaches; the crux is the proportions of the two types in each individual. The KAI index specifies where an individual lies on the range from adaptor to innovator.

Groups composed of individuals from across the spectrum as described by Kurtin tend to perform well. They tend to be very good at defined tasks but less good at a continuing relationship. This is not hard to explain. Men and women with a markedly different approach to creativity are unlikely to get on very well together socially. Thus a management team created on these lines might prove to have serious built-in frictions even though it would tackle problems well.

So, if one were creating a task force to deal with a specific project or investigation, this approach could be very valuable. Highly innovative individuals tend to look at the world as if composed entirely of variables. It is their task to mould and shape it. Ideas and solutions flow like water but no work gets done and no report written. Highly adaptive individuals see a world of parameters. They seek to make sense of what is. They put a high emphasis on analysis and order. Their solutions are usually conventional and predictable but the report gets written and the work is completed on time.

Put the two together under the leadership of an individual who is neither an extreme innovator nor adaptor and the outcome is likely to be good. The group may be relieved when it is over but a good job will be done.

Another aspect of group working concerns the issue of 'management style'. Important though relationships within management teams are, there is also the relationship between the manager and his subordinates. It is our view that a management team should pursue a consistent style. Such styles can be identified using situational leadership tests.[3] Each of us approaches the problem of managing others differently. By describing various 'management situations' and inviting the respondent to describe how he would behave it is possible to construct a picture of his management style. Such a picture is again developed by the manager himself and while it may surprise him, the insights revealed in facing the fictitious 'situation' provide hard evidence.

A group constructed of those with varying management styles will even spend its time arguing about how to organise itself. So in this case we should bring together those with similar leadership styles. In the artificial environment of a management training programme, the comparison in performance of the different styles is likely to be less obvious than in the real world. Nevertheless the styles themselves will be apparent. Within the company itself, the identification of different styles of management will enable sensible management teams to be created who share a management style, and those that differ from the company culture may be coached through the necessary changes.

There are other self-administered assessments and tests and

each has validity insofar as it enables managers and their bosses to understand current behaviour and be able to plan for change. While we have considerable reservations about tests and assessments, we recognise that some way has to be available for sorting out the different behaviour and styles of management so that individuals can recognise themselves. We are convinced that in this matter of constructing successful management teams such an approach is not only useful, it is essential if real change is to be achieved.

References

1 BELBIN, R. M. *Management Teams*. London, Heinemann, 1981.
2 KURTIN, M. 'Adaptors and Innovators: a description and measure'. *Journal of Applied Psychology*. Number 61, 1976.
3 HERSEY, P. and BLANCHARD, K. H. *Management of Organisational Behavior: Utilizing group resources*. Englewood Cliffs N.J., Prentice-Hall, 1977.

Appendix VI
Examples of Role Descriptions

1. *Export Services Assistant*

Role:

1. To handle customer queries, complaints and requests either personally or by referral; to ensure referred queries are followed up until an answer is received.

2. To receive orders from customers, ensuring all necessary information is translated and recorded accurately; to input details into the business scheduling system and complete all documentation.

3. To update customers on any delays or problems in filling their orders immediately.

4. To deal professionally and courteously with customers.

5. To contact and inform the relevant Export Sales Representatives of all new developments concerning customers and their orders and to pass other information to them as necessary.

6. To complete accurately all export documentation for orders and prepare invoices.

What will be happening when this role is performed satisfactorily?

A. 95 per cent of customers get a full and accurate response to their query, request or complaint (or a full explanation of why one is not available) within four hours.

B. There are no reasonable complaints from customers about the manners or attitudes of the Export Services staff.

C. When contacting the company, customers will want to deal with Export Services staff and will ask for them by name.

D. Orders are never delayed, wrong orders are never sent and customers never dispute prices because of errors in information [provided by Export Services Department].

E. Orders delivered are never abandoned or delayed because

of incorrect or inadequate export documentation.

F. Export Sales Representatives are kept up-to-date on their customers and their orders, any complaints, problems and other market intelligence.

G. The Sales Management is able to pass information and documentation quickly to its Export Sales Representatives.

2. Safety Officer

Role:

1. To enable managers to adopt standards of safety, in the operation of which they will be responsible as laid down in the Company Safety Manual.

2. To undertake inspections, and to advise managers how to achieve the standards laid down in (1) above.

3. To investigate serious lost-time accidents and to write reports for the Factory Inspectorate.

4. To report on the causes of recurrent minor accidents.

5. To ensure that the Health and Safety Committees function effectively.

6. To take visitors round the factory ensuring that they receive the relevant information.

What will be happening when this role is performed satisfactorily?

A. Accident trends will be favourable and there will be no major criticisms from factory, insurance and fire inspectors.

B. Managers will ask for advice on safety matters and be willing to implement it.

C. After accidents, and within a short time, all relevant facts and figures will have been assembled and other information collated.

D. Statistical series concerning accident trends will have been maintained and all anomalies investigated.

E. Findings and resolutions of the Health and Safety Committees will have been implemented and notices of the meetings circulated.

F. Information for visitors will be pitched at a level which enables

276

them to feel that they have increased their knowledge of the company as a result of their visit.

3. *Personnel Manager – Engineering Operations*

Role:

1. To ensure that personnel practices within the Engineering Directorate are consistent with the company's overall personnel policy, while allowing maximum flexibility for each of the businesses within the Directorate.

2. To provide professional personnel advice to the Engineering Operations Director and to ensure that he is forewarned of any personnel problems.

3. To provide personnel advice for all units in the Directorate as requested and to assist them in taking decisions for which they are responsible; where appropriate to assist in the development of personnel resources within the units.

4. To ensure that the specific requirements and circumstances of the Engineering Operations Directorate are taken into account in the company's development of personnel policy.

5. To ensure that all managers within the engineering function have the necessary skills and knowledge to do their jobs.

What will be happening when this role is performed satisfactorily?

A. All personnel records pertaining to contracts of employment will be current.

B. Procedures will be in place to enable managers to control unauthorised absence.

C. Unit Personnel Officers will be playing a full part in budget preparation and business plans.

D. The Director of Engineering Operations will be fully and accurately briefed at all times on all personnel issues.

E. Unit Managers will be making increasing use of their local personnel resources and only referring to the job holder on 'substantive' matters.

F. 20 per cent of Personnel Officers will be undertaking study leading to professional qualifications at any one time.

G. Company personnel policies do not unduly limit the Directorate in the achievement of its business targets.

H. Training matrices have been established for each managerial activity and individual training plans are being implemented based on these.

Bibliography

ARGYRIS, C. and SCHON, D. A. (1978). *Organisational Learning: A Theory in Action Perspective*. Reading, Mass: Addison Wesley.

BARHAM, K., FRASER, J., and HEATH, L. (1978). *Management for the Future*. Final report to the Foundation for Management Education. March. Ashridge: FME.

BELBIN, R. (1981). *Management Teams*. London: Heinemann.

EDMONSTONE, J. (1990). 'What price the learning organisation in the public sector?' In M. PEDLER, J. BURGOYNE, T. BOYDELL and G. WELSHMAN (eds). *Self-Development in Organisations*. London: McGraw-Hill.

GARRATT, B. (1987). *The Learning Organisation*. London: Fontana.

HAYES, R. H., WHEELWRIGHT, S. C. and CLARK, K. B. (1988). *Dynamic Manufacturing: Creating the Learning Organisation*. New York: The Free Press.

KEPNER, C. and TAYLOR, B. (1965). *The Rational Manager*. Provincetown, N.J.: Kepner-Tregoe Inc.

PETTIGREW, A. M. and WHIP, R. (1991). *Managing Change for Competitive Success*. Oxford: Blackwell.

KENNY, J. P. J. and REID, M. (1988). *Training Interventions*. London: Institute of Personnel Management.

MCGREGOR, D. (1960). *The Human Side of Enterprise*. New York: McGraw-Hill.

REVANS, R. W. (1980). *Action Learning*. London: Blond and Briggs.

BALL, C. (1991). *Learning Pays: The Role of Post-Compulsory Education and Training*. London: Royal Society of Arts.

SENGE, P. M. (1990). *The Fifth Discipline: The Art and Practice of the Learning Organisation*. New York: Doubleday/Currency.

SINGER, E. J. (1974). *Effective Management Coaching*. London: Institute of Personnel Management.

Index

DEVELOPING SKILLS

Other titles in this series

Turning People On
The motivation challenge
Andrew Sargent

How does the manager gain the positive commitment of the workforce? What measures are necessary to motivate employees and make them effective members of the organisation?

Andrew Sargent explains the issues, the theories expounded by behavioural scientists, the barriers to motivation, the crucial influence of the personnel expert and, through description of actual case studies, the role of supervisors. He offers positive, practical and informative guidance to achieving harmonisation and motivating the team.

Above all, the book focuses on constructive analysis of the challenge of motivation and practical help in making it happen.

0 85292 444 5

Raising the Profile
Marketing the HR Function
David Clutterbuck and Desmond Dearlove

HR departments *know* they provide a vital service to their internal customers – so why do they often enjoy only grudging **respect?**

Largely, suggest David Clutterbuck and Desmond Dearlove in this stimulating handbook, because they neglect basic *marketing* skills. By segmenting their 'client base', developing the 'key accounts', soliciting and responding to feedback, creating an HR brand and constantly communicating the key messages, personnel practitioners can soon transform the way they are perceived. A commitment to quality and customer care is no optional extra, but clear evidence of HR professionalism; this invaluable book explains the essential techniques involved.

0 85292 526 3

Job Analysis
A practical guide for managers
Second edition
Michael Pearn and Rajvinder Kandola

Job analysis offers a series of invaluable techniques for assessing how work is done – and how it could be done better.

Whenever managers try to define excellence or draw up job descriptions, identify career paths or evaluate a training scheme, job, task and role analysis count as vital tools. In this well-established text, two leading occupational psychologists examine the most effective modern methods and illustrate their use with fascinating real-life examples. Their extensively revised second edition includes full discussion of recent developments like the Work Profiling System and the competency framework. For all personnel specialists and many other managers, it offers a superb introduction to a crucial (but often neglected) area of expertise.

'This is essentially a practical text that focuses on an area which is of crucial importance to a manager and demonstrates how much more there is to 'job analysis' than time and motion study. It is brief, clear and to the point.'

Modern Management

0 85292 542 5

The Institute of Personnel Management is one of the leading publishers of books for personnel professionals, general managers and students. For further information on the full range of IPM titles please contact

The Publications Department
The Institute of Personnel Management
IPM House
Camp Road
London SW19 4UX
Tel: (081) 946 9100